Abortion

*Between Freedom and
Necessity*

JANET HADLEY

Abortion

*Between Freedom and
Necessity*

TEMPLE UNIVERSITY PRESS
PHILADELPHIA

363.4
HAD

Temple University Press, Philadelphia 19122
Copyright © 1996 by Janet Hadley. All rights reserved
Published 1996
Printed in the United States of America

First published in Great Britain by Virago Press

The author and publisher are grateful to Lyndal Ryan, Marge Ripper and Barbara Buttfield
for permission to quote from *We Women Decide: Women's Experiences of Seeking Abortion in
Queensland, South Australia and Tasmania* and to the World Health Organization, Maternal
Health and Safe Motherhood Program, for permission to reproduce the maps on pages 41
and 42.

Text design by Kate Nichols

Library of Congress Cataloging-in-Publication Data
Hadley, Janet.
    Abortion : between freedom and necessity / Janet Hadley.
      p.   cm.
    Includes bibliographical references and index.
    ISBN 1-56639-506-2 (cloth: alk. paper).—ISBN 1-56639-591-7 (pbk: alk. paper)
     1. Abortion.   2. Abortion—Moral and ethical aspects.   3. Feminism. I. Title.
HQ767.H23   1996
363.4′6—dc20
                                              96-26850

For my dear friend Sue O'Sullivan

Contents

Acknowledgments

L IVING WITH THIS BOOK for almost two years would not have been possible without the encouragement and support of friends, colleagues and family. It has brought new friends too, and I have been overwhelmed by the generosity with which some people have lent me their time and their skills. First and foremost I have to thank Rita Ward, librarian at the International Planned Parenthood Federation (IPPF), whose ferreting talents, wry humor and peerless knack of knowing the color of every book I have ever needed has made the research as painfree as ever it could be. Grateful thanks too, to Ann Furedi at the Birth Control Trust, and Rupert Walder, also at IPPF, both of whom have generously played a more significant part in this project than they perhaps can guess.

There have been a few special friends who have particularly shared in the travails of early drafts and whose comments and involvement I have valued so much: thank you Debby Yaffe, Caroline Beatty, Gail Lewis, Anne Davies and Sue O'Sullivan for unleashing your critical talents on this project. Thanks as well to my family: my boys, Patrick and Martin, and above all to Terry—for keeping faith with the project and sharing it with me.

I also want to thank Pat Agana and Lambeth Women and Children's Health Project, Gautam Appa, Marge Berer, Paul Bekkering and Willem Boissevain of Arnhem, whose descriptions of their philosophy and their work made for one of the most inspiring interviews of my professional life, Bing Sum Lau, all the staff at the Birth Control Trust, Sarah Boston, Elizabeth Clements, Philip Crow, Victoria Daines, Catherine Dawson, Rosemary

Dodds, Henk Doppenberg, Lesley Doyal, Len Doyal, Nel Druce, Sara Dunn, Barbara Einhorn, Hilary Everett, Mary Hickman, Ed Hillman, Hanna Jankowska, Jenny Keating, Evert Ketting, Rob Kievit, Margaret Kirkby, Barbara Klugman, Gill Knight, Karen Knorr, Hope Massiah, Jon O'Brien, Sue Olley, Elke Pluijmen, Jany Rademakers, Lisanne Radice, Rayna Rapp, Jane Roe of the Abortion Law Reform Association, Melanie Silgardo, Christine Sanders, Beatrijs Stemerding, Joan Walsh, Susanna Wight, Sarah White and Nira Yuval-Davis.

Finally I want to acknowledge this book's debt to Rosalind Petchesky's towering, brilliant, complex book, *Abortion and Woman's Choice*. The analytical solecisms which may follow are entirely my own, but on almost every issue I kept finding that Petchesky had something illuminating and incisive to say.

Introduction

IN 1953 THE EDITOR OF *WOMAN'S HOUR,* the BBC's flagship radio magazine show for British housewives, wrote from BBC Broadcasting House to abortion law reformer Alice Jenkins, regretting that she was "a little doubtful about our being able to touch this subject in *Woman's Hour.*" Times have changed. Today, features about abortion appear regularly in newspapers and on television. When this book was first published in Britain, I was at once invited to talk on *Woman's Hour* about abortion and the issues it raises. Everyone has an opinion about abortion. It's a stock element in the roundabout of soap opera crises—will she, won't she? The U.S. soaps *Days of Our Lives, General Hospital* and *All My Children* have all breathlessly featured the dilemma of unwanted pregnancy.

In recent years in several countries abortion has been in the headlines, sometimes for months on end. In Ireland in 1992, the harrowing case of the raped fourteen-year-old girl, forbidden to go to England for an abortion, absorbed the entire country for almost a whole year, putting a human face on what had in the past seemed a remote and lofty issue of life. In the aftermath of communism, Poland likewise found itself in the grip of a debate about the rights and wrongs of abortion. And most bizarrely of all, the United States has become a country where doctors who perform abortions wear bulletproof vests as they journey to work, because since 1993 no less than five people working in abortion clinics have been gunned down by anti-abortion fanatics. By the time this book is published the issue of abortion may be polarizing the politics of other nations and dominating their headlines. New twists to the story are occurring every week.

Yet abortion is still not talked about much in everyday conversation. Few women admit to having had one without being sure they are among friends. It is too personal, it is still taboo. Often, in the last two years, I have been asked, "what's your book about?" and have had to take a deep breath before I say the word, and wait to see if I get a hard stare, an embarrassed smile, or a transparently dissimulating story about a "friend who had one." Yet this intimate personal issue has become sensationally and bewilderingly public. It has even brought down governments—a paradox which I found intriguing enough to start me on the project of this book.

There is a polarity of views and values on the question of abortion. People speak of the abortion "debate," implying that some sort of dialogue is going on. What is actually happening is more akin to a slanderous cacophony. The pope's battalions stand on picket lines outside hospitals and clinics yelling at pregnant women as they go in, "murderer, you are killing your baby." The language has cut loose from its moorings—life versus murder; motherhood versus infanticide; family values versus selfish individualism; the rights of the fetus versus the rights of the woman. Slogans on a badge. Linguistic feats are performed with words such as choice, life, rights—and even more extraordinary things happen to statistics.

This loose cannon which has politicians running for cover is a fairly recent phenomenon in politics. The public "debate"—there is no other word, it will have to suffice—only emerged in the early 1970s. At that time, thousands of vocal and active women, not all of whom called themselves "feminists," were demanding that abortion no longer be a crime. They marched and organized, many with stories of their own illegal abortions, or those of their friends, fresh in their minds. Yet today's feminists have little to say about abortion and the new issues which have impinged on it, such as the prospects offered by prenatal testing for genetic abnormalities. There is far more interest in the politics of infertility, the new reproductive technologies and whether women have a "right" to have children. The availability of legal abortion has been central to the development of much of the new reproductive technology. New genetic knowledge and artificial reproductive techniques have played a hand in the abortion controversy, as the hardline anti-abortion movement exploits new knowledge about the very early stages of embryo development. But feminist voices on abortion are fading.

Memories of illegal abortion are fading too, and few younger doctors have ever seen women with temperatures of 106°F and septic abortions. Women's experiences of abortion—legal or illegal—are invisible, their stories largely unheard.

Abortion has been legal in the United States and most of Europe for ten, fifteen, twenty years and yet it is as explosive an issue as ever. Being at the center of such a controversy has profoundly affected the way it is perceived and discussed. I have tried to peel away the carapace of battle-hardened slogans, to explore what is happening to women today who are unwillingly pregnant, whether their pregnancy was totally unintended or was originally planned. I have also tried to weigh the influence of some of the new factors impinging on abortion, which were not around twenty-five years ago. It has been a journey around the world, featuring Brazil, Russia, Zambia, China, India, Poland, Morocco, Ireland, Germany, Japan, Holland, Australia, the United States and Britain. All yield stories about abortion today and about women's access to good reproductive health care and their "reproductive rights."

Reproductive rights: a vital concept, which opens the door to a much wider perspective on women's health than abortion alone. There will be those who accuse me of focusing too much on abortion as a single issue. I have tried to avoid that pitfall: such a narrowing of focus happens all the time in the public arena when people claim it's a question of choice, or life or reducing teenage pregnancy or maternal mortality. But at the same time there is no detaching abortion from a central role in women's reproductive experience. It seems to me that access to abortion is pivotal to women's reproductive freedom and can never be taken for granted. Women in postcommunist Eastern Europe have recently learned that to their cost. For many women there and in much of Africa, Asia and Central and Latin America, it remains a fundamental health issue, sometimes a question of life or death.

The abortion controversy "may begin with reasons, proceed to statistics, but it always comes down really to stories" (Wilt 1990). True, but as well as stories, there have to be reasons and there have to be statistics. This book offers them all with a viewpoint—that the decision to end an unwanted pregnancy has to be unflinchingly claimed for women. Most women, given the choice, would not seek the experience of abortion, but if they do, it should be available to them as a safe, legal, accessible and affordable service.

Among the early campaigners for abortion law reform in Britain before the Second World War, was Stella Browne, a socialist and an unmistakable feminist. Her combination of views placed her apart from some of her campaigning colleagues, some of whom pursued an implicitly eugenic agenda, and almost all of whom found it repugnant to link abortion with the notion of women seeking sexual pleasure, free from the fear of pregnancy. Their ideological descendants are alive and well in the "pro-choice" movement. Stella Browne was different; she said:

Abortion must be the key to a new world for women, not a bulwark for things as they are, economically nor biologically. Abortion should not be either the perquisite of the legal wife only, nor merely a last remedy against illegitimacy. It should be available for any woman without insolent inquisitions, nor ruinous financial charges, nor tangles of red tape. For our bodies are our own.

(BROWNE, LUDOVICI AND ROBERTS 1935)

There cannot be a more concise and lucid statement.

1

The United States: Back to the Crusades

A WOMAN'S DECISION to terminate an unwanted pregnancy is, seemingly, a personal and private matter. To find this transformed into a public issue which has the power to convulse or even paralyze a nation's politics for weeks or even months on end is a bewildering spectacle. We expect the re-sounding economic issues of the day—law and order, or national security—to dominate public affairs or to make or break governments. But like it or not, abortion is a political issue. It influences party politics, local politics, even international politics, and is itself profoundly influenced by political events far removed from the individual dilemma of unwanted pregnancy.

This is not because politicians court the treacherous cross-currents of abortion politics as a promising political issue. Most want nothing to do with the matter. Time and again—in Canada, Holland, Australia, Germany, Ireland, the United States—they have tried to steer clear until the issue seemed too politically dangerous to ignore any longer. Even then they usu-ally try to pass the buck. They argue that abortion is a medical matter which doctors must decide, or a question for the courts to umpire. Some profess it to be a purely moral issue—a question of conscience—not a political mat-ter (Fox and Murphy 1992).

Nowhere has the abortion controversy twisted the tail of national poli-tics more than in Ireland and the United States. In Poland too after the fall of communism it eclipsed the economic upheavals of the fledgling democ-racy (see Chapter 3). In Germany it became so intractable a stumbling block in the political unification, that it seemed as if the entire enterprise would collapse. Twenty-five years ago, as Britain pioneered the first abortion law reform in a democratic state, only the wildest Cassandra could have foreseen such a phenomenon.

The unremitting fury and stridency aroused by abortion in the United States baffles outsiders. Besides the words, a low-intensity civil war has been conducted for almost twenty years, the battleground reaching from the Supreme Court to Congress and the state legislatures, out to the sidewalks outside abortion clinics, where women have been systematically terrorized and, latterly, doctors have been gunned down and killed.

It began in the summer of 1969 when Norma McCorvey became pregnant. She did not belong to any women's organization and was not politically active. She was 21, living in Texas, a divorcee with little money and an unpromising future. Abortion was banned in the state of Texas, except when it was necessary to save the life of the pregnant woman. McCorvey had no money to travel to California or any other state where abortion was available—she was forced to have her baby. The lawyer who arranged for Norma McCorvey's child to be adopted introduced her to two young lawyers, who took up her case. They challenged the constitutionality of the Texan law all the way to the highest court in the United States, the Supreme Court (Craig and O'Brien 1993).

The case is *Roe v. Wade,* a case easily as famous as the trial of O.J. Simpson, and far more significant. There is "probably no decision that has had so profound and pragmatic an impact on women's daily lives" as the case of *Roe v. Wade* (Copelon 1990, p. 34). In court, Norma McCorvey was known only as "Jane Roe." Henry Wade is a real name—of a Dallas county prosecutor, taking on scores of cases for the state of Texas. In 1980, McCorvey revealed her identity, volunteering that she had been gang-raped on her way home. Years later still, she confessed that the gang-rape story was a fabrication— she had merely "gotten into trouble," been unable to face the grim prospect of single parenthood with three children—she already had two—and ashamed to tell the world her real name. Throughout the 1980s, McCorvey worked hard to make abortion services available for other women. She appeared on demonstrations—a loyal symbol of the pro-choice movement— and even worked in a Dallas abortion clinic as the marketing director. But in 1994 Operation Rescue, the fundamentalist anti-abortion group, set up an office next door to the clinic, which it regularly picketed, making Norma McCorvey a special target. In August 1995, McCorvey, now 47, announced that she had become a born-again Christian and had been baptized by none other than Operation Rescue's current leader, Flip Benham. She said "I'm pro-life, I think I've always been pro-life, I just didn't know it," and said she had always felt exploited by the pro-choice lobby.

McCorvey's conversion to the ultra-conservative "born-again" Christian movement has demanded from her more than an about-turn on the abortion question. Until recently, there has not even been that commitment on her part. She still supports, she says, abortion in the first twelve weeks: hardly a dedicated pro-life stance there (Jeffreys 1995). In her personal life, however, the conversion has created turmoil, impelling her to declare that the relationship with her life-long lesbian partner, Connie Gonzales, is now platonic. McCorvey tours the country under Flip Benham's watchful eye, denouncing her former allies and their cause. It remains to be seen whether the legendary intolerance of the anti-abortion movement will provide a safe haven for this former icon of the campaign for safe, legal abortion.

Back in 1973, the case for "Jane Roe" was that making a crime of abortion was a violation of her constitutional right of personal privacy. The judges of the Supreme Court declared that the "right of privacy" in the United States constitution is not only fundamental but is also broad enough to protect the personal decision of whether or not to seek an abortion (or use contraception). They decided by a majority of seven to two to sweep away almost all state laws on abortion. The court also said that the fetus was not a legal person "in the whole sense," and not entitled to the law's protection, at least not for the first twelve weeks of pregnancy.

The ruling did not concede an unqualified right of privacy. It said that once a fetus was "viable" (capable of being born alive), the state could regulate or even ban abortion, provided the life or health of the mother was not in jeopardy (Gold 1990). Ever since, in courtrooms across the nation, the nuances of a "right to privacy" have been challenged, again and again and again.

The court ruled on *Roe v. Wade* on 22 January 1973, the day following the death of former President Lyndon B. Johnson, amid news of possible peace in Vietnam. It was a day which catapulted abortion onto the national political agenda of the United States. Today everyone has a well-rehearsed opinion about abortion, but in the 1960s, the years leading up to *Roe,* campaigners for abortion law reform in California, asking people to sign petitions, had found that no more than four or five names could be gathered in an afternoon, because people took such a long time thinking and talking, to work out where they stood (see sidebar). Before *Roe,* Catholics had assumed

SHERRI FINKBINE

"Baby-deforming Drug May Cost Woman Her Child Here," said the 1962 headlines. The slow-burning fuse towards *Roe v. Wade* may have been lit when Sherri Finkbine needed an abortion. She was the mother of four children under the age of seven. She worked as the host of a children's television program in Arizona and was impeccably married, white, middle-class, and content to be expecting another baby. With her previous pregnancies, she had suffered badly from nausea but this time the symptoms of constant sickness were relieved by the medicine which her husband brought her back from a business trip to Europe.

Then she heard about the deformities in babies whose mothers had taken thalidomide—cases were coming to light in Europe—and discovered what she had taken was thalidomide. Her doctor advised an abortion, and although she did not approve, she booked at her local hospital, with her doctor's recommendation. A hospital committee had to approve each request for abortion and the committees' interpretations of the law varied widely across the country. In some, opponents of abortion put every request under the microscope, putting the strictest construction on what threatened a woman's life. Others were far more lenient. Finkbine's request was approved. As the day for Sherri Finkbine's abortion approached, she worried that other women might be as ignorant of the horrors of thalidomide as she was. She called the newspapers and explained what had happened to her. Alarmed by the publicity, the hospital canceled her abortion, because in the strict eyes of Arizona law, Finkbine's life was not in any danger.

Sherri Finkbine did not get her abortion in the United States—she had to go to Sweden. Her case strengthened the reformers' case for abortion to be legal on the grounds of fetal abnormality and quietly began the public debate about abortion.

Source: Luker 1984, Chapter 3.

that everyone shared their moral abhorrence of abortion precisely because there was no public debate about it. But *Roe v. Wade* made abortion "a public and moral issue of nationwide concern" in an entirely new way, questioning a deeply held set of beliefs held by people accustomed to thinking theirs was the majority opinion. "A day of infamy," is how the opponents of abortion recall that 1973 January day. Overnight, the opposition mobilized, and people who had never joined an organization in their lives flocked to protest against the court's decision.

The 1970s was a period of increasing conservatism in the United States. The goal of overturning *Roe v. Wade*—a woman's right to abortion—gave the forces loosely known as the New Right something positive to fight for— a Manichean struggle between good and evil. "The politics of the family, sexuality and reproduction—and, most symbolically, of abortion, became a primary vehicle through which right-wing politicians sought to achieve state power in the late 1970s and the 1980 elections" (Petchesky 1984, p. 242). The ultra-conservative campaigners appealed to Christian fundamentalists to vote for candidates solely on their attitude to abortion, in order to get them behind the tough Republican campaign. The burgeoning far right of the Republican Party was also happy to stir up other fears about the moral and social order of the United States harbored by many opponents of abortion. A sample appeal for funds in 1976 urged supporters to dig deep to reform a political order in which, they said, "your tax dollars are being used for grade school courses that teach our children that *cannibalism, wife-swapping* and the *murder* of infants and the elderly are acceptable behavior" (McKeegan 1992, p. 9). They saw the federal government as a supine accomplice of policies such as no prayer in schools, busing programs and welfare handouts for single mothers. Their New Right policies added up to a frontal assault on feminism, driving women back towards their traditional roles in a male-dominated, private domain, untrammeled by state "interference" (Petchesky 1984, p. 247).

Gradually the New Right, including the anti-abortion lobby, established and consolidated the power base which, in 1980, brought them into the White House itself with their champion, Ronald Reagan, elected president for the first time.[1] Since the 1980s the "born-again" fundamentalist Christian sects have been as militant and visible among US anti-abortion activists as Roman Catholics, but it was the Catholic Church which was first into action after *Roe*. It poured millions of dollars into setting up campaigning groups, such as the National Right to Life Committee, which held its first national convention, in Detroit, just six months after the Supreme Court announcement. What aroused the evangelical section of the population, which saw the growing threats of gay rights, women's equality, and abortion as inextricably linked, were liberal attempts to amend the constitution in the late 1970s with an Equal Rights Amendment. In 1979, Jerry Falwell founded the misleadingly named Moral Majority, on a "pro-life, pro-family, pro-moral and pro-American," platform, of which the center-piece was abortion. According to political analyst Michele McKeegan, "no other social issue had the political potential to galvanize the evangelical Protestants" (McKeegan 1992, p. 21).

The anti-abortion lobby in Congress first tested its political muscle in 1977 with the Hyde amendments (named after a then-novice congressman,

Henry Hyde). Hyde and his allies said abortion was immoral and it was therefore wrong for taxpayers' money to be used to promulgate immorality. Hyde did not expect to do more than test the strength of anti-abortion feeling, but his amendments were passed—after intense and prolonged debate in Congress. They banned the use of Medicaid funding (paid for with federal money) for almost all abortions, including some deemed necessary by doctors, such as abortions for fetal abnormality. Around a third of all legal abortions had been funded in this way since *Roe,* but now not even a woman whose pregnancy would cause long-lasting and severe damage to her physical health could get an abortion paid for out of federal funds. The Hyde amendment painfully exposed the fragility of *Roe,* which granted the "private" right to abortion, "but no more required the state to fund abortions than the right to bear arms obliged it to make guns freely available" (Brodie 1994, p. 136).

Hyde's opponents countered that refusing poor women abortions would drive them deeper into poverty and welfare eligibility and it was wrong to make constitutional rights subject to ability to pay.[2] Bluntly, if you can't afford an abortion, they said, it may as well be illegal. But memories of anti-Vietnam liberals arguing that tax dollars should not be used to finance napalm bombing in a war they held to be immoral were fresh in everyone's mind. It was hard for *Roe*'s defenders to make inroads on the case against "immorality." Many members of Congress were also realizing that they were under close political watch from their constituencies and many no doubt hoped that even if Congress approved the Medicaid ban, the Supreme Court would throw the regulation out and do the dirty work for them. On this crucial public health issue, the American Medical Association and the American College of Obstetricians and Gynecologists remained disgracefully silent.

It seems ironic and illogical to find the New Right prohibiting Medicaid from paying for poor women to have abortions, when a central element of its mission is to reduce welfare handouts to single mothers. For in 1978 alone an estimated 20,000 indigent women were compelled to undergo births they would otherwise have terminated with Medicaid abortions (Sommers and Thomas 1983, pp. 340–6). It has also been estimated that every dollar of taxpayers' money spent on abortion for low-income women could avert four dollars of public spending in just the first two years after birth (Torres et al. 1986, p. 111; Donovan 1995). But cutting Medicaid was the thin end of a potent *ideological* wedge, not only undermining the feminist notion that women's right to abortion is fundamental, but also hammering out the vital political message of the New Right coalition, that there is a moral (as opposed to a fiscal) argument for cutting spending on social services. Hyde's amendments successfully tapped into a vein in "middle ground" public thinking, that women should not be allowed to "get away" with something (that is, sex) and expect a "free ride." It was this argument, more than the killing of fetuses, that made it hard to oppose Hyde, especially for any politicians uncomfortably aware that they were seen as unfashionably "soft" on welfare issues.

Reagan and the New Right

But neither religious fervor nor political expediency is enough to explain the remarkable pressure and momentum which built up behind the "pro-life, pro-family" movement. The New Right is a conservative response to the personal fears evinced in a great many Americans—male and female—by fast-emerging social changes, such as increased economic independence for women. When people are feeling dislocate—worrying about growing evidence of teenage sexuality, the loss of traditional motherhood roles within the "protection of the family," fearing that homosexuality and feminism will wipe out the "differences" between women and men—the promise of a politics of moral absolutism (offering itself as essentially patriotic) as a counter to "godless liberal [treacherous] philosophies" is highly attractive.[3] Coalitions of disparate groups worked together in the 1980 elections. To oppose senior Democratic Senator McGovern in South Dakota, for instance, antiabortion groups took part in a coalition which also included the National Conservative Political Action Committee, Committee for the Survival of a Free Congress, Eagle Forum, John Birch Society, Gun Owners of America, Committee to Defeat Union Bosses, and the Committee to Save the Panama Canal. But among them all it was the anti-abortion groups, with their plastic fetal models and their "righteous fire," which attracted most of the television coverage and newspaper inches. The bewildering power of the single-issue voters (that is, people prepared to back a candidate *solely* on whether he/she opposes abortion) to sway the outcome of elections, at whatever level, is partly due to the fact that very few people actually bother to go to the polls in the United States. Scrutiny of votes, where turnout, even in presidential elections, averages a scant 40 per cent, accords the single-issue voting block the power to determine the results by tiny critical margins.[4]

The 1980 Republican convention fulfilled the far right's wildest dreams for a moral offensive and an anti-social welfare backlash. It lambasted the Equal Rights Amendment, condemned the spending of public money on abortion, and with the election of Ronald Reagan the anti-abortion advocates gained open access to the White House. The Christian fundamentalists had helped to elect Ronald Reagan largely on the promise that he would change the composition of the Supreme Court in order to throw out *Roe*. As the 1980s dawned, and their true friend Ronald Reagan entered the White House for the first time, things could not have looked rosier.

Reagan made abortion irrevocably part of presidential politics. He crudely embellished his anti-abortion rhetoric with a gloss of patriotism. He wrote a book, *Abortion and the Conscience of the Nation*—with a foreword by one of the architects of Britain's moral backlash, Malcolm Muggeridge (Reagan 1984). And he urged Americans to ban abortion because "it debases the underpinnings of our country" (Craig and O'Brien 1993, p. 170). At the annual "March for Life" demonstrations, Reagan rallied the anti-abortion troops. He was pointedly tardy in condemning the growing violence against abortion clinics.

The 1980s backlash against the gains of feminism and women's reproductive freedom has been exhaustively charted elsewhere—notably in Susan Faludi's book *Backlash* (Faludi 1992). By the end of the decade the courts at all levels were dominated by judges appointed for their readiness to turn back the clock on abortion rights.[5] By making views on abortion a litmus test for all senior government appointments, Ronald Reagan and his successor George Bush ensured that their staunchly anti-abortion officials would harass reproductive health care programs and starve them of funds. When Marjorie Mecklenberg was appointed head of the Office of Family Planning, she was asked how she would handle the problem of teenage pregnancy. Teenagers should "postpone sexual involvement" was her answer. Things came a little unstuck with the report on abortion by Surgeon-General Everett Koop, Reagan's top public health official. Koop, a Reagan appointee precisely on account of his ardent opposition to abortion, had been commanded by the president to investigate the health consequences of abortion. In the anti-abortion camp it was confidently expected that his report could be used as scientific ammunition against *Roe*. But Koop fulfilled his brief in strict medical terms and reported that, in his professional judgment, the risk to women's health was "minuscule" (See Chapter 3).

Abortion, nonetheless, was hemmed in by God's bullies on all sides. Susan Faludi, for instance, reports the fate of a script for the television show

Cagney and Lacey. In "Choices," as the early 1980s' episode was to be called, Cagney—the single woman in the feisty female cop duo—becomes pregnant. CBS programming executives went berserk at the mere idea of abortion (even as an option to be rejected). They demanded numerous rewrites until, in the final version, Cagney only mistakenly thinks she is pregnant. "Lacey . . . tells her that if she had been pregnant she should have got married. Abortion is never offered as a choice" (Faludi 1992, p. 186).

Election candidates could not escape an inquisition on their stance on abortion, whether they were aiming to be president, state governor or simply to chair the local school board. Anti-abortion single-issue voters are now an expected occupational hazard for politicians at every level. Republican Senator Robert Packwood, a veteran defender of abortion, sees them as "a frightening force . . . They are people who are with you 99 per cent of the time, but if you vote against them on this issue it doesn't matter what else you stand for" (Tribe 1992, p. 150). Through single-issue voting, the anti-abortion movement built up majorities in many states and restrictions on abortion became more and more boldly challenging to the basic principles of *Roe.* It was only a matter of time, seasoned observers reasoned, before the Supreme Court finally jettisoned *Roe* altogether.

In 1988, however, after two terms of office, Reagan's presidency itself had not actually delivered much, at least not to the satisfaction of the militant wing of the anti-abortion movement. Operation Rescue and other direct-action organizations were a frustrated response to what the extremists saw as establishment pussy-footing. They pointed out that women were still obtaining abortions (at much the same rate from about 1980 onwards). Prospects did not improve when Reagan was succeeded in the White House by his former vice-president, George Bush. Not only was Bush a far less skilled polemicist than his former boss, but many anti-abortion activists could not forget the days when George Bush had been known as a defender of *Roe v. Wade.*

Fissures began to appear in the anti-abortion movement's pact with the Republican Party. The coalition of secular right-wingers, eager to reduce state intervention, with the anti-abortion moral absolutists, anxious to stem the tide of moral decline, was proving a volatile mixture for Republicanism. There were many Catholics, including the powerful bishops, who were not the Republicans' natural allies on questions of social justice and welfare. Catholics and non-Catholics alike were disturbed by the obtrusive crisis of homelessness in the streets and a feeling that welfare cuts were perhaps too heartlessly cavalier towards the vulnerable and poor. The picket-line aggression outside clinics and the increasing resort to vandalism, arson and bombing were alienating many moderate Republicans, especially women. The Republican Party was beginning to see that by courting the anti-abortion votes, it had become hostage to the Christian Right, and that this might well prove an electoral millstone.

It was the Supreme Court's turn to enter abortion politics yet again, and while Bush was in the White House two judgments—*Webster v. Reproductive Health Services* and *Planned Parenthood of Southeastern Pennsylvania v. Casey*—dramatically turned the political weathercock. *Webster* featured a law enacted in Missouri which, among other things, stated that life begins at conception, and prohibited abortion in all public institutions. The Supreme Court dismissed the challenge that such restrictions were in conflict with *Roe,* and by giving *Webster* its seal of approval the court all but withdrew its protection of the constitutional right to abortion (Tribe 1992, pp. 173–91). Emboldened by this judicial invitation, a number of states revived the harshest nineteenth-century laws. Louisiana, for instance, made abortion illegal except to save the mother's life, or after rape, provided it was reported within a week, with a punishment of up to $100,000 and ten years' hard labor. It made Romania's anti-abortion law look lenient by comparison.

After *Webster* there was jubilation in the anti-abortion camp. *Roe*'s days were surely numbered, the leaders happily assured the media. Such celebration was a profound tactical blunder, and the "pro-choice" lobby saw its chance to make people realize at last that abortion rights were on the ropes. The National Abortion Rights Action League (NARAL) warned, "The Court has left a woman's right to privacy hanging by a thread and passed the scissors to the state legislatures." Indeed in only nine states were both houses of the legislature in favor of protecting access to abortion (Tribe 1992, p. 178). The streets were filled with marchers defending abortion rights. "Take our rights, lose your job," they warned their representatives, and many Republicans took stock, seeing that the hardline stance on abortion could now be their undoing. It had always been uphill work for even the most loyal Republican to explain the pitiless measure of denying poor women abortions on Medicaid, even for health reasons, and increasingly people's imaginations were turning to the crisis of the unwillingly pregnant poor woman. As one (Republican) congresswoman put it: "Those who are helpless are condemned." After years of annually rubber-stamping the ban on Medicaid funding Congress suddenly agreed to allow Medicaid funding after rape or incest. When George Bush threatened to veto the amended bill, the party rift exploded.

As jockeying began for the 1992 presidential elections, abortion was causing trouble not only for the Republicans but left, right and center. In elections for state congresses at least ten anti-abortion Republican candidates ran television advertisements containing photos of bloodied fetuses, which appeared in the middle of sports programs and even cartoons. And at the Republican convention the hardliners swept the field, voting overwhelmingly to ban abortion, even for victims of rape or incest. Good news for hardliners. But in the same week the president's wife, Barbara Bush, told *Newsweek* that she considered abortion to be a "personal choice." Also, party funds were feeling the pinch because moderate Republican wives, offended by the extremism of the right-to-lifers, were damagingly persuading their wealthy husbands not to donate to party coffers. Not such good news for hardliners. But party strategists also feared that going "soft" on abortion would drive many of their single-issue supporters "back to voting their economic interests, which are decidedly not Republican," (McKeegan 1992, p. 174). Republicans soldiered on, endorsing a regulation, known as the "gag rule," which forbade staff in all federally funded family planning clinics not only from referring women for abortions, but from even mentioning it as an option. The symbolism of the gag rule, in a country which attaches so much symbolic importance to free speech, was not lost on the Democratic campaign. The Democratic presidential contestant, Governor Bill Clinton of Arkansas, played his hand in April by attending a 500,000 strong "pro-choice" rally in Washington.

With only a few months to go before the presidential election, the Supreme Court's June 1992 ruling on *Casey* hardly extricated Bush. The court did not, as some had expected, finally dismantle *Roe* but it sanctioned states to create a further raft of restrictions, provided they did not impose an "undue burden" on a woman seeking abortion. The criteria for an "undue burden" appeared to be something that a well-heeled middle-class woman would not find too irksome.[6]

Clinton:
A "Pro-choice" President?

Clinton became president and abortion rights advocates held their breath. For the first time in twelve years, there was a president not threatening to make abortion illegal. His "pro-choice" record was far from unsullied—he had approved Arkansas state curbs on abortion for minors and opposed

Medicaid-funded abortion. Nonetheless, he had cautiously ventured that abortions should be "safe, legal and *rare*" (my emphasis), and in January 1993, within days of taking office, Clinton demonstrated a clear break with the past. He lifted the gag rule and the ban on abortion in US military hospitals, he ordered a review of the medical evidence on the "abortion pill," RU 486, and also did away with the policy which had crippled US overseas-aid funding of abortion—the "Mexico City policy."[7]

And that was about all. Although the White House announced that the flagship of Clinton's election campaign, the promised health-insurance reform, would contain provision for abortion, by the end of 1994 the health reform had come to nothing. The anti-abortion groups had vowed to torpedo it, but it had other equally powerful enemies. The president's main achievement on abortion was the Freedom of Access to Clinic Entrances Act, which made it an offense to obstruct or threaten to use force against women entering clinics.

Merely having Clinton in the White House was enough for the anti-abortion camp to feel that its crusade was all but lost. Militants stepped up the violence. Within two months of the Clinton presidency, the first death occurred among abortion-clinic doctors, and within the next two years the death toll rose to five and violence against clinics escalated. Firms supplying bullet-proof windows were busier than ever, meeting clinic requirements.

Clinton might at least have been expected to lend some muscle to getting rid of the notorious Hyde amendment, but he remained silent when moves were made in Congress to achieve this, plainly hoping to avoid the quicksands of abortion politics. In 1995, the bungled nomination of Dr. Henry Foster as Surgeon-General—the US chief medical officer—demonstrated how even the wariest politician could be ensnared by it.

Foster, a black 61-year-old Tennessee obstetrician-gynecologist had devised a nationally acclaimed health education programmed to discourage pregnancy among teenagers, which preaches sexual abstinence, personal responsibility and esteem. He was nominated to replace the controversial Jocelyn Elders, dubbed the "condom queen" for her forthright advice on safer sex. Clinton sacked Elders for publicly speculating about the public health merits of teaching schoolchildren about masturbation. If there was one thing he was anxious for after that furor, it was a "safe pair of hands."

Foster looked squeaky clean, but the "gynecologist" tag should have been enough to set warning lights flashing to the White House vetting staff. For the very first question the press asked about Foster was, how many abortions has he performed? A hapless White House spokesman hazarded, "about a dozen in his entire career . . . almost all in cases of rape or incest or where the mother's life had been threatened." With predictable glee, the anti-abortion lobby excavated the record of a 1978 meeting in which Foster admitted around 700 abortions. With the further revelation that he had also sterilized a number of severely retarded women in the 1970s, the White House ordered a full FBI check on decades of Foster's medical records and a delay in seeking Senate confirmation of the appointment. A furious Clinton blamed sloppy White House staff for the mess (Turque and Cohn 1995). Three months later, with would-be Republican presidential candidates vying to outstrip each other in their public displays of anti-abortion zealotry, Dr. Foster was a dead duck.

The Foster fiasco was not without some comfort for Clinton. It took place in the spring of 1995, with the 1996 election campaign thundering over the horizon, reawakening the Republican Party's internal feud—between the standard-bearers of moral absolutism and the more pragmatic Republicans, who blamed abortion and the religious ultra-conservatives for derailing them in 1992.

Throughout 1994 and 1995, the Republican Party stressed how keenly it wished to avoid divisions on abortion. In the party's high councils, it was agreed that the wrathful biblical tones of the 1992 Republican convention—such as the speeches of television evangelist Pat Robertson—may have cost George Bush the election and now the right-to-life should take second place to simply getting back into power. "The political situation has changed in this country," declared Bush's former vice-president Dan Quayle as he hopefully eyed the presidential nomination for 1996. "There is not the political support to make abortion illegal, so we should focus on reducing the number and we want to change attitudes" (Walker 1994). Around the time of Quayle's speech, Nancy Reagan, the former first lady, said on a public platform, "I don't believe in abortion. On the other hand I believe in a woman's choice. So it puts me somewhere in the middle." And after sweeping Republican victories in the congressional mid-term elections of 1994, which propelled the house speaker, Republican Newt Gingrich, into apparently almost as powerful a position as the president, the Republican's legislative blitz on federal welfare spending—*Contract with America*—was notably silent on abortion as such. But the issue surfaced anyway, when the Catholic bishops condemned the *Contract*'s plans to stop welfare payments for children born to single mothers already receiving federal support. The bishops said such a cut would pressure women towards abortion. How such abortions would be paid for, with the Hyde amendment still in place, the bishops did not speculate.[8]

1996: Republicans Divided over Abortion

In 1996, with the race for the White House fully underway, no other issue was as contentious or divisive for the Republican Party. Hopes of avoiding the potentially lethal splits of 1992 had been moondust. In the wake of the 1994 congressional elections, it was clear that the powerful Christian Coalition—founded by Pat Robertson to infuse Christian values into Republican politics—wanted its reward for sending God's battalions out to vote Republican. Evangelical Christians make up 42 per cent of Republican primary voters.

Senate leader Robert Dole, the lackluster front-runner for the Republican nomination, tried to square the wheel, to steer a course that would satisfy both the anti-abortion social conservatives and also the more moderate wing of his party. It was an impossible feat, as his fire and brimstone rival for the nomination, former White House speech writer for presidents Nixon and Reagan, Pat Buchanan, was ever ready to point out. But if Dole is perceived as giving the merest hint of compromising his party's anti-abortion stance, he knows he risks the loss of the well-drilled, single-issue voters who decide their voting preference solely on the abortion question. There are clear threats that if Republican pursuit of "pro-life" policy wavers, the implacable Christian soldiers may well defect.

They may have a ready-made political home in the U.S. Taxpayers Party (USTP), whose platform combines radical libertarianism, obscure conspiracy theories, militant opposition to abortion and some whose world view includes the conviction that Reagan's White House was full of Trotskyists. Their simple goal is abolition of the state and its replacement by biblical law. The USTP already embraces Operation Rescue founder Randall Terry and Matthew Trewhella, leader of the anti-abortion armed militia, Missionaries to the Pre-Born (see Chapter 9), and its very existence is a pressure on the Republicans.[9]

The so-called "partial-birth" controversy, which kept abortion sensationally in the media spotlight throughout the winter of 1995–96, may well have been part of the Republican Party's game plan to keep the God-fearing militants within the fold. The medical term—dilatation and extraction—for this extremely rare late-term abortion procedure was ditched by the anti-abortion campaigners in favor of "partial birth," a far more jarring concept. It seemed for a while as if President Clinton, severely hampered in his political agenda by the right-wing Congress, might use the powers available to him to thwart the bill.

The early pro-choice gestures of the presidency were almost all eroded or reversed by the Republican-driven congressional juggernaut as Clinton sacrificed them to purchase Congress' support for other policies (see below). Having a Democrat in the White House certainly did nothing to reverse the fact that 83 per cent of counties in the United States have no abortion provider, despite containing nearly one third of women between 15 and 44 (Alan Guttmacher Institute 1993). But eventually, faced with clear opposition from defenders of abortion and from organizations such as the American College of Obstetrics and Gynecology, Clinton changed his mind and vetoed the bill, calculating that in doing so he would deepen the rift within the Republican Party. The nation's Catholic cardinals, whose other concerns, such as welfare and immigration, incline them to support Clinton, at once threatened to make their outrage a public issue among Roman Catholic voters.

Whatever gains the Republican Party may have calculated on making from the "partial-birth" issue, the grandees and senior advisers within the party had not forgotten the lesson of 1992, when strident anti-abortion fanaticism had cost the party the White House. The fact is that abortion is as potent a vote-loser as a vote-winner, as the primaries showed in state after state in 1996. Among Republican voters, almost half actually favor tolerance of abortion and leaving the decision up to a woman and her doctor.[10] The more ground the Republican mainstream concedes to the Christian Coalition, the easier it is for the Democrats to convince moderate Republican voters that the party is hostage to a bigoted fringe, who imply that women who demand equality are violating their fundamental natures and every woman who has an abortion is a murderer (Quindlen 1994).

The Christian Coalition's ferocious grip on the Republican Party has showed little sign of loosening: rumors of a retreat from the demand for a constitutional amendment were swiftly denied. Even if the constitutional amendment were not pursued—it has after all been Republican policy since 1976—pro-choice observers view the possibility of a Republican victory as a dim prospect for women seeking abortions in the United States.

Thanks to the tireless grassroots organizing of the Christian Coalition, single-issue voting is still reliably delivering anti-abortion state governors and anti-abortion majorities in state legislatures. And thanks to *Casey,* local legislatures have free rein to block access to abortion.[11] In Congress, the Republicans are pushing almost a score of bills aimed at virtually eliminating abortion in practice while leaving it constitutionally intact. There with be more twenty-four-hour and even forty-eight-hour waiting periods, more "informed consent" requirements, designed to intimidate, together with all manner of restrictions devised to make abortion as unobtainable as possible and to "chip away" at what the anti-abortion movement regards as the liberal abortion culture. The Republicans have promised to halt efforts to get FDA approval for the drugs needed for medical abortion in the United States (see Chapter 7) and to reinstate the gag rule, which forbade abortion counselling in publicly funded family planning clinics. And once again, as under presidents Reagan and Bush, only people hostile to abortion will succeed in being appointed to sit as judges in the Supreme Court. And the prospect of a second term for Clinton raises little more than two cheers, judging by his highly flexible "defense" of abortion rights from 1992 to 1996. The self-styled "pro-choice president" has already approved a ban on abortion as a health benefit for federal employees, and a fresh ban on abortions in overseas military hospitals. He also signed a "compromise" reduction of overseas aid funding for family planning, cutting the budget from $546 million in 1995 to $72 million in 1996. How cutting the budget for contraception would meet the goals of those wishing to eliminate abortion is a mystery. What's more, when veteran anti-abortion campaigner Henry Hyde revived the infamous Comstock Act of 1873 (used to prosecute the pioneers of the birth control movement) in an obscure section of the 1996 Telecommunications Act, to criminalize sending or receiving information about many aspects of abortion on the Internet, Clinton mutely approved the gagging measure.

The newest tactic in anti-abortion campaigning is an organization called Life-Dynamics, which organizes malpractice suits against abortion-clinic doctors. Its stated aim is "to force abortionists out of business by driving up their insurance rates." Even if a case is never won, the mere fact of the claim may make the doctors claimed against look like an insurance risk, and drive up premiums of their professional indemnity to such a point that they cannot continue to practice.

Meanwhile violence against clinics and providers of abortion services is undiminished, with death threats on the increase as a strategy of terror.[12]

And the tragedies roll on. In Florida, a young woman is facing charges after shooting herself in the stomach when six months pregnant, because she could not afford an abortion. The charge may be murder, it may be manslaughter, because although the shooting did not mortally wound the fetus, it was delivered and died two weeks later, from lung and kidney failure. The case of this young woman, Kawana Ashley, is dragging almost every aspect of the pro-choice/anti-abortion argument into a grotesque legal slanging match. Whatever one might say about the narrow pigeon-holing of these questions into courtroom semantics—"Is it murder?" "Does she have a 'right' to shoot herself when pregnant?"—the case is a blazing indictment of the failure to provide public funding and facilities for early, safe abortions (Hunt 1995).

The law's hounding of this desperate young woman bleakly symbolizes the effects of the inward-looking parochialism which characterizes the ever more bizarre "abortion debate" in the United States. The story of U.S. abortion politics, threading its way through this book, can only be told to mid-1996, with a presidential campaign in full swing. But whoever wins, in 1996, in 2000, in 2004, there seems little hope that the arguments for and against abortion, as presented to the American public, will ever reach beyond the chauvinistic, parish-pump mentality to witness and comprehend the reality of eliminating legal abortion, as has happened in Poland, and is the case for more than a quarter of the world's population beyond American borders.

2

Ireland and Germany: Constitutional Brutality and Legal Twilight

THROUGHOUT 1992, after the Irish High Court banned a raped 14-year-old girl from travelling abroad for an abortion, the *Irish Times* published hundreds of intense letters on the rights and wrongs of abortion. When the Irish Supreme Court gave its judgment in May 1995 on whether or not it was constitutional for women to be given addresses of abortion agencies in England, the Irish newspapers printed every word of the judgment, over several pages. Irish politics has been transfixed by the abortion question—resulting in unparalleled displays of political chicanery. In Germany, not only was the unification process placed in jeopardy by the abortion feud, but the precariously unified nation continued to be divided over the matter for almost four years.

Ireland: The Silent Export

Abortion is a reality in Ireland today. "A pregnancy which was conceived in Ireland, agonized over in Ireland, but terminated in England, is without doubt, an Irish abortion," said Tony O'Brien, former director of the Irish Family Planning Association. Every year thousands of pregnant Irish women muster their courage and scrape together the money to take the ferryboat, to "visit relatives" over in England.[1] They call it the silent export. There is no typical case: the women range from 16 to 40, some married, some not. They travel silently and usually alone, in every sense of that word. They must tell lies or remain mute about their journey, for they cannot speak safely to anyone. The sense of guilt is so great for some women, steeped in the legacy of hell-fire sermons against the sin of abortion, and remembering the images of the anti-abortion film *The Silent Scream,* shown to them in school science lessons, that they sometimes ask the English clinic to perform the operation without pain-killer, as punishment. The caul of enforced silence exacerbates the guilt and shame within. If a parish priest should discover what they have done, it could affect every aspect of their lives—the chance to send their children to a local school, to get a job, even to be admitted to hospital. Yet to hear the churchmen, jurists and politicians of Ireland arguing about abortion, such women and their experiences count for nothing. The focal point of all debate is the fetus and its value. That is what lies at the roots of the "X" case crisis, which exploded over an already highly volatile Irish political scene early in 1992 and gripped Ireland throughout the year. The shock waves caused legal mayhem and political instability, which even threatened the nation's participation in the European Community. In its midst stood a convent-educated, 14-year-old girl from a law-abiding and devoutly Catholic family, living in a well-to-do Dublin suburb.

The girl had been raped by the father of her best friend, who had been sexually abusing her since she was 12 years old.[2] In great distress the girl finally confided in her parents, telling them over and over that she must have an abortion. After much heartsearching they agreed that they would take her to London to terminate the pregnancy. But first they went guilelessly to the Irish police, the Gardai, explained that they were going to England for an abortion and inquired if they should request DNA analysis on the fetal tissue, which would prove the culprit's paternity and minimize the trauma for their child of a rape trial. The police conferred but said that such evidence would probably be ruled inadmissible in court, so the family quietly departed for London.

But, in the course of seeking guidance on the DNA question, the police had notified the Irish attorney-general's office of the family's plans. The attorney-general decided to seek an interim injunction in the Irish High Court, restraining the girl from seeking an abortion in England. When the injunction was granted it referred to the Irish constitution, which since 1983 had defined abortion as an unconstitutional act. It was from then on a case of real life versus the law.

The abortion had not yet been performed when the police broke the news to the girl's father in London. The officer explained simply, "You have to come home." Flouting the order could mean jail or an immediate fine. On the return journey, the girl threatened to throw herself under a London tube train. A full High Court hearing was scheduled, to decide whether it was indeed the attorney-general's constitutional duty to prevent an Irish fetus being legally and safely aborted in a British clinic. A journalist caught wind of the story. On 12 February, a shocked Irish public learned that in 1983 it had passed a law which required a raped child to be treated in this way.

Surely, people asked themselves, the 1983 anti-abortion amendment loftily reflected a national aspiration? Guaranteeing the rights of the fetus under the constitution was admirable, but it was never meant to sanction such legalized torture and flint-hearted cruelty? Most of the mail to the *Irish Times* spoke of horror at Ireland's "descent into cruelty." But at the full High Court hearing, despite expert evidence that the girl's mental health would be devastated if the pregnancy continued, Justice Costello ruled that the girl must continue to be pregnant and must not leave Ireland for nine months. He considered that any risk of the girl's suicide was "much less and of a different order of magnitude" than the certainty "that the life of the unborn will be terminated."

Many ardent anti-abortion activists, who had campaigned so hard for the 1983 amendment, were as appalled as anyone by the attorney-general's action. Could he not have lost the file, asked one anti-abortion campaigner, or performed some legal alchemy to ward off this crisis? The wave of public sympathy for the girl looked unmistakably like a threat to Ireland's staunch consensus against abortion. Throughout the 1980s, using the 1983 amendment, voted for by a two-to-one referendum majority, the anti-abortion lobby had set in train a carousel of court cases, harrying anything and anyone trying to help Irish women needing abortion. But they had always accepted, tacitly and hypocritically, that abortion was available in England and it was a shock to find the law now being used to prevent someone travelling.

Ireland's prime minister, Albert Reynolds, who had only been in office a few days, found his government embroiled in a legal and political morass—the stuff of politicians's nightmares. Nothing, of course, to compare with the nightmare of the girl herself, a prisoner in her own land. Her lawyers, having decided to appeal on her behalf to Ireland's Supreme Court, found themselves having to become experts on abortion law, the Irish constitution and even European regulations on citizens' rights to travel and obtain services in other member countries.

The 1983 amendment to the constitution, Article 40.3.3. stated:

The state acknowledges the right to life of the unborn, and, with due regard to the equal right to life of the mother, guarantees in its laws to respect, and as far as practicable by its laws to defend and vindicate that right.

(HOLDEN 1994, p. 30)

Now those words were being tested to their limits. In their sympathy for the girl, people realized what a black-white code on abortion they had voted for. Men and women looked at their daughters, nieces, sisters, who could now be imprisoned in the constitution of Ireland: "If 'X' was my daughter . . ." they said to each other, and saw that abortion was not that simple. Meanwhile the alleged rapist, out on bail, was free to come and go as he pleased. On every street corner in the early spring of 1992, Irish people debated the issue. One commentator observed the mood of the time as "Ireland riveted by its own barbarism." Foreign commentators compared Ireland to the Iran of the ayatollahs—cruel and despotic. The absolutist position seemed coldly indifferent to the trauma of the girl in the "X" case. As the country waited for the case to be heard in the Supreme Court, there were growing calls for a new abortion referendum.

Back in 1983 the campaign for Article 40.3.3. had been marked by "unprecedented levels of bitterness, bigotry, intimidation and raw emotionalism." People compared it to a civil war.[3] According to the anti-abortion lobby, a vote against the constitutional amendment would be nothing less than a vote in favor of killing babies (and probably chopping them up too, if the propaganda pictures were to be believed). It had appealed to people to "prevent the direct and deliberate killing of individual, unique, human beings." The amendment was packaged as a pre-emptive vote against the contaminating tide of foreign liberalism. Even sex education was denounced as an "alien philosophy." Women's groups and other opponents of the clause had warned that its "flabby, imprecise and dangerous wording" could be used to infringe personal liberty.[4] But as narrow-minded Catholicism rallied, Article 40.3.3 was carried by a two-to-one majority, and Ireland became the only country to have voted a ban on abortion into its constitution.

Oddly, the Pro-Life Amendment Campaign took pains to tell everyone that Article 40.3.3. would change nothing. It certainly did not stem the flow of women crossing the Irish Sea to British abortion clinics (Conlon 1994).

A few months after the vote, a newborn child and her 15-year-old mother died in a wintry field, after a birth of unimaginable, lonely terror. No one knew she was pregnant.

For almost ten years, Ireland's ultra-conservatives, operating from their shadowy world of secret societies, hounded a range of counselling organizations and others, dragging them through the courts in the name of Article 40.3.3. One such case brought by Ireland's Society for the Protection of the Unborn Child (SPUC), led to the closure of one counselling center for pregnant women and an end to counselling activities in another. No one was sure what the amendment really meant. The High Court declared that non-directive counselling was illegal, because it infringed the constitutional rights of the unborn. The issue of whether women could be prevented from leaving the country to seek legal abortions abroad was already raising its head, as perplexed and frustrated judges tried to weigh the equal rights of fetus and mother. The centers' lawyers had argued that under European law, a person had an absolute right to go to another country for services which were legal there, and if they had a right to services then they also had a right to information about such services (O'Reilly 1992, pp. 110–19).

As a result of court wrangles such as these, student unions in Dublin were forbidden to include abortion information in their handbooks. Public libraries even agonized over removing their London telephone directories from public display. Adverts for abortion advice or clinics in Britain had to be censored from the pages of *Cosmopolitan* magazine before it could be sold on Irish bookstalls. *Our Bodies, Ourselves,* a respected women's health guide, could not be sold in Ireland because it mentioned abortion. Radio and television stations sought costly legal advice on what they could and could not discuss on air. The big court cases, meanwhile, sluggishly worked their way to the European Court of Human Rights and the Court of Justice, where the labyrinth of regulations was expensively traced and retraced by the lawyers.

In December 1991, in the same month that the girl in the "X" case was raped by her friend's father in his car in Rathmines Park, Dublin, the government of Ireland, together with eleven other European nations, signed the historic Maastricht Treaty, aimed at bring the European Community member states closer together. Irish law demanded that the treaty had to be ratified by a referendum of Irish voters and this was scheduled for June 1992. But no one had reckoned on the "X" case, which brought the most bizarre twist yet to the stew of European affairs and Irish abortion politics, when it dragged the secret Maastricht "protocol" on abortion into the limelight.

For hardly anyone in Ireland, not even the parliamentary opposition, knew that the Irish anti-abortion lobby had secretly engineered the insertion into the treaty of a sort of "electric fence" around Ireland's abortion laws, in which the European Community promised that it could never override these particular laws. Had it not been for the case of *The State v. Miss X,* Irish people might never have known about the secret protocol and how it consigned Irish women forever to fewer rights than other female Europeans.

But because the attorney-general's lawyers mentioned the protocol in court while seeking their injunction against "X," the fate of Ireland in Europe and the issue of abortion became inextricable. Throughout 1992 the government floundered, trying to save its skin and the Maastricht Treaty by appeasing its extreme anti-abortion right wing, while having to face a reopening of the abortion debate in the most harrowing and urgent circumstances. Trying to get itself off the hook it first implored the "X" case family, reluctant for further public trauma, to appeal to the Supreme Court for the injunction to be lifted. It announced it would pay their legal costs. A government which only weeks before had pressed for the secret Maastricht protocol to prevent Irish women ever having abortions, now appeared desperate to spirit a pregnant young woman to England for an abortion. The Supreme Court, preparing to hear the "X" case appeal, picked up the urgent drift on the political airwaves. It released the girl from the injunction. Miss "X" could quietly leave the political bullring and end her pregnancy.[5]

The government may have expected comfort from the Supreme Court, but its final judgment in March 1992 merely impaled the politicians on the horns of a fresh dilemma. The court explained to an astonished Irish public that some abortions were now legal in Ireland—and the raped girl could have hers in Ireland if she so wished—because death did not have to be imminent to permit termination, and "the equal right to life of the mother" would be infringed by denying her the right to travel abroad. The government's new dilemma was that it had either to accept the judgment and legislate for abortion, or to face the minefield of yet another abortion referendum, to see if people agreed with the new interpretation of the constitution.

But. There was a "but." Only those women whose continued pregnancy threatened their *lives* like the "X" case girl could be allowed to travel abroad. Anyone else could still find themselves under threat of jail or fines for disobeying a court injunction not to travel. The government still could not shrug off the charge that it was presiding over a police state, which incarcerated its citizens within its borders.

More shocks were to come. The protocol to the Maastricht Treaty had been turned inside out by the Supreme Court. Far from ensuring that Ireland's ban on abortion was watertight, safe from any European change, as things *now* stood, if Irish people gave a "Yes" vote to the Maastricht Treaty in the June referendum, they would also be voting "Yes" to limited abortion in Ireland, and "Yes" to a travel ban and "Yes" to a ban on information to women with unwanted pregnancy. Both the pro-choice and the anti-abortion groupings found themselves speaking as one, calling on the Irish people to say "No" to the Maastricht Treaty and its infamous protocol.

The pro-choice groups said it would be quite wrong to ask Irish women to support a treaty which, as it stood, denied them the basic right to travel and to information about abortion. On the other side, subtle as ever, the anti-abortion fundamentalists said that a vote for Maastricht was a vote for the murder of babies, nothing less. At every anti-Maastricht meeting, they showed *The Silent Scream.* "Don't be Maas-tricked," said their posters. There was no end to the confusion.

Less than a month before voting day, however, Ireland was stunned again when Bishop Casey of Galway admitted that he had fathered a child and had secretly "borrowed" church funds to pay for his son's schooling. The bishop's transgression made a mockery of the pope's exhortations to safeguard Ireland as "a beacon of Christian virtue in a corrupt world." A popular T-shirt slogan caught the public's scepticism: "Wear a condom, just in Casey," mordantly referring to the other campaign, for contraceptives to be available in Ireland.

As the June referendum date approached, the government seemed as bemused by the legal morass as everyone else. Abortion looked set to put Ireland's economic future in jeopardy. The prospect of losing billions of pounds of European aid because of losing the referendum was unthinkable. Frantic to salvage the treaty, Prime Minister Reynolds' government pleaded in vain with European colleagues to be allowed to withdraw the protocol. With Irish ratification plainly in the balance, the European Parliament offered "a solemn declaration" that it would respect Article 40.3.3. "Words writ on water," retorted the critics. Finally the government faced up to the fact that to win the vote for Maastricht, it would also have to offer a further referendum on the abortion questions. Reynolds offered a three-part referendum, hoping to erase the Supreme Court edict that abortion could be performed legally in Ireland, but securing women's access to information and their right to travel. It was enough. Irish voters said a battered but convincing "Yes" to the European treaty and Euro-subsidies.

The show moved on. Punch-drunk from the Maastricht match, abortion protagonists mustered their strength for a second referendum featuring abortion in the space of six months. As one pro-choice pamphlet observed, if "X" happened again, Reynolds' answer would be to let the girl commit suicide in Ireland or export the problem: "An Irish solution to an Irish problem," if ever there was one.[6] Women's groups urged people to vote "Yes" (to travel), "Yes" (to information) but "No" to the substantive issues of abortion in Ireland. Getting across the message—"Yes, Yes, No"—in a tripartite referendum was a fraught business.

The bishops, aware that Church meddling was increasingly resented in many quarters, refrained from browbeating the faithful to the ballot box. But the curious wording of the main clause on abortion—which callously differentiated risks to health and risks to life—once again backed the anti-abortion campaigners into the same corner as the feminists and the pro-choice groups. To the anti-abortion groups the microscopic loophole in the ban on abortion was nothing less than a "licence to kill" (Boylan 1992). A new and sinister flank of the anti-abortion movement—Youth Defence—made its presence felt among the marchers and at the meetings. This thuggish band of abortion vigilantes, sporting brass knuckles, was given to mounting "pickets" outside the homes of prominent pro-choice campaigners. Dispassionate debate was not their style.

Meanwhile Albert Reynolds' ramshackle coalition was tottering. Three weeks before the second referendum, to settle—in the light of the "X" case—what Article 40.3.3 was to supposed to mean, it was announced that it would also be general election day. Amid the frenzy of the campaign the European Court of Human Rights ruled that Ireland's efforts to stop the counselling services giving women information about abortion—a case which had been started back in 1986 was a breach of Irish women's human rights. So the clause on information was virtually redundant and Reynolds' government was further embarrassed. Nevertheless, the vote, when it came, plumped in favor of travel and in favor of information, but once again rejected abortion in Ireland.

Four years later, "the legal situation of abortion in Ireland is complex, restrictive and dismissive of the health, rights and bodily integrity of Irish women" (Conlon 1994, p. 20). Ireland could be faced with another "X" case tomorrow, and there is no prospect of substantial abortion law reform. As many Irish women come to Britain as ever. But there has been a real shift in consciousness. As Ruth Riddick, founder of Open Line Counselling says, the calamity of the "X" case, "was the first time that a human face had been put on abortion in this country." There is a different mood in Ireland today. It now has for its head of state, a woman, Mary Robinson, whose track record includes vocal campaigning against the 1983 anti-abortion amendment and representing the student unions in court in 1989, free of charge. In 1993 it became legal to buy condoms—now classified as AIDS prevention devices— over the counter, and in 1994 homosexuality was legalized.

In early 1995 a bill was passed, supposedly to formalize the referendum decision on access to abortion information, but the government predictably fudged things. Whilst it said doctors could give women information, it criminalized the act of referral, a measure which would hit hardest at women without the resources to contact distant clinics. When the bill was forwarded for assent to the president, Mary Robinson, she asked the Supreme Court to decide whether it was "repugnant to the constitution." The constitution itself had been amended by the "Yes, Yes, No" referendum and, said the court, the bill was not "repugnant." Mary Robinson signed it, and one more tiny piece of the Irish abortion jigsaw slipped into place. Later that year Ireland voted, albeit narrowly, to permit its citizens to divorce.

If reform is steadily seeping across Ireland, rending the state and the Church apart, it is the girl in the "X" case who unwittingly triggered the events which cracked the mold. "The personal is political" declares a well-worn feminist slogan. In the "X" case the personal was never more political.

And Bishop Casey also helped ease Ireland down the road towards a secular society. In his wake there have been a steady stream of revelations to shatter the Irish public's long-held belief in the unshakeable morality of the Church—alcoholic bishops, child-abusing monks and tales of gothic horror and cruelty in orphanages run by nuns.

Stereotypes of Catholic Ireland's quaint and callous bigotry are tempting bait for all commentaries on abortion politics. In such a frame, Europe comes up as a modernizing, liberal influence. Yet Europe's politicians lost no time in granting Ireland its protocol to the treaty, furtively consigning half of Ireland's population to permanent second-class status. Nevertheless, the potency of anti-abortion absolutists of Ireland's right wing should never be underestimated: there is a complex shroud of Catholic lay groupings, including Opus Dei, whose threads reach far into the Irish establishment and whose leaders are adept at pulling political strings and manipulating the febrile, short-lived coalitions which have been the story of Irish government for two decades. The taunt of going "soft" on abortion has been the kiss of death for

Irish politicians and has been used time and again to preserve the status quo. With ample finance, raised both in Ireland and in the United States, the fundamentalists' energy and ingenuity are far from spent.

Germany: Cold Winds of Change

As 1989 drew to a close the sight of jubilant Germans on top of the Berlin Wall signalled a unique, heady moment in the history of twentieth-century Europe. Few could imagine the dramatic changes ahead. For months afterwards, people and politicians on both sides of the old, hated divide worked feverishly towards a united Germany with an agreed deadline of October 1990. The pace of change was breathtaking as the two lumbering systems of government came alongside each other, merging their disparate laws and economic processes.

There was one glaring exception, where agreement seemed impossible—abortion. The two Germanies had had fundamentally different laws on abortion. In the east, access to abortion was unhindered. Women had the right simply to request it. The law in the west, which dated back to the 1871 penal code drawn up by Bismarck, was much more restrictive.[7] Among the west's ten, relatively independent states, those dominated by Catholicism often made access to abortion so difficult that many pregnant women were forced to travel across the country, or even to Holland, in order to get the help they needed, especially for abortions on social grounds (Thoss and Baross 1995). Few in the east wanted to turn the clock back to that kind of law.

Throughout 1990, accord was being reached at breakneck speed on matters vital to the state, such as monetary and economic union (Mushaben 1993). But in meeting after meeting the health ministers and ministers at the justice departments failed to harmonize the laws on abortion. It was plain deadlock. "The gap between the two positions is clearly unbridgeable," said a spokesman at the West German Justice Department (Lader 1991). In practice, unification meant that the states of former communist East Germany would adopt the laws and practices of the *Wessis* (westerners), their more powerful neighbors. But on abortion, this seemed impossible: neither side was willing to import the laws of the other. Some states, such as Saxony, in the former East Germany, were threatening the entire accession treaty, if they could not agree to terms for a new abortion law. It really looked as if the differences might derail the entire process and the extraordinary political opportunity could slip away.

The German officials and politicians in the negotiations sidestepped. They specifically wrote into the historic treaty of unification that it excluded abortion. The two parts of the country agreed to preserve their own laws, and told the future all-German Parliament to formulate a new law, which was to be in place by 31 December 1992. The treaty committed the Parliament to finding a policy that

> would ensure better protection of unborn life and provide a better solution, *in conformity with the constitution,* of conflict situations confronted by pregnant women, notably through legally guaranteed entitlements for women-first and foremost to advice and public support—than is the case in either part of Germany at present.
>
> (KOMMERS 1993, MY EMPHASIS)

Everyone was aware that in 1975 the (western) Supreme Court had ruled that the state is obliged under its constitution to protect unborn life at all stages of pregnancy.

With the treaty of unification signed and a new government of united Germany in place under the conservative leadership of Helmut Kohl, the former chancellor of West Germany and a devout anti-abortion Catholic, campaigners of all persuasions were under starter's orders for a battle royal. On both sides of Germany, they grasped that they had a fleeting chance to put in place the reforms they desired. The stakes were high, time was short. The anti-abortion lobby wanted more stringent controls. Ireland offered a reasonable model, they felt.

In former East Germany, access to abortion had been guaranteed under a law passed in 1972, which was part of a package of "equal opportunity" measures for women.[8] It was available on request up to twelve weeks of pregnancy. Because contraception was hard to come by and there was considerable mistrust of the Pill, particularly on the part of doctors, the abortion rate was high. A third of pregnancies ended in abortion. Women having abortions went to hospital, the procedure was performed under general anesthetic and entailed a minimum of three days' hospital stay. For many East German women it was a very routine healthcare procedure.

In the former West Germany, abortion law had had a more checkered recent history and attitudes were much more polarized. The law passed in

1976 said abortions could only be legally performed if a doctor considered it was specifically indicated, under a number of categories—medical, genetic, ethical (after rape), or because of "social hardship." Counselling was mandatory. The law had caused political trouble for many years. In states governed by conservative parties, such as the Christian Democrats, or Christian Social Union, it was very difficult for women to find doctors prepared to certify a "social hardship" abortion. Doctors were afraid they would be prosecuted, an anxiety which was considerably increased when Dr. Thorst Heissen, a doctor in the Bavarian town of Memmingen, had his medical records seized by the police and was convicted early in 1989 of carrying out illegal abortions.[9] The case caused an outcry and was very much alive in the public memory when the East German regime collapsed later that same year.

For a woman in West Germany, access to abortion depended on which state she lived in. Many had to consult several doctors before they could get a referral, travel considerable distances for counselling and sometimes further for the operation itself. Many women went abroad, even though it was not legal to do so without undergoing the counselling process. The German border police were in the habit of stopping women returning from Holland, having been told to look out for travelers looking "pale and emotional." On the pretext of investigating drug smuggling, they often trapped these women into admitting the abortions. Abortions were less prevalent than in East Germany, around one in ten pregnancies ended in abortion, and contraception was more freely available. Many feminists groups, aspiring to decriminalize abortion altogether from the cumbersome West German law, hoped that with added support from their new allies in the east they might tip the scales towards something approaching the rights to which their compatriots in East Germany had been entitled (Clements 1994).

In the first post-unity year, 1991, abortion politics roared through the already precarious coalition politics. Parliament considered proposal after proposal, none of them able to command sufficient support, and the debate within the ruling center-right coalition, led by Christian Democrat Helmut Kohl, became increasingly heated. Kohl stressed in public that the matter was one for personal conscience but brought enormous pressure to bear on party colleagues to toe the Christian Democrat anti-abortion line. The Christian Democrats from the east looked as if they were determined to back a more liberal law, closer to the old East German law, and this infuriated the strongly Catholic Bavarian Christian Democrats. Of all the high-tension issues requiring solutions in unified Germany, such as immigration, the collapse of the east German economy, and so on, abortion was proving the trickiest.

Meanwhile, women continued to be governed by the laws valid where they lived. Few west Germans went east for abortion: grim conditions in east German hospitals were deterrent enough and women feared that such abortions might land them in court. The politicians seemed agreed on one point: the sooner they could find a solution and shelve this febrile element in their midst, the better. For the pressure groups, picking a path of compromise and negotiation between the rocks and whirlpools of the coalitions was an intense and exhausting process. One open question was whether abortion should be removed from the criminal statutes altogether, where it had been placed in Bismarck's time. Some feminist activists, such as Alice Schwarzer, who had long campaigned for this, decided instead to go for a more pragmatic approach and concentrate on ensuring that it would at the very least be possible for all German women to get abortion on request up to twelve weeks, whether the criminal law remained or not. Public opinion polls showed that three-quarters of Germans favored a more liberal law (Gow 1992).

Eventually, in June 1992, after a 14-hour debate, during which the Catholic Church held special masses and tolled church bells, as if for a national emergency, a new law was passed with a clear majority (72 votes). It brought some improvements for women in west Germany. But for women in the east, despite the rueful consolation that things could have been worse, it was a severe blow. After almost twenty years of being free to decide about abortion for themselves, they now faced prosecution if they did not submit to mandatory counselling, among other things.

The new law kept abortion in the penal code, but permitted women to seek abortion on request up to twelve weeks, *provided* they submitted to counselling and a waiting period of three days. It also included a package of measures designed to encourage the woman to continue the pregnancy, such as help with maternity-care costs, day-care provision and a monthly child allowance. The federal president signed it and it became law. The Parliament had done its duty by the treaty of unification, or so it seemed to many (Kommers 1993).

The vote was, however, a bitter personal defeat for Kohl, and almost at once the Christian Democrats declared that the law contravened the 1975 ruling which said that abortion was unconstitutional and they would be referring it to the German Supreme Court. Meanwhile, the legal twilight of separate laws would have to continue. In May 1993, by a six-two ruling, the judges declared that abortion was indeed unconstitutional, could only be considered "in exceptional circumstances," recriminalized it, *for the whole nation,* and threw Parliament's hard-won settlement out on its ear. Public health insurance would no longer pay for terminations and state-funded hospitals would not be allowed to provide them, since they were, after all, illegal.

There were some concessions: women were to be allowed their illegal abortions in the first twelve weeks of pregnancy, *provided they could pay for them,* said the court. To obtain an abortion in the first twelve weeks of pregnancy all women would have to undergo counselling which would not be "merely informational" but an active effort to dissuade, and there would be a three-day waiting period. *If all these conditions were met,* doctor and woman would not be prosecuted under criminal law for their illegal act. The court's decision became all-Germany's new abortion law.

There was uproar. Kohl praised the court for "truly protecting unborn life." In the hours that followed, protesters took to the streets in Cologne, Potsdam and other cities, despite the fact the announcement came just before a public holiday weekend. The six judges had destroyed "what is the clear wish of the parliament and the people," said Irmgard Adam-Schwaetzer, the Free Democrats' deputy leader (Gow 1993).

The business of obtaining an abortion has become a fraught experience for German women, and the women of east Germany have lost out in particular. Pre-abortion counselling has become a predictably hot issue. Many counselors are resentful of the new law whose explicit and sole purpose is "protection of the unborn life" especially, it is implied, from the woman herself. "It hurts me to give the impression that I am the enemy of the woman seeking advice or that I want to manipulate her," says Hanna Havemann, a counselor at a new east Berlin advice center (Tomforde 1993). Counselling and abortions cannot be provided by the same organization under the same roof. Some of the new organizations establishing themselves as counselling and advice centers, particularly in east Germany where there is no independent family planning network, are even based in the Catholic Church.

And for women on low incomes—which means far more women in east Germany, where women make up the majority of the unemployed—abortion will become a two-tier affair. There will be means-tested public funding for abortions which are deemed constitutional, but in order to get the money a woman will have to apply for state aid and have her application approved on financial and constitutional grounds before she can go ahead. As well as being a total breach of her confidentiality this will inevitably cause delays, as well as acting as a deterrent for women who are ashamed of claiming state aid, or of revealing that they have an unwanted pregnancy, or both. And in east Germany, the only abortion provision has been in public hospitals and these are now prohibited from performing abortions. There is no network of clinics or private doctors: "choice" in the first twelve weeks has a pretty hollow ring.[10]

The winds of political change have blown coldest on the women of east Germany. The communist regime had made it easier for women to combine work and parenthood, although women's everyday lives may have fallen far short of the proclaimed ideals of communist emancipation of women. But reproductive choice was more of a reality in East Germany than it ever was for their western sisters (Einhorn 1992). Now the social programs have been withdrawn, day nurseries have closed, and rising prices are making it harder for women to contemplate childrearing. Maternity wards stand empty and the birth rate has dwindled by two-thirds since 1990. More and more women are asking to be sterilized, before they have even reached the age of 30. An unplanned pregnancy must seem a far greater disaster today in east Germany than it would have been ten years ago, yet the criminal law looms over abortion.

Three years later the court's ruling remains in force and a series of new proposals, designed to comply with the court's constraints, have been drafted and abandoned. Women seeking abortions are finding that doctors are refusing to help them, because they are fearful of breaching the law or of having a new law applied retrospectively. In 1994, in a cynical and alarming move, Helmut Kohl appointed to the post of Minister for Women and the Family, Claudia Nolte, a 28-year-old Roman Catholic woman from the former eastern state of Thuringia, who says that women who have had abortions should be forced to work in a hospital for a year, "to make amends." Nolte's appointment was seen by right-wingers as a shrewd move to appeal to younger women, and she talked about finding a "compromise" on abortion. But she belongs to no fewer than three anti-abortion organizations and, said Alice Schwarzer, her appointment was "a slap in the face for every woman in Germany" (Staunton 1994). Nolte was entrusted with overseeing yet another commission to come up with an abortion law acceptable to Germany's politicians, churchmen and doctors. At the end of 1995 the German Parliament finally passed abortion legislation which complied with the frame set down by the Supreme Court. Whether this will quell the politicking or will produce anything to meet the real needs of German women is another matter.

3

The Specter of the Backstreets

L EGAL ABORTION—IN THE UNITED STATES, Europe and Australia—is
something that people have got used to. Memories of abortion as a crime
are fading. As British obstetrician and gynecologist Wendy Savage points
out, "Ninety-eight women died from illegal abortion in the three years 1964
to 1966, but younger doctors have never seen these tragedies" (Savage 1995,
p. 84). Young women of the 1990s are frankly astonished by tales of the days
when being single and pregnant meant you "had to get married . . ." Was
marriage the only option, thirty, forty years ago? Yes, pretty much, and
often, as an immediate prospect, much less terrifying than trusting yourself
to the mercies of the backstreet abortionist. The press no longer carries headlines such as "Fiancé gave girlfriend tablets," "Good nature led to prison,"
"Sister found dead in kitchen." The dimming of the folk memory is a boon
for the anti-abortion lobby: it is not too hard to ridicule the symbolic coat-
hanger and knitting needle as fatuous and definitely far-fetched. Yet illegal
and unsafe abortions still kill and maim thousands of women every year. If
the pope, the leaders of the fundamentalist Islamic world and the Christian
anti-abortion militants were able to achieve their ideal, what would happen
to women and to children world-wide?

The Oldest Method of Fertility Control

Abortion is probably the oldest, most common and universal method by
which women have controlled their fertility, long before the law regulated
it. Women determined to end their pregnancies have always known a wide

variety of ways to do so. Until relatively recently it has certainly not attracted the shame or stigma which clings to it today.

The word *abort* comes from Latin, meaning "to perish" or "to fail to be born." In the ruins of the Roman city of Pompeii, dilators and curettes almost identical to modern instruments have been discovered. Abortion was widely approved in ancient Greece. A medieval European book of herbs gives a recipe for a Chinese abortifacient from almost 3000 BC. In the year 1200 the pope decreed that abortion was permissible within eighty days of the conception of a female and within forty days of that of a male: how sex was determined is somewhat mysterious, but what counted was that until these days had passed, the fetus was not "ensouled" and did not count as a human life. Until the middle of the nineteenth century, the Roman Catholic Church's view oscillated and it was not until 1869 that Pope Pius IX forbade all abortion and declared that the soul was present from the instant of conception and not merely from the moment of "quickening." Quickening—the moment when the pregnant woman becomes aware of fetal movement—had been an obvious and therefore popular marker point in pregnancy, and until 1803 common law in England did not regard abortion as a crime.[1] Abortion "before quickening" was legal in all U.S. states until 1821.

In the nineteenth century, the laws of Europe and the United States began to prohibit and regulate abortion. The image of abortion was transformed from a common method of birth control into a crime—against the laws of God and men. In the 1870s an estimated one fifth of all pregnancies in the United States were being terminated and it was the American Medical Association, the voice of the rising young profession, which led the campaign to criminalize abortion state by state (Petchesky 1984, p. 80). The British anti-abortion legislation of the Victorian era, the Offences Against the Person Act of 1861, was never enforceable: remedies for "menstrual blockages"—which warned, knowingly, that "married ladies should not use"—were openly available through newspaper advertisements. Such "remedies" were regarded as much more respectable than "artificial" birth control. The cheapest was diachylon, a form of lead, though swallowing it ran the risk of poisoning, insanity, blindness and paralysis. In 1914, in Burnley, Lancashire, a cotton mill town, a pharmacist was found to have sold 500 doses of diachylon.

After the First World War, when birth-control pioneer Marie Stopes set up her clinic in north London to provide birth control to working-class

THE TRIAL OF DR. ALECK BOURNE

The predicament of a pregnant 14-year-old girl, raped by officers of the Royal Horse Guards, with such violence that she suffered serious physical injuries, prompted Dr. Aleck Bourne of St. Mary's Hospital, Paddington, to perform an abortion on 14 June 1938. The case had been referred to Dr. Bourne by Dr. Joan Malleson, a stalwart campaigner for abortion law reform and birth control. The girl's middle-class parents had brought her to Dr. Malleson, suffering from extreme nervous symptoms at the prospect of bearing a child and being reminded by her pregnancy of her terrible experience. A doctor at St. Thomas's Hospital had already refused an abortion, saying that because the girl had been raped by officers, she might be carrying a future prime minister of England. Bourne was known to have performed a previous abortion in similar circumstances and to be looking to challenge what he regarded as an inflexible, harsh law. Dr. Malleson asked him to help.

Bourne observed his patient carefully in hospital for a week and, having satisfied himself that only an abortion would save her from mental collapse, he operated. She was in very early pregnancy. The charges he faced at the outset of his Old Bailey trial carried a maximum penalty of twenty years' imprisonment. In his defense he compared the "ordinary, decent" girl's mental anguish to the symptoms of shell-shock in victims of the 1914–1918 war.

The judge, Mr. Justice McNaghton, compared Bourne's decision to that of a surgeon who believes it necessary to save a patient's life by removing the appendix. If it is found that the appendix is normal—the surgeon should not be blamed, because the decision was made "in good faith" for the patient's welfare. In such circumstances, the surgeon and Dr. Bourne had a duty to operate. Dr. Bourne had acted not to save the patient's life, but to preserve her mental and physical health, and this was a valid interpretation of the law. The jury's acquittal was greeted with public acclaim. Bourne had single-handedly brought about a massive shift in English abortion law.

In the years that followed, Bourne was forever turning pregnant women away from his consulting rooms. He supported the traditional medical framework for abortions and thirty years later became a member of the Society for the Protection of the Unborn Child (SPUC), because he thought that the 1967 Abortion Act would lead to "abortion on demand."

Source: Holden 1994, Chapter 12

---

women, she was shocked to receive 20,000 requests for abortion and abortifacients in the first three months. She concluded that the women asking for her help were not even aware that abortion was a crime. Despite the fact that it was now a criminal activity, abortion was not shunned, indeed it was widespread. In the 1930s one-third of all maternal deaths in Scotland were due to septic abortion and, according to an official report into the very high death rate caused by illegal abortion in Britain, the typical woman seeking one was a "respectably married woman of modest means with two or more children," who wanted to end an unwanted pregnancy for the sake of her own health and that of her existing children.[2] Among wealthy women, it was common knowledge that abortions were performed by "medical practitioners of the highest skill," and as the gynecologist and campaigner for abortion law reform Joan Malleson observed, the difference between a "therapeutic abortion" and a criminal abortion was often no more than the patient's ability to pay (Brookes 1988).

By far the most dramatic landmark of Britain's abortion history was the trial of Dr. Aleck Bourne, an eminent London gynecologist, acquitted in 1938 for performing an abortion on a 14-year-old girl, who had been the victim of a multiple rape. The jury found him not guilty after the judge indicated that an abortion could be lawfully performed, not only to save the mother's life, but also if the doctor believed in good faith that it was necessary to prevent the woman becoming "a physical or mental wreck."[3] The case set an important legal precedent, because from then until 1967 it was up to the prosecution to prove that a doctor had not been acting "in good faith" (Holden 1994, ch. 12). Dr. Bourne was no advocate of abortion on demand or women's rights, but he believed that women who had been raped were in a special category. (The parallels between Dr. Bourne's young patient and the raped Irish girl in the "X" case, more than fifty years later, are impossible to ignore.) After the Second World War, until the reform of the abortion laws in 1967, illegal abortion was the main cause of maternal death in Britain. The scale of illegal abortion in Britain was estimated variously at between 20,000 and 100,000 a year.[4] In the early 1960s forty-four women in Holloway prison, jailed for having performed illegal abortions, reflected on their offenses and typically observed, "I knew it was against the law, but I didn't feel it was wrong . . . women have to help each other" (Woodside 1966).

Methods of Illegal Abortion

Drinking a bottle of gin, possibly containing iron filings; sitting in a scaldingly hot bath; douching with a solution of very soapy water; or throwing yourself downstairs; these were just a few of the favored home remedies for self-induced abortion in Britain. The women jailed for performing abortions (see above) had mostly used soapy water and an enema syringe. World-wide, methods vary as widely as every other cultural practice. Traditional herbal methods have given way to commercial preparations—in Africa herbs have been superseded by "blue-bag," the laundry bleach; in Britain, herbs such as pennyroyal gave way to gin and quinine tablets. In contemporary Thailand, where abortion is officially so restricted that it hardly reaches 100 a year, there are an estimated 250,000 abortions every year, mostly by traditional abdominal massage. Women risk hemorrhage and pelvic infection.

In Morocco, despite the fact that interpreters of the religious law declared in 1975 that the fetus only acquires its soul forty days after conception, the government has remained unmoved; pregnancy can only be terminated if a woman's life is in danger *and,* in the case of a married woman, her husband consents to the operation. The traditional *qabla* or midwife is trusted and cheap. In 1984, a small survey of Moroccan married women revealed that around four out of ten had had an abortion and it is not uncommon for women to undergo as many as three abortions in a lifetime. The Moroccan midwives use herbal potions, or even a cocktail of contraceptive pills; sometimes they stimulate the uterus with a stem of parsley, or get the woman to squat over a dish of smoking herbs, which brings on bleeding. It may work but it is very risky. Wealthier women go to doctors who welcome the fees. When tragedies have come to light, as happened in 1991 when a young woman died and her parents sued the abortionist, the Moroccan media's outrage was reserved for the doctor, who was accused of encouraging premarital sex among young women: "if they did not know they could have an abortion, girls would be better behaved" (Naamane-Guessous 1993).

Not all illegal abortions are equally unsafe. In Belgium, until 1990, abortion was as illegal as in Ireland or Malta but it was openly available—not only in hospitals but also in specialized clinics—and was safe and inexpensive. Sometimes doctors were prosecuted, but abortions continued despite the ban for fifteen years, until 1990, when the law was liberalized (Donnay et al. 1993). In Tanzania, in the 1970s, where grounds for abortion are very narrow, doctors working clandestinely used sterile instruments to rupture the membranes, after which they dispatched the woman to a hospital, which was obliged to complete the process. In Brazil, trained midwives operated with considerable skill and often dispensed antibiotics to combat possible infection (Liskin 1980).

But usually the methods used, either by women themselves or by untrained practitioners, are patently hazardous. Women may use drugs, chem-

"JANE"

A woman phoning the Chicago women's abortion collective, "Jane," was told that she was speaking to "Jane, from women's liberation." Everyone was anonymous, protected by the name Jane. At first the network operated purely as a feminist referral service. The man employed by Jane to perform the abortions—dilation and curettage operations costing US$375—was someone whom the collective believed to be a qualified doctor. When it was discovered that despite his demonstrated competence and responsibility, the man was not in fact medically qualified, the women concluded that if he was not a doctor and he could do it, then anyone could learn. They decided to acquire the skills themselves.

"It's like making canteloupe balls," reported one "Jane," "the same motion with the curette . . . quick and sure." The greatest skill needed, they discovered, was in safely and gently dilating the cervix. At its peak, "Jane" was providing 300 abortions a week, having succeeded in reducing the price of an abortion to US$40. Once abortion became legal in New York State, Jane became a service for poor women, many of them Black and Hispanic, who could not afford to leave Chicago and travel to New York, even for a day. In 1973, after the Supreme Court ruled that abortion was a constitutional right for women, Jane ended. They had done more than 11,000 abortions.

Sources: National Women's Health Network 1989; "Jane" 1990

---

icals or herbs, either by mouth or in the vagina. Pushing a catheter or wire or needle into the womb to provoke bleeding risks tearing or even puncturing the womb. Scraping the womb or undergoing heavy abdominal massage are also widespread methods. It is not surprising to find that at least some of the modern world's dazzling range of pharmaceuticals have been adapted as abortifacients—a drug, called Cytotec, manufactured for the treatment of gastric ulcers, is being bought by women in Brazil, on a huge scale, at considerable risk to themselves (see Chapter 7). Pain and danger are the hallmarks of unsafe abortion.

Women solve their difficulties in ways appropriate to their time and place. In the late 1980s in the United States, when the right to abortion seemed so perilously close to being lost altogether, feminist campaigners speculated that they might have to revive schemes such as "Jane," the Chicago self-help abortion collective. "Jane" was an underground abortion network from 1969 until the bench-mark 1973 Supreme Court judgment, *Roe v. Wade*, made abortion legal. It became the best-known secret in Chicago, though its founders had no inkling of making history when they started up in 1969 (see sidebar, "Jane").

Today, for many women in the United States, getting an abortion is as hard as it was in the 1960s. The Supreme Court judges of the 1990s have weakened the laws at the same time as the anti-abortion fanatics have tried to shame and harry pregnant women on the sidewalks outside the clinics. In 1989, a Quaker group in Philadelphia set up what they call the Overground Railroad, to help pregnant women who live where abortion is virtually unobtainable. The Quakers help with transport, accommodation and escorts for women to travel to states where they can obtain safe, legal terminations.

The specter of illegal abortion could well revisit the United States. In the 1960s the kickbacks from illegal abortion made it the biggest racket after narcotics and gambling. More than half the women who were recently asked what they would do if abortion was once again totally outlawed, said they would have an illegal abortion, somehow. Since there are around 1.6 million legal abortions a year in the United States, that works out at a demand for around 900,000 secret operations.

Neither the law nor the strictures of religion will stop a woman who desperately needs an abortion. In the Philippines, a devoutly Catholic country, where the bishops rail against contraception, Sunday mornings see a brisk trade in herbal abortifacients, outside Quiapo, the busiest church of the capital, Manila. There are little stalls, stocked with candles, religious pictures and, quite prominently, bottles of "remedies," selling openly to women entering or leaving mass. Almost every village has a similar trade. In Latin America too, where abortion is outlawed, 40 to 60 per cent of pregnancies are unwanted. The poorer the woman, the more likely she is to induce an abortion herself or to go to an untrained person. Little wonder that the law and the Church have been powerless to stem the tide of up to four million illegal abortions every year in Latin America (Alan Guttmacher Institute 1994).

A Lethal Epidemic

A clandestine abortion is rarely a single event, but rather a series of ever more dangerous and probably more costly steps. Women often start with a simple home remedy that they believe may work. If that fails, they try something more drastic and more expensive until they achieve their goal or run out of money or get too scared. Whatever the laws say—whether abortion is permitted or not—a total of up to 55 million abortions are performed each year. Something approaching half of these are performed in unsafe conditions, usually because safe abortion is illegal or inaccessible (World Health

Organization 1994). One quarter of the world's population live today under laws which either regard all abortion as a crime or only permit it in severely restricted circumstances. If women cannot get the help they seek locally and they have money or can at least scrape some together, they journey to where abortion is available. If they are poor, they take whatever steps they can.

Because abortion is so often a secret business, no one knows how many women lose their lives from it. The estimates are riddled with uncertainty. The number of women dying each year as a result of botched abortion may be 70,000 (World Health Organization 1995). It may be as many as 200,000. That means between 190 and 550 women, many of whom will be very young, dying every single day.

Unsafe abortion is to blame for more "maternal deaths" world-wide than any other single cause.[5] (Maternal deaths are deaths from childbirth, pregnancy complications, and abortion.) These deaths are needless: almost all could be prevented if women had access to decent health care. Because of them perhaps half-a-million young children each year lose their mothers. And after the death of their mother, their prospects for survival plummet still further.[6]

Unsafe abortion is the leading cause of maternal deaths in countries as varied as Ethiopia, Colombia and Bangladesh. In Romania, from 1966 to 1989, when abortion and contraception were banned by communist dictator Ceausescu and harshly policed, around 10,000 women lost their lives from unsafe abortion. The most common cause of death was bleeding or infection, often resulting from self-inflicted abortion or attempts at abortion. Besides the deaths, many women endured permanent damage to their cervixes, chronic infection or severe chronic anemia. Such problems could cause low birthweight or premature birth in later pregnancies, or could well result in permanent infertility. The measures failed to achieve Ceausescu's objective of boosting the Romanian birthrate. They did succeed in turning otherwise law-abiding women and their partners into criminals (Stephenson 1992). Each year an estimated 1.2 million secret abortions were taking place—in a population of 23 million people. (The United States, with a population of around 243 million, has around 1.6 million abortions every year.) By 1992, when abortion had once again been legal in Romania for three years, the maternal death rate plummeted—from 170 deaths per 100,000 live births, to 60 such deaths—thanks to a 60 per cent drop in abortion-related deaths.

In Zimbabwe, unwanted pregnancy, especially among adolescents, is leading to an estimated 70,000 illegal abortions a year and complications from unsafe abortion—hemorrhage, and sepsis—are claiming women's lives. Not only

Unsafe abortions per thousand women aged 15–49

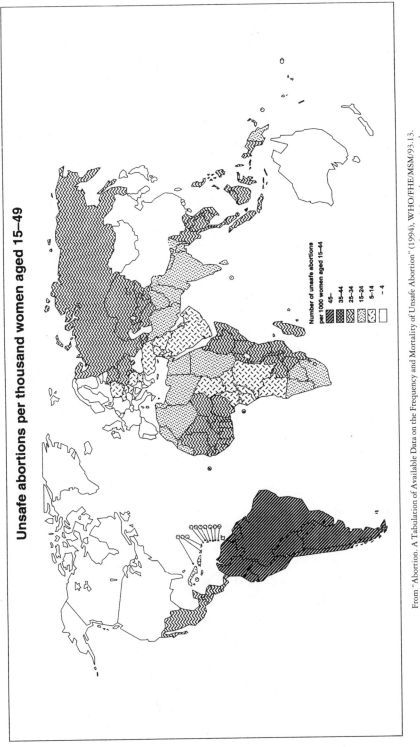

Number of unsafe abortions per 1000 women aged 15–44

- 45–
- 35–44
- 25–34
- 15–24
- 5–14
- –4

From "Abortion. A Tabulation of Available Data on the Frequency and Mortality of Unsafe Abortion." (1994), WHO/FHE/MSM/93.13. The designations employed and the presentation of material on this map do not imply the expression of any opinion whatsoever on the part of the World Health Organization concerning the legal status of any country, territory, city or area of its authorities, or concerning the delimitation of its frontiers or boundaries. Dotted lines represent approximate border lines for which there may not yet be full agreement.

Abortion deaths per 100 000 live births

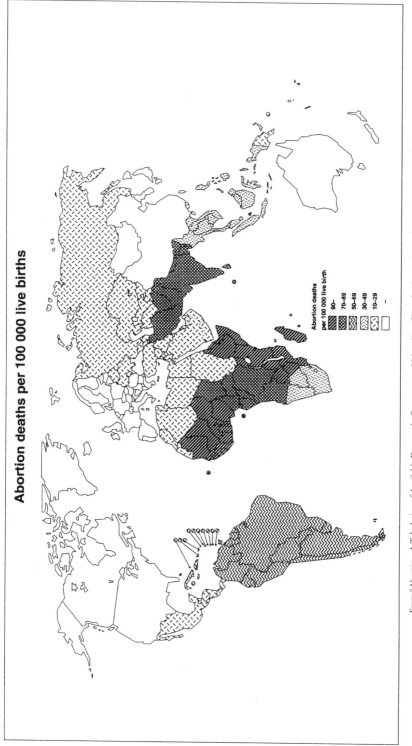

**Abortion deaths
per 100 000 live birth**

90–
70–89
50–69
30–49
10–29
–

From "Abortion. A Tabulation of Available Data on the Frequency and Mortality of Unsafe Abortion" (1994), WHO/FHE/MSM/93.13. The designations employed and the presentation of material on this map do not imply the expression of any opinion whatsoever on the part of the World Health Organization concerning the legal status of any country, territory, city or area of its authorities, or concerning the delimitation of its frontiers or boundaries. Dotted lines represent approximate border lines for which there may not be full agreement.

are grounds for abortion very restricted in Zimbabwe, but the excessively bureaucratic procedure for getting permission compounds the difficulties for women. Illegal abortion thrives, women are killed and maimed. The Zimbabwean minister of health's blinkered response to this state of affairs? In November 1993 he announced a "crackdown on backstreet abortion."

Laws against abortion succeed in making it painful and dangerous. When an abortion is legal and can be performed early in pregnancy by a skilled person, using modern techniques, with ready access to emergency facilities in case problems arise, it is safer than having your tonsils out. In the United States, the risk of death from having a legal abortion is far smaller than continuing the pregnancy, or childbirth itself (Council on Scientific Affairs, American Medical Association 1992). For illegal abortions, the risk of death is magnified 100 to 1,000 times (see sidebar on health risks of abortion at the end of this chapter).

For every woman who dies, many more pay a ghastly price, their bodies and their psychological well-being traumatized and mangled. Indeed for many women some complications of unsafe abortion, such as sterility, may amount to a fate worse than death, in cultures in which barren women are treated as unmarriageable outcasts. The commonest problem is incomplete abortion, leading to pelvic infection, hemorrhage, shock. Poisoning, perforated wombs and injury to the cervix engender a lifetime of permanent ill-health, pain and weakness. Staff at a clinic set up in Romania, after the fall of Ceausescu in 1989, found four out of five of patients were suffering as a result of past incompetent abortions.

Governments wishing to make abortion a crime have to ignore all this somehow. But when they ban abortion they face two alternatives. Either an illegal abortion business will spring up and thrive under their noses, or the problem of unwanted pregnancy will be "exported" as pregnant women slip quietly out of the country to end their pregnancies. Ireland for instance, deals with abortion by exporting it: Irish women "take the boat." Often, as in Poland, both happen.

Poland: Reagan's Dream Come True?

Nowhere has abortion been made more dramatically illegal in recent years than in Poland. The speed at which the hallmarks of illegal abortion have emerged in Poland highlights what President Ronald Reagan's 1980s pledge could really mean for women, if his allies achieve their goal.

In a survey conducted since the fall of the communists, almost three-quarters of Polish women said they had experienced an unplanned pregnancy. Contraception has always been hard to obtain, and has been of notoriously poor quality. The pressures on women under communism to have abortions were very strong, with appalling housing conditions and low wages. In the 1970s and 1980s, without contraception, abortion was the main method of birth control.

Under Poland's new abortion law, passed in 1993, only 3 per cent of the abortions previously performed in Poland are now deemed legal (Novicka 1993). The new law allows abortion when a woman's life or health is in danger, after rape or incest, or if there is suspected fetal abnormality. But prenatal testing is only permissible if there is a proven history of genetic disorder in the family (Jankowska 1993). Industrial pollution in Silesia, southwestern Poland, is now causing a soaring numbers of babies to be born with birth defects. One in four infant deaths in Silesian hospitals are the result of genetic abnormality. Even before President Lech Walesa signed the new abortion law, a harsh new code of medical ethics which doctors had voted for in 1992, was having its effect. The code threatened to take away the license of any doctor who performed abortion, except in cases of rape or incest or when the woman's life was in danger. This effectively ended all hospital abortions and prenatal testing: some institutions put up signs, "No Abortions."

By the end of 1992, the Warsaw police morgue had already begun to receive the bodies of women bearing witness to botched abortions. Deaths are certainly being outnumbered by injuries. For the last three years, cases of infanticide have steadily increased. A helpline set up in Warsaw by the pro-choice Federation for Women and Family Planning is receiving calls from men seeking advice because their wives are refusing to have sex any more. Women are phoning in to say that even in circumstances which comply with the new law, they are being refused operations. In Poland's deeply Catholic south, a pregnant Krakow woman, furnished with a police report confirming that she had been raped, was refused help at the hospital. Twice as many babies are being abandoned at the Warsaw maternity hospital as before the clampdown; dead newborns are turning up in fields and woods; and miscarriages have started to increase again—after years of falling steadily. In 1994, two Polish lawyers were arrested on suspicion of trading babies to Western Europe.

All the standard symptoms of outlawed abortion quickly surfaced in Poland. In the newspapers small ads appeared: "Gynecologist: Interventions." The price for such an illegal abortion in Poland is US$350–1,000: the average monthly wage is $200. The private clinics are often unsanitary. For well-off women, "medical tours" can be arranged—to Lithuania, to Kaliningrad (a Russian enclave next to Poland), even to Holland. A specialized travel agency, set up near the border with Kaliningrad, offers "a full range of gynecological services," a return mini-bus trip and a four-day hospital stay; the price—US$200—roughly one month's salary. The trips are well organized, and the Polish women are treated well. Russian surgeons are probably getting a welcome boost to their meager salaries and the Polish organizers are making a mint. Poland's southern neighbor, the Czech Republic, has been less accommodating. Scarcely a month after Poland's law was passed, the Czechs banned abortions for foreign visitors (as well as pricing abortion beyond the reach of all but the wealthiest Czech women). A Czech doctor is now in prison awaiting trial after Czech police raided a clinic in Cieszyn, found two Polish women having abortions and notes naming scores of others, plus large amounts of money in U.S. dollars (Novicka 1995).

The Polish Ministry of Justice has admitted to Parliament that it is having difficulty enforcing the law. People make false or even malicious denunciations and women who are not even pregnant find themselves being investigated. Scores of investigations have come to nothing (David and Titkow 1994). It seems that the police are generally reluctant to take action unless there is a specific complaint; thus the newspaper advertisements appear regularly and with impunity and the underground services develop steadily. It was not until 1995 that the first trial took place. Barbara Pawliczak, aged 37, had been refused an abortion by a public hospital in Katowice—the pope's home town—and pleaded with Dr. Wincenty Kroemeke to help her. "I insisted, begged and cried and promised nobody would learn about it," said Mrs. Pawliczak, a divorcee with a 10-year-old daughter to support on a clerk's scant wages, who met her lover by answering a "lonely hearts" advertisement. The doctor faced two years in prison and the loss of his medical license for ten years. He denied ever seeing Mrs. Pawliczak or performing the abortion, but Mrs. Pawliczak's jilted lover, embittered by her decision to have the operation, had informed on him to the police, because he wanted to "teach her a lesson, so she won't have anything to do with other men." Asked about contraception, Mrs. Pawliczak said she had tried to take the Pill, "each time, before intercourse."[7]

on abortion, practice is in fact even more restrictive than the law itself. The Federation for Women and Family Planning says that women with legal grounds for abortion are often being refused, the wealthy are getting abortions and the poor are resorting to soapy water and vinegar. The Federation estimates that around 50,000 illegal abortions are taking place each year, both in and outside Poland. Women seeking a legal abortion in Poland face a lottery of the desperate; the influence of priests on hospital policies or doctors' fears that their decisions may be used against them, is creating an atmosphere in which women are refused abortions which are actually sanctioned by this, the harshest of laws. In 1995 a woman pregnant with her eighth child and in rapidly deteriorating health, due to a suspected brain tumor, had her scheduled and medically sanctioned abortion thwarted by a priest. The cleric persuaded the doctors to withdraw their support. The woman attended another hospital where her illness was treated as if she was not pregnant. Finally the baby was born. The woman was too sick to care for her baby and her children, but was terrified that the aggressive treatment she had received might have injured her child. The father has had to give up work and the family faces poverty (Novicka 1996a).

Outside the law, doctors have turned into peddlers: one Warsaw doctor offered a choice of abortions. For a lower price a woman could have an abortion but no guarantee of future fertility. For more money he could give an assurance that she could look forward to bearing a child in the future. There is nowhere else in Europe where the hands of the clock have been wrenched back so viciously. A more liberal law was passed by the parliament in 1994, but Poland's staunchly Catholic president, Lech Walesa, blocked it. However, with the election of president of former communist, Alex Kwasniewski in 1995, the Federation for Women is hoping to restore abortion rights. In 1996 a parliamentary committee was debating yet another proposal, which would permit abortion during the first twelve weeks of pregnancy on social grounds, but only after a three-day waiting period and mandatory counselling, intended to intimidate the woman in the new German style. To help the public debate along, the main TV channel broadcast *The Silent Scream* in prime time. To defenders of abortion rights, this proposed "liberalization" is so glaringly imperfect that it is hard to know which way to argue. One thing is certain: this issue of longstanding and deep dispute in Poland is not going to fade away.[8]

Exporting Abortion

In the Republic of Ireland early in 1992 a raped pregnant 14-year-old girl who was threatening to commit suicide, found herself at the center of what became a *cause célèbre*. The political crisis provoked by her case is described in Chapter 2. It hinged on whether the right of female Irish citizens to move freely across state borders should be restricted if the purpose of their journey was to seek an abortion.

The case highlighted the plight of thousands of Irish women with unwanted pregnancies. Each year a growing number—perhaps 100 a week—cross the Irish Sea, "to visit relatives." Even finding out where in England to go for help requires great determination and resourcefulness: in Dublin, stickers in women's toilets displaying phone numbers are defaced within hours. Financing the journey and the operation may require as much as £500. To fulfill the requirements of the law in Britain, women must wait one day to receive counselling and must therefore stay overnight.

Official figures suggest that in 1992, more than 4,000 women who were prepared to admit that they came from Ireland had abortions in British clinics. The real "export" statistic is doubtless higher, some say 15,000. The 1967 Abortion Act does not apply in Northern Ireland. It has only recently been liberalized in the Channel Islands by very narrow votes. In 1992, almost 1,800 women came to mainland Britain from Northern Ireland alone, where abortion is unavailable except in rare incidences of fetal handicap. In the waiting rooms of British clinics, they are sure to meet others who have travelled long distances.

A glance at the abortion statistics of Britain since the beginning of the 1970s gives an instant reading of the trends in Europe's abortion laws. In 1973, for example, of all abortions performed in England and Wales, one in three was for a woman who did not live in the country, and more than 35,000 women came from France to British clinics. But following an easing of French law in 1975, permitting abortion up to twelve weeks, the numbers from France plummeted and by 1977 only 4,000 French women made the trip. Liberalization of the law in Spain produced similar results. Today less than one in ten abortions in Britain is for a foreigner.

The pattern for Holland has been very similar. Although most abortions in Holland are still for non-resident women, there are far fewer than during the 1970s and early 1980s. In 1994 I visited an abortion clinic in Arnhem, not far from the border with Germany: as soon as I gave the name of the clinic to a taxi driver at the railway station, he assumed that I was from Germany. Around 4,500 German women came to Holland for abortions in 1993 and in the past, when the numbers were much greater, the German authorities stopped many on their return at the German-Dutch border.

The massive differences in abortion rates in the various states of the United States shows that access to safe abortion depends on where you live: if you are unlucky a long journey awaits you. Women all over the world travel for abortion: in the 1960s, Swedish women took the ferry to Poland, and today women in Hong Kong cross the Chinese border for abortions in Shenzhen. Financing and organizing a trip of this kind inevitably causes delays and increases the hazards and the stress of the abortion itself. In a major survey of women's experiences of abortion in Australia, where the law is chaotic and huge journeys may be required, women often said that making the arrangements to ensure the abortion was the most stressful part of the whole episode (Ryan, Ripper and Buttfield 1994). Further delays, such as statutory "waiting periods" between requesting the abortion and getting it, ostensibly to prevent hasty decisions, simply create more tension and extra cost. In the largely rural state of Mississippi, a twenty-four-hour waiting period increases the cost of an abortion either by the price of a tankful of gas—for two trips—or by the price of a motel room for an overnight stay, not to mention arrangements for the care of children or lost wages. For the youngest and the poorest the journey itself may be an insuperable hurdle. Women with means can usually find a way. The rest have to fend for themselves and the poorer a woman is, the greater the risks of unsafe abortion for her—she may be malnourished and anemic and have little or no chance to rest afterwards and combat any threat of infection.

Teenagers: Too Scared, Too Poor

Adult society's discomfort with teenagers' sexuality and young women's own lack of information and confidence make it very hard for them to get hold of contraceptives. Often adolescents do not recognize the early symptoms of pregnancy. What's more, telling an adult and seeking help may incur heavy punishment for the admission of having had sex—being expelled from school or thrown out of the family. A pregnant teenager or young woman rarely has access to money, cannot travel, wouldn't know where to go even if she could. If she does find someone to help her illegally, or induces an abortion herself, she is often too scared to seek medical help afterwards until it is too late.

In developing countries, teenagers who have unsafe abortions suffer even more severe complications, a higher rate of infection, and a greater risk of mutilation and death (Dixon-Mueller 1990). The rates of unwanted pregnancy among young, single women are rising—in Latin America as many as 60 per cent of the pregnancies occurring to women between 15 and 19 years old are unwanted. In Kenya, at the Kenyatta National Hospital in Nairobi, one of the largest public hospitals in sub-Saharan Africa, women suffering from incomplete abortions account for around half the gynecological admissions. Nearly all of them are under 25 years old. Kenya's strict laws against abortion and the prospect of ostracism for any unmarried woman who has a baby combine to drive young women to desperate measures— washing powder and herbs are popular "remedies." Most schools are run by religious orders, the government opposes classroom sex education and there is little practical information or access to contraception for young people. The main hazard of unsafe abortion is infection leading to sterility. How ironic that in order to postpone the start of their childbearing years young pregnant women are forced to take such risks that it may become impossible for them to get pregnant ever again.

The muddle and hypocrisy about teenage abortion and sexuality run deep. In the United States the anti-abortion lobby has taken advantage of public disquiet about teenage promiscuity and "easy" abortion to press for specific curbs on teenage confidentiality in abortion. And with considerable success: "Pro-choicers admit defeat in teen abortion battle," say the newspapers. Thirty-six states now require teenagers under 18 either to involve one or both their parents in their abortion decision or to appear before a judge for an assessment of their maturity to decide for themselves. Under such "parental notification" clauses, youngsters must even defer to a parent who has abandoned them, whether emotionally or financially. A court appearance often looks more like a ritual shaming and judges demand far more knowledge about the side-effects of an abortion than anyone would reasonably ask of an adult. Some ask ludicrous questions: one was partial to asking teenagers how much they knew about the physics of electricity. In 1989 in Idaho, a father murdered his teenage daughter after she sought his permission to have an abortion, as required by the state's laws of "parental consent."

Piously breaching teenagers' confidentiality is consistent with a vision of a patriarchal family as the bedrock of moral order and has political appeal— pro-choice President Clinton supports parental notification clauses—but it serves young women very poorly, both imperiling their health and worsening family tensions. Its main effect is later and riskier abortions for those who can face the hurdles, and since many cannot, a huge leap in the birthrate (Brodie 1994). In Mississippi, where teenagers have to get the written consent of both their parents, the number of adolescents having abortions within the state has dropped significantly, but the number of terminations performed on minors outside the state has jumped. The operations themselves are taking place later, a telling fact indeed (Henshaw 1995b). In Michigan, an anti-abortion judge delayed hearing a plea by an 11-year-old girl until she was twenty-four weeks pregnant. Then he told her she was too late. Some American teenagers are resorting to illegal abortion rather than face these formidable obstacles and there have already been some deaths. The anti-abortion campaigners say that abortion is too momentous to be left to youngsters to determine but the hypocrisy of this posturing is highlighted by the fact that virtually none of those states has been lobbied by the pro-life, "family values" camp to order a teenage mother to have mandatory adult guidance or support in deciding whether or not to have a baby adopted— surely an equally momentous life-event. And once the child is born, the crusaders have precious little to offer—there is no equally aggressive lobbying for maternal and infant health care services, day-care or housing support (Jacobson 1990). The public is duped into supporting restrictions such as this, which are packaged as "compromises," but these restrictions protect neither fetuses nor access to abortion. They merely produce bizarrely cruel and unintended ordeals (Henshaw 1995a).

In Britain there are almost 4,000 abortions a year performed on girls under the age of 16, and, as the law stands, some would argue that these operations could, "in the absence of parental consent or knowledge . . . constitute an assault" (Mason 1989). A doctor under such an attack would however cite in defense, first, the principle of patient-doctor confidentiality, and secondly the judgment in the Gillick case, which concerned doctors' prescription of contraceptives to minors. In 1983 Mrs. Victoria Gillick, an ardent Catholic, mother of ten children, and talented self-publicist, challenged the legal basis on which doctors prescribed contraceptives to young people under 16 years old. Mrs. Gillick argued that it was improper for doctors to give out contraceptives to her daughter without her prior consent. The case was finally heard by the House of Lords, the final arbiter of legal uncertainty in the United Kingdom. The judges decided that as long as people under 16 are fully able to understand what is proposed and its implications, they are competent to consent to medical treatment, and that doctors would be committing no offense, provided they considered the treatment to be in the young person's best interests and had tried to persuade the patient to tell her parents.

Young women's secrets might be safe with doctors, but the issue does not die down. (See Chapter 8 for more on British policies on contraception and abortion.) The fact that Britain's teenage pregnancy rate is nine times that of Holland, where wide-ranging sex education has been shown to delay the onset of sexual activity, makes no impression. Crass efforts at deterrence are the only thing that strike a chord for the "moral majority" enthusiasts.

To what lengths can deterrence be taken? For some, nothing can be too harsh, no price too high to discourage young women from abortion. As Phyllis Schlafly, a veteran celebrity of the U.S. New Right sees it:

> It's very healthy for a young girl to be deterred from promiscuity by fear of contracting a painful, incurable disease or cervical cancer or sterility or the likelihood of giving birth to a dead, blind, or brain-damaged baby (even ten years later when she may be happily married).[9]

But they are not deterred. Inculcating young women to fear sex and to shudder at the mention of abortion is hypocritical as well as utterly futile. In the swathe of southern states of the United States known as the Bible Belt, where True Love Waits campaigns, run by the born-again churches urge young people to wait till marriage and even teach classes in how to dance "purely," the abortion rate at colleges attended by the daughters of Christian fundamentalist families mirrors the U.S. national average. Guilt about sex (and strong feelings against abortion) keeps these young, church-going, college women not from sex itself, but from using contraception effectively. But, faced with unwanted pregnancies, they seek abortions, as millions of women before them have done.

The Price of Restricting Abortion

Unsafe abortion exacts an exorbitant toll on the health budgets of many developing countries. A woman who needs hospital treatment for a botched abortion may need two to three days occupying a bed, plus operating theater time, anesthetic and antibiotic drugs, and possibly a blood transfusion. In some places, treating abortion complications may eat up as much as half the entire hospital budget, demanding not only far more money and equipment but also far more of the priceless time of scarce skilled people than would be needed to carry out a far higher number of safe abortions. The cost of treating the illness and injury caused by unsafe abortions in Africa is making it much more difficult to meet the challenge of that other health crisis, AIDS. The logic of the economics of abortion points unwaveringly towards removing the obstacles—bureaucratic, geographic or financial—which might prevent women from obtaining early legal abortions. Not only is early abortion safer, it costs far less to provide.

Without safe affordable abortion, unwanted pregnancy means either a risky abortion or unplanned births. Whilst the birth of a wanted child is greeted with rejoicing, to be born an unwanted baby—perhaps born "too early, too late, too many or too close"—is a far from promising beginning. If the odds are already stacked against your survival—as in Africa, where in 1990 nearly five million children under 5 years old died from disease and malnutrition—being unwanted may seal your fate. There is plenty of evidence that unwanted children are at an extra disadvantage, wherever in the world they happen to be born. In Thailand children wanted by one or neither parent were twice as likely to die before their first birthday as children wanted by both parents.

Unwanted, children may be abandoned, as they used to be in the foundling hospitals of pre-industrial Europe. In the eighteenth century, the philosopher Jean-Jacques Rousseau abandoned all five of his children in this way. In twentieth-century Romania as many as 150,000 to 200,000 children were abandoned in overcrowded, understaffed orphanages after communist dictator Ceausescu decreed childbearing a compulsory duty in 1966, in an attempt to boost the falling birth rate. (Only two in a hundred were actual orphans.) Every month women were forced to undergo internal examinations, ostensibly for cancer, but in fact to check whether they were pregnant. Those found to be pregnant were warned that if they did not give birth at the time expected, they would face heavy penalties. Informers for the dreaded security police were stationed in maternity hospitals. But with food shortages so bad that families could spend up to four hours a day trying to obtain food, no heating in winter, and a chronic lack of medicines and health care, the pronatalist Ceausescu regime left many families with little option. Children were left in cold and primitive human warehouses, because their parents could not care for them.

The effect of denying abortion is a grim picture of long-lasting disadvantage for the children subsequently born. Children suffer, from being raised in exactly the circumstances which their parents had sought so desperately to avoid (Dagg 1991).

The opponents of abortion say adoption is the alternative. They regularly plead that there are thousands of infertile couples wanting babies. To view adoption as a straightforward, rosy alternative to abortion flies in the face of reality. A study of women refused abortion in the United States, showed that almost half found another way to get an abortion and an alarming number reported "miscarriages." The rest gave birth, but only one in five of the babies was adopted.

During the 1980s it was official U.S. government policy to encourage adoption, as part of bolstering the institutions of marriage and the family. The government, along with much of the anti-abortion movement, assumed a glib stereotype of the woman who is accidentally pregnant—they only saw her as young and single, and, with scarcely a backward glance, able to relinquish a baby for adoption. In fact half of the women who seek abortions are mothers already—they have children and would have to weigh the emotional impact on those children of seeing their mother carry a pregnancy to term and then, "give the baby away."[10]

Refusing women abortions casts a long, dense shadow over the prospects of the children they are forced to bear, whether they are raised by their biological mothers or adopted. And adoption is not a smooth ride, for anyone involved. Few women see it as an acceptable way of resolving an unwanted pregnancy. It is possible though that if the anti-abortion tactics of systematically shaming and harassing women at abortion clinics continues, adoption will appear an easier option.

Making It Legal Is Not Enough

Despite opposition, there is a world-wide trend towards recognizing the need for safe legal abortion. Around 40 per cent of the world population lives in countries where abortion is widely permitted, at least in the first trimester. Restrictions and conditions may range from limiting abortion only to women whose health is endangered, to requiring teenagers to obtain the consent of their parents, or married women the permission of their husbands. But the statute books are no guide to the availability of abortion (Henshaw 1990). Abortion may be legal, and yet unsafe abortions still rife. In India, for example, abortion has been legal since 1971, but acute shortages of medical

THE HEALTH RISKS OF ABORTION

Scientific and medical conflict about the hazards of abortion has been as fierce as the political and moral controversy. Of course they fuel each other. The charges against abortion are that it is dangerous for women; it makes it hard for women to get pregnant in the future; and it increases the risk of ectopic pregnancy, miscarriage, even breast cancer. Women who have abortions become depressed. They might even kill themselves. In 1987 anti-abortion psychiatrists in the United States began to write about "post-abortion stress syndrome." The media quickly took up this new "fact" about the risk of abortion. President Ronald Reagan promised the anti-abortion movement that he would order his top public health official, United States surgeon-general C. Everett Koop, to prepare a "comprehensive report" on the impact of abortion on women's health.

Koop was known for his fervent "pro-life" stance, and the opponents of abortion were confident such a report would detail the terrible effects of abortion and forge a path towards an utter rout of abortion rights. Koop duly reviewed more than 250 published research articles, but his conclusion came as a shock. Far from bolstering the president's anti-abortion prejudices, Koop declined to issue a report at all, saying that "the scientific studies do not provide conclusive data on the effects of abortion on women."[a] Eventually in 1989, a congressional committee compelled Koop to release his report and ordered him to testify. Koop told the committee that the problem of adverse psychological effects on women was "miniscule from a public health perspective."

Koop was right about the difficulties with the evidence—a great deal of the research is flawed. According to one exhaustive trawl of the literature the defenders of abortion seem to rely on better-conducted research. But studies of women's attitudes, for example, rarely distinguish between *unwanted* pregnancy and *unplanned* pregnancy, and sometimes paid no heed to women's circumstances and motives for seeking abortion. Delayed reactions are especially hard to study. Often important questions are not even asked, for instance: if post-abortion syndrome exists, how does it compare with post-natal depression? What's more, is there a difference between the "mental impact of having an abortion" at eight weeks and having one at eighteen weeks? Does the method of abortion affect physical and psychological responses? Common sense tells us it all makes a difference, especially when it comes to the psychology, and yet many of the studies do not separate out all the influences. The information below comes from Britain and the United States, where standards of health care are relatively high.

Complications of the Operation

In the **first twelve weeks (the first trimester)** infections are the commonest hazard. Most are mild and prompt treatment can prevent further problems. Other possible hazards include blood clots retained; damage to the cervix; incomplete abortion;

continued

and—extremely rarely—perforation of the uterus or other organs. Between 1 and 5 per cent of women suffer from a complication and most are very minor (Savage 1995).

After thirteen weeks the hazards are the same but the risk is greater and general anesthesia brings an additional risk. (In most countries general anesthesia is not used in first-trimester abortions: Britain is the exception.) Different methods of abortion carry different risks. In general, from thirteen to sixteen weeks the dilatation and evacuation (D&E) method is significantly safer and more effective than other methods. After sixteen weeks, the different methods carry about the same complication rates.[b]

The most important factors influencing the risks of legal abortion are good, prompt services; the skill of the doctor; gestation; and the woman's age and general health.

Physical Hazards

Providing post-abortion infections are thoroughly treated, there is no link between abortion and future **fertility**.

Legal abortion has "little or no influence" on **ectopic pregnancy** after abortion.

There is "no relationship" between induced abortion and **subsequent miscarriages**.

Abortion did not affect the outcome of subsequent pregnancies, in **miscarriage, ectopic pregnancy, stillbirths, low-birthweight** or **premature births,** according to a large and rigorous long-term study by the Royal College of Obstetricians and Gynaecologists and the Royal College of General Practitioners. In a following pregnancy, there may be an increased risk to newborns of an infection picked up during the birth itself (Germain et al. 1995) The only area of any dispute is premature birth and this risk seems to be related to the technique used for the abortion, and possibly the number of abortions the woman has experienced (Frank et al. 1991)

Breast cancer: There may be a link between abortion and an increased risk of breast cancer before the age of 45, especially for women who have had an abortion in their teens, according to a study in *The Journal of the National Cancer Institute,* published in a blaze of publicity (Daling et al. 1994). Ignoring an editorial in the same journal which observed that "neither a coherent body of knowledge nor a convincing mechanism has been established," anti-abortion activists rushed to the television studios to claim, an abortion "*can cause* breast cancer." This is unscrupulous and exploitative, although clearly no one should dismiss the evidence out of hand. It is now clear that the difficulties of investigating the link between breast cancer and abortion are considerable and other studies have shown no increased risk (Gammon et al. 1996, Newcomb et al. 1996). Besides, if telling a 19-year old woman with an unwanted pregnancy that she runs an increased risk of breast cancer is enough to change her mind, than an abortion was probably not what she really wanted in the first place.

continued

Finally, as one experienced American doctor observed, "feelings and attitudes of those providing abortion services have a profound effect on the quality of care the patients receive" (Hern and Corrigan 1980).

Mental Health Hazards

Unwanted pregnancy is a stressful life event, however it is resolved. A woman's response to whatever decision she makes reflects the pregnancy's meaning for her. The feeling most often expressed by women who have recently had an abortion is "relief" although regret, sadness and guilt may be mixed in as well. The most stressful time for them is before the abortion, not after it.

What about delayed reactions? A group called Women Exploited by Abortion says that almost all women who have had an abortion suffer moderate to severe emotional and psychological stress. And then there is "post-abortion syndrome," defined as a type of post-traumatic stress disorder.[c] There is a dearth of evidence about long-term hazards—studies seldom compare the impact of an abortion with the impact of childbirth on women's mental health. One recent, authoritative study which did make such a comparison showed that rates of total reported psychiatric disorder were no higher after an abortion than after childbirth (Gilchrist et al. 1995). Studies claiming "post-abortion syndrome" are fatally flawed (Holden 1989). The balance tips in favor of abortion, when it is freely chosen: "severe negative reactions are rare" (Adler et al. 1990)

Among women who do suffer mental health problems after abortions, there are some discernible patterns. Women who had mixed feelings about the pregnancy, who were in conflict about the abortion itself, who blamed themselves or felt ashamed of their need for abortion, or who had no one to turn to for support, were all more likely to have difficulties. Other pointers to possible distress were abortions for medical or genetic reasons, a history of mental illness, and abortions later in pregnancy. The more difficult the decision, the more likely there were to be negative feelings—a fairly simple guideline for counselors to help them make sure that women get offered as much time as they need before the abortion, and, if they decide to go ahead, extra help and support afterwards. No one has tried to weigh up the effect of the anti-abortion campaign's systematic attempts to shame and stigmatize women who have abortions—a new factor in the balance.

Finally, whether or not mental health problems are "minuscule" as the U.S. surgeon-general stated, society still has to make its judgment as to what level of risk is acceptable and what women should be told, in order to give their informed consent (Wilmoth et al. 1992).[d]

Effects of Refusing Abortion

"The psychological responses to abortion are far less serious than those experienced by women bringing their unwanted pregnancy to term and relinquishing the child for adoption," according to two Canadian studies which found the majority of such

continued

mothers still grieving, ten years or more after the event. By comparison, after abortion, such long-term effects were very rare (Sachdev 1993). A third of women refused abortions who subsequently brought up their children said they feel negatively towards them. And crime studies reveal that more than eight out of ten newborn babies who get murdered by their mothers are from unwanted pregnancies. Children born unwanted are at serious developmental risk. They have more insecure childhoods, more psychiatric care, less schooling, and are more at risk of delinquency, even after important factors such as social class are taken into account. Of course, not all unwanted pregnancies end this way, but the idea that every woman is transfigured into a loving mother, once her baby is cradled in her arms, is the myth it always was (Dytrych et al. 1975).

In the opinion of C. Everett Koop, only a five-year prospective study, costing US$100 million would yield unalloyed evidence about the hazards of abortion. But even in the face of a tidal wave of irrefutable scientific evidence about psychological damage, one side would attribute it to the frightening climate of anti-abortion bigotry and guilt-tripping: the other would claim it as evidence of trauma about baby-murder. Science has never held the key to consensus.

NOTES

[a] Adler et al. 1992. Koop may have been frustrated to find that, due to pressure from the anti-abortion lobby, the government's own monitoring organization, the Center for Disease Control, had stopped collecting data comparing the safety of abortion with childbirth.

[b] Chapter 7 looks in detail at medical abortion—using RU 486, the "abortion pill." Most studies on safety reported here concern surgical abortion—by scraping the womb or sucking out its contents.

[c] Speckhard and Rue 1992. It was Speckhard and Rue who coined the term "post-abortion syndrome" in a paper written in 1987 at the request of the United States National Right-To-Life Committee.

[d] Wilmoth and Alteris 1992. The authors question whether if counselling is to include information on the health risks of abortion, it should not also include the emotional and physical risks of giving birth.

facilities and trained personnel mean that, for a great many of India's women, safe abortion is still beyond reach, especially in the countryside. Illegal abortions may outnumber legal operations by more than ten to one and may be responsible for the deaths of as many as 25,000 women every year.

Abortion may be strictly prohibited, yet widely practiced in acceptably safe conditions, as it was in Belgium in the 1970s and 1980s. Bangladesh also has laws which threaten harsh penalties for abortion, unless a woman's life is in danger. But in 1979, when women were dying at the rate of 8,000 a year from illegal abortions, the government recognized the practice of "menstrual regulation" (see Chapter 7) as an "interim measure of establishing non-pregnancy." On the whole, however, if the law allows abortion, it is likely to be safer for women. One point alone illustrates this.

When performing abortion is a crime, there is no safe forum for doctors, other health professionals, and providers of services to learn from each other. Only when it is above board can doctors acquire safer techniques, teach students, discuss how to control pain, write papers, hold conferences. Only when it is legal can health services work towards developing lower-cost, more accessible and local provision. Likewise, all counselling has to stop. Poland proves the point.

A wall of silence grimly surrounds abortion when those who seek it and perform it are branded as criminals. There is no room for hesitation, exploring feelings or ambivalence when seeking an abortion means breaking the law.

4

The Fetus Factor:
Ethics and Arguments

A BORTION AS A MORAL QUESTION insistently confronts us. Deciding about abortion is in a different league from a woman's decision to change her job because "the question of what beings it is seriously wrong to destroy" is one of the central questions of ethics (Tooley 1983, p. 95). The politics and policies of abortion are one thing, but many people on both sides of the divide on abortion agree that it is at heart a "moral issue."

And because abortion connects with the ethics of life and death, there is unease. Opinion polls consistently reflect the uneasy view—"permit but discourage." Opponents of abortion rights have moved in on that ambivalence, with language such as "baby," "unborn child" and even "murder" and "murderer" to bolster their essential message—that the fetus is a person, with an independent existence and the *same* moral rights as an adult person. And abortion, therefore, is a form of murder.

Sometimes defenders of abortion rights have tried publicly to challenge the anti-abortion murder thesis within the parameters set by the claim that the "fetus is a person." This has pushed them into assertions that abortion is of no more consequence than visiting the dentist for a tooth extraction, because after all, they say, physically the embryo or fetus is no more than a "clump of cells," and no more a full human being than an acorn is an oak tree. But many others who defend abortion, including many feminists, feel uneasy with such a claim, especially when it comes to later abortions. As one troubled feminist put it: "Nobody *likes* abortion. The right to have one cannot be fought for with the same zest as the right to equal pay or universal day-care" (McDonnell 1984, p. 28).

Campaigning for abortion today as a practical and ideological issue of women's oppression requires feminists to have a firm grasp of their own moral code and thoroughly to understand their opponents' underlying philosophies, however crude and distorted they may sound by the time they have been through the mill of propaganda leaflets. This chapter focuses on the ethics and the ingredients of the moral philosophy that underlies that anti-abortion argument and sets out the *ethical* defense of abortion.

But there is no balanced, universal "moral truth" about abortion, waiting to be discovered somewhere along the spectrum of views between flat-out feminism and the pope himself. It is startling, considering the Roman Catholic Church's current vehemence against abortion, to find that even church doctrine has oscillated. The early founders of Christianity were against abortion but Tertullian describes abortion as a "necessary cruelty."[1] It was not until 1869 that the pope proclaimed that "ensoulment" took place at conception and forbade all abortion. In the previous six centuries Catholic notions of permissible abortion centered around the moment of "quickening," when fetal movement is first felt. At that instant the soul arrived but before that moment abortion was not a sin.

Intuitions about what is distasteful or acceptable are not a secure reference point either, especially at a time when medical and biotechnological advances are rapidly shifting the goal-posts, for instance, inching back the age at which premature infants can be said to be viable. Such intuitions, or what we "take for granted," are historically fickle. Not so very long ago, slavery, torture and public execution were perfectly respectable along with the view that women and black people were less than human beings and therefore not persons in the eyes of the law. The framework of concepts such as humanity, personhood, murder (and maternalism) shifts in the sands of time. "Morality cannot be separated from the social conditions and concrete situations in which moral judgments take place" (Petchesky 1984, p. 356).

Awareness of the limitations of the narrow ethical focus is one reason why campaigners for abortion have concentrated on practical arguments about women's health and rights. They have distanced themselves from debating the morality of abortion and concentrated on trying to counter the "awfulization" of abortion. But reluctance to engage in close debate about morals has paid dividends for the anti-abortion movement, who present themselves to the public as the only people with any sense of concern about the fetus (McDonnell 1984; Himmelweit 1988). They claim the "moral high ground," casting abortion as "bad" and the simple but vague "right to life" as "good." It has been a stunningly successful strategy, putting advocates of abortion rights onto the defensive.

The problem is that there are two arguments going on at the same time, and the emotive simplicities of "abortion is murder" have proved almost impervious to challenge, especially in a culture of thirty-second soundbite debates at the microphone. It seems to me that the anti-abortion camp's moral arguments inform a much wider political and ideological strategy, which many defenders of abortion struggle to highlight, but are at a loss how to counter as long as they are pinioned to arguing about "life." For the narrow moral focus prises abortion out of context, away from a woman's reproductive health and sexual identity in all its complex richness—pregnancy, childbirth, sexuality—and away from the individual woman's life. Feminists are quite right to say that beneath the cloak of the moral issue many opponents of abortion share deep-seated hostility to women's rights in general. Conveying the idea that to have an abortion is heartless and *unwomanly* is part of a wider strategy to push women back into traditional roles or simply keep them there. The "right-to-life" case also drives a wedge between the pregnant woman and the fetus, and makes anyone who tries to tackle these wider ideological issues look like a strident, callous extremist. That is why the mainstream strategy is "pro-choice," a defensive and an innocuous-sounding message, with attractive resonances (of freedom, anti-coercion, and so on), avoiding the risk of offending middle-of-the-road supporters by any talk of power, oppression of women, and so on. The other "pro-choice" retreat has been into the health arena, in which there are powerful practical arguments to be made about the consequences of unsafe abortion for women's health.

I do not discount the question of the fetus's moral value as a potential person. But for me, attributing a potential moral status to the fetus does not instantly close down the argument about the position of a woman seeking to end an unwanted pregnancy. A woman must have the power to decide to have an abortion, because the corollary of *refusing* her an abortion is coerced pregnancy and childbirth. I also believe that women themselves, because of their unique relationship to the fetus (not the same thing at all as "owning their own bodies"), are more likely to make a morally informed judgment than anyone else about an abortion and the other moral claims in their lives.

The ethical arguments against abortion hinge on the "personhood" of the fetus. Traditionally, the *law* pinpoints birth—the observable separation of mother and infant—as the moment at which personhood begins. From then onwards, all persons must be considered of equal value before the law. There

WHEN DOES THE EMBRYO/FETUS BECOME
MORALLY SIGNIFICANT?

Are any of the markers of embryo/fetus development individually robust enough to be the dividing line between those with a right to life and those who lack such a right (Bok 1976)? Many Roman Catholics follow the Vatican view that from the moment of fertilization the embryo has the same moral claims as any other human being. Other moments of moral significance have been suggested, and can contend with the moment when the pregnant woman first feels movement—the age-old marker of "quickening"—the traditional moment of "ensoulment." Most controversially of all, there is viability, the point at which the fetus is "capable of being born alive."

Fertilization provides biological evidence of the advent of human life. It is the moment of fusion between sperm and egg, when the genetic packages are fully assembled. But by the time women have a period, four out of ten of them have lost a fertilized embryo and most miscarriages occur before the twelfth week of pregnancy. Does this imply that we should be searching for a drug to prevent this and ordering women to take it in order to save lives? Making conception the moral marker creates ethical difficulties with fertilized eggs which fail to implant and with spontaneous abortions—miscarriages—which occur later. In law, and generally in medicine, the beginning of pregnancy is defined as the stage at which the fertilized egg, having travelled along the Fallopian tubes, becomes implanted in the wall of the womb (Cook 1985).[a]

The first anatomical feature—the **"primitive streak"**—develops at around fourteen days after conception and is the precursor of the backbone. The Warnock Committee, which looked into the ethics of human fertilization and embryology, chose this as the instant when human life acquires moral importance and banned embryo experimentation after this point.[b]

Now that we are able to see inside the womb with ultrasound scans, a case is being made for the fetus having **moral human properties when it looks human**—arguably at six weeks' gestation. In 1980 the state of Louisiana passed a law requiring women seeking an abortion to see an ultrasound scan, on the grounds that seeing the tiny human form would cause a woman to bond with the fetus and so prevent the abortion (Gold 1984). There has been considerable mileage in such images of "proof" for the anti-abortion movement. See it suck its thumb, they say, see its beating heart—a fetus really is a baby.

All the stages above are only discernible because of modern science. The fact that at between sixteen and twenty-two weeks' gestation, the pregnant woman can feel fetal movement, makes this a very attractive, technology-free marker. Early Christian writings on abortion assumed that a fetus did not possess a soul until the **moment of "quickening"** and it has a similar significance in Islamic teaching. For many women, quickening is a critical moment in pregnancy. It makes sense, at last, of all the previous symptoms. But judged as a moral marker it is an arbitrary event, and we know from ultrasound that an embryo actually moves as early as six weeks after conception.

continued

Most people would understand **"viability"** as the point at which a premature infant has a reasonable chance of surviving. In 1973 the United States' Supreme Court's famous *Roe v. Wade* judgment on abortion held "viability" to be the point at which the state should offer a fetus the same protection as a premature infant. Britain's law, dating from the 1929 Infant Life Preservation Act, makes it illegal to destroy a child "capable of being born alive," except to save the pregnant woman's life. Doctors' interpretation of this law was that after twenty-eight weeks a child was capable of breathing and therefore abortion was illegal from then on.

In 1929, twenty-eight weeks was a reasonable age for viability: nowadays, there are doctors who consider that infants born at twenty-three to twenty-four weeks may be viable—capable of breathing, with or without a ventilator (Chervenak 1995, Greaves 1992). It is an area of great ethical uncertainty, for even with sophisticated life support, only a handful will live. In a study of 342 babies, only a third of those born before twenty-nine weeks survived until the age of four (Johnson et al. 1993). Is a premature infant non-viable just because it is born miles from medical help, with breathing difficulties which could have been helped *if* the medical equipment and skill had been at hand? The logical and somewhat unreal implication would be that the fetus is "viable" in Britain earlier than in, say, sub-saharan Africa. Viability is an unstable concept, dependent on the medical skill and technology available.

A paralyzed elderly person might be completely dependent on others for his or her survival: dependence cannot be the key to "personhood" and moral rights. It is hard to see how the personhood of fetuses can hinge on viability, even if it is a useful yardstick for doctors specializing in intensive care for babies.

In practice, doctors assume a gradual road to personhood and work with a general rule of thumb—"the ascending slope"—though this may give them little comfort in deciding what to do in specific cases. What the slope acknowledges is the hopelessness of trying to locate a sharp moral cut-off point on the developmental path.

NOTES

[a] Thousands of millions of sperm are lost for every one that achieves fertilization of an egg. Less than half the eggs which are fertilized succeed in becoming implanted. Of those which do, around 5 per cent have serious chromosomal abnormalities, but by the time of birth, miscarriage has reduced this proportion to less than 1 percent. Human reproduction involves staggering wastage (Birth Control Trust 1991).

[b] *Report of the Committee of Enquiry into Human Fertilisation and Embryology,* (1984) [Warnock Report] Cmnd 9314, London, para. 11.

have been a number of recent cases strengthening the legal status of the fetus in English law, but the law continues to regard a fetus as an integral part of the pregnant woman until the moment of birth and not as a person in its own right. This is a practical device for courts, but it does not tell us when a human fetus has *moral* status—and therefore the moral rights of a person, which require protection.[2] I have tried to summarize as objectively as possible the case against, and in defense of, abortion, without in the first instance commenting on the merits of either.

Arguments Against Abortion

- "Thou shalt not kill." **Abortion is murder.** Although the taking of human life can sometimes be morally justified—for example, in self-defense—the human fetus is innocent and helpless. There is no difference, morally, between killing a 7-year-old child and destroying a 7-week-old fetus and it is especially wrong to destroy *human* life.
- **Abortion is wrong because the fetus can feel it.** Morally it is worse to destroy an organism, say, a horse, with a central nervous system, capable of feeling pain, than an organism such as a lettuce. At some stage, maybe at around twenty-two weeks, perhaps not until thirty weeks, the fetus is capable of feeling pain (Dworkin 1993, p. 17).
- With the characteristics above—life, humanity, capacity for feeling pain—**the fetus is above all a person.** It is therefore as wrong to destroy it as to take the life of an adult. For some opponents of abortion, there can be no compromise, even to save a pregnant woman's life. Many Roman Catholics believe that all human development, from the moment of **conception,** is the "process of becoming the one he already is" and any other moment for attributing "personhood" is artificial. The fertilized egg contains all the necessary chromosomes within the single cell. Others elaborate this with arguments such as those above concerning life, capacity to feel pain, and genetic humanity.[3]
- Even if, for the sake of argument, the fetus is *not* a person in the full moral sense, **it is undeniably a *potential* human person.** After all, from the moment of fusion between sperm and egg, the genetic blueprint of the crucial forty-six chromosomes is in place. This is what fuels the opponents of abortion in their hostility to experiments on embryos and research into fertility.
- **Widespread abortion is the top of a slippery slope** which dulls the public conscience towards other assaults on the sanctity of life. If abortion is ethical, say those who oppose abortion, there remains no moral defense against infanticide—killing of newborn babies

(Singer 1993, p. 169). If destroying a severely abnormal fetus at twenty-six weeks' gestation is not wrong, how can we prevent a doctor giving a lethal injection to a severely abnormal newborn?

- **Fetuses today have more right than ever to be protected.** As recently as ten years ago, nothing could be done to help a baby born prematurely, at say twenty-two weeks. It had no chance. The minimum age was perhaps twenty-six weeks. Today the borderline has edged back and there are specialist units willing and able to care for tiny premature infants of as little as twenty-two weeks, clinging to the edge of life. This, plus the leaps in our knowledge of embryological development, fetal life, and also the possibilities of giving treatment to babies still in the womb, make a compelling case for recognizing the fetus's independent existence and claim to have rights of its own.

We know that a pregnant woman's drug-taking, alcohol and smoking all harm the chances of a fetus being born healthy; we know that some workplace hazards can also be harmful. It would be wrong not to protect the fetus against the possible dangers which the mother's behavior and environment might pose to its health and welfare. And if we believe it is right to protect a fetus when its future healthy development is desired, how can we deny another fetus its moral rights just because the pregnant woman seeks an abortion?

The arguments above are those of absolutist Christians. Not all are so fundamentally opposed to abortion. In a response to *Evangelium vitae,* the Vatican's most recent condemnation of abortion (and euthanasia), the former archbishop of York, Dr. John Habgood, argued that sometimes abortion is the lesser of two evils, especially when the mother's life is in danger. He criticized the pope for ignoring the facts of biological gradualism and thus erasing the moral differences between contraception, abortion, embryo research, and euthanasia. Other Christians, including Catholics, distance themselves from fundamentalist condemnation of abortion (Habgood 1995).

How Anti-abortion Activists See the World

Anti-abortion activists interviewed in the United States described how offended they felt by the "casual" way in which women sought abortions for their own "convenience," and by the idea that a woman's decision could outrank the weaker rights of the embryo or fetus. "If a child [sic] can't be safe in his mother's womb," they asked, "where can it be safe?" (Luker 1984). In a world which they viewed as a place where men and women are intrinsically different, motherhood is seen as a natural role for women. Abortion demeans women's special role as bearers and raisers of children and also diminishes men's duty to be sexually responsible. It also oppresses women, because men can simply have sex and walk away from a resulting pregnancy, but women must "pay the price."

As with motherhood, anti-abortion activists perceive parenting as something natural, not something which can be planned for and learned. To talk of planned parenthood, like planning to buy a car or going to parenting classes, and of being "ready" for parenthood is as unfathomable to them as it is repugnant. Sex itself is natural and procreative—it creates life and should be sacred and within marriage. Contraception and sex education (especially for teenagers) encourages sex outside marriage and threatens the breakup of the family.

Lastly, the anti-abortion cause itself: like the fight against slavery, fighting abortion is about defending a helpless section of persons in society from being rendered "less equal than others" and from having their lives disposed of.

Arguments in Defense of Abortion

In moral philosophy the defenders of abortion concede that a morally crucial dividing line along the path of fetal development between fertilization and birth does not exist, but this leads them to very different conclusions. Nevertheless, when challenged to pinpoint the moment when "life begins," liberals have felt obliged to contest the ethics of the anti-abortion case, line by line, as follows.[4]

- Reverence for life cannot be the crucial plank in the anti-abortion argument. **Abortion is not murder,** even if it takes helpless and innocent human life. Neither the Christian nor the Jewish tradition gives absolute value to human life. There are cogent moral arguments justifying war. While laboratory rabbits and rats are helpless and innocent, their lives are taken, albeit controversially, in order to benefit humanity. Animals are killed for meat. What is more, scientists still have no consensus on when human life actually begins

(Moore 1990, p. 38). No one yet has suggested that we attribute moral rights to unfertilized eggs or to sperm, which may also be "alive."

- Does the fetus feel pain? In 1994, British newspapers reported the "Pain of the Unborn Baby." Research published in *The Lancet* had recorded the hormonal responses to a blood-transfusion needle in fetuses of twenty-three to twenty-nine weeks. (The blood was given because of life-threatening anemia.) Although the rise in the level of two hormones resembled that in conscious individuals who are in pain, the fetal response, "cannot be equated with the perception of pain," said the study. Until this is resolved beyond doubt, later abortions are more of a problem. **But the *morality* of abortion cannot pivot on the pain issue.** We do not eradicate the moral rights of people in a coma or under anesthetic and kill them, solely because they *cannot* feel pain (Warren 1985, p. 94; Birth Control Trust 1994a).

- **Fetuses are not persons** and it is therefore not morally wrong to destroy them. The defenders of abortion have looked at personhood not as a biological state but as a social phenomenon, involving "the capacities for reason, self-awareness, and social and moral reciprocity" (Warren 1991). These seem to develop only after birth. Liberal philosopher Michael Tooley lists the elements of personhood—the capacity for self-consciousness; to think; for rational thought; to envisage a future for oneself; to remember a past involving oneself; to use a language; and finally, for being a "subject of non-momentary interests" (Tooley 1983, p. 349). The last point is the cornerstone, argues Tooley, and means having "a sense of time, of a concept of continuing mental states, and of a capacity for thought episodes." Citing evidence about the development of the brain during the final stages of gestation (and even for a few weeks after full-term birth), Tooley argues that a fetus is not a person and cannot have the same moral claims as an adult.

- Undeniably, **the fetus is *potentially* a person.** But this does not tell us the moral value of that potential being at a given moment in its development. No one would say that placing a hen's egg—a potential hen—into boiling water is the same as dropping a live hen into the pan, but the case for potential personhood would collapse that difference. Around four out of ten fertilized human eggs are lost before the expected next menstrual period. We cannot even say, until around fourteen days after fertilization, whether a fertilized human egg is going to yield just one individual or two—that is, twins. How far back does potentiality go—to the individual sperm or egg? No anti-abortion advocates have yet proposed rescuing eggs or sperm in order to save life. And how can a potential person, a fetus, have greater moral claim than an actual person, the pregnant woman?

- **The contexts of abortion and of infanticide are totally different.** Once a baby is born—separated from the woman's body—their relationship is changed forever, however dependent the baby still is on others for its survival. "Birth makes it possible for the infant to be granted equal basic rights without violating anyone else's basic rights" (Warren 1991, p. 312). Whereas inside a single human skin "there is room for only one being with full and equal rights" (Warren 1985, p. 103).

- The argument that **abortion heralds a slide into moral decline,** which is followed stealthily by infanticide, is contradicted by the experience of Japan, which has moved from widespread infanticide to abortion as the main method of birth control in the post-war era. In Japan the Pill is still not authorized for sale, because of worries about side-effects, and abortion is commonplace: women can expect to have at least two. It is not a secretive, stigmatized business but neither is it treated lightly. The Japanese do not share the religious belief that a fetus is a human being, but some Buddhist temples provide a religious ritual, *mizuko kuyo,* and people put up baby-size statues in temple gardens, for which they knit little scarves or bibs, or give them baby toys. *Mizuko* means "water children." The parents apologize to the statue to assuage their guilt. Critics say the temples are commercially exploiting people's fears of retribution and there is also a small, mostly Christian movement, the House of Life, calling for abortion to be criminalized. But moderate Buddhists make a moral space for abortion, believing that too many children weakens the family unit and that unwanted children are a tragedy. Women's rights hardly enter the debate. Feminists in Japan have been fighting for access to the Pill in order not to have to depend on abortion, and since March 1996 low-dose contraceptive pills have been available on prescription. One does not need to subscribe to anything so crass as a ladder of moral progress to see that legalized abortion in Japan did not lead to further stages of moral turpitude (Lafleur 1992, pp. 205–6).

- **"It is impossible in practice to grant equal moral rights to fetuses without denying those same rights to women,"** says moral philosopher Mary Ann Warren (1991, p. 311). First, pregnancy makes considerable physical and emotional demands, and injury, even death, might arise from childbirth or an illegal abortion. Secondly, the imposition of pregnancy and involuntary childbirth is an infringement of a woman's moral rights to liberty and to self-determination. Pregnant women are not merely ingenious containers for growing babies. Motherhood is a conscious and demanding activity. It demeans motherhood to conflate it with pregnancy in this way. The ultimate corollary of fetal personhood is nothing other than forced motherhood.

How Defenders of Abortion See the World

In the United States, activists for what they call the "pro-choice" lobby believe that men and women should be equal. What's more, for women to achieve their full potential on a par with men, they must be able to control their fertility. Sex is seen as a good, pleasurable thing in itself, and objections to contraception are regarded as "medieval." Parenting is something that should not be lightly undertaken, and abortion plays a part in making it a chosen activity. Defenders of abortion rights stress that in the long run it will be better for children if parenthood is an option and not simply a state, which at present too many people stumble into before they are "ready."

They do not advocate abortion as a routine form of birth control, for both health and moral reasons, and many feel offended by what they see as capricious and repeated use of abortion. Whilst they acknowledge that a fetus, especially at later stages, must have some moral rights, they emphasize that an embryo or fetus is not the same as a child. Most important of all, they believe that abortion should be something about which people should be allowed to follow their own conscience, not subject to an external moral code (Luker 1984).

Late Abortions: A Case for Fetal Rights?

As the weeks go by abortion becomes a riskier and more traumatic business for all concerned. Pro-choice campaigners know that it is much harder to defend late abortions than early ones. In anti-abortion publicity, gory pictures of late abortions mislead the public into thinking that not only are such abortions typical but also that they are insouciantly undertaken at this stage.

Clear use of terms is crucial here. Although early abortions are generally agreed to be those in the first trimester, that is, before twelve weeks, sometimes all abortions after the first twelve weeks are described as late abortions, at least in the medical journals. In general parlance, however, a "late abortion," implies sometime after about eighteen weeks of gestation, that is, after "quickening."

The 1967 Abortion Act for England and Wales permitted abortion, on the grounds of the risk to a woman's physical or mental health, up to *twenty-eight* weeks. In 1988 the Roman Catholic Liverpool MP David Alton tried and failed to persuade Parliament to prevent abortions after eighteen weeks. In 1990, in an amendment to the Human Embryology and Fertilisation Act, the time limit was eventually reduced and the law now states that after *twenty-four* weeks abortion is only permitted if the woman's life is in danger or if there is a serious risk that the child will be handicapped. Neither is defined and doctors are confused about the rules.

Medical advances in saving the lives of very premature babies (and in maintaining the pregnancies of women injured in accidents who are technically "brain-dead," until the infants are mature enough to be delivered) affect the ethical framework surrounding later abortions. With more and more premature babies surviving, it is not surprising that people ask why there should be abortions at twenty-three weeks' gestation, if there are doctors trying to keep alive infants prematurely born at the same stage. Ideologically, the driving force underlying the controversy is the idea of "fetal rights," which has burrowed deep into medical, legal and moral thinking.

The 1980s witnessed much discussion of the rights of the fetus. The anti-abortion lobby provided some of the most vocal opposition to research and treatment for infertility and genetic abnormality. In 1984, an attempt was made to get Parliament to grant "civil personhood" for embryos—in order to protect them against experimentation.[5] The motives are not hard to find. By talking up the status of the embryo or fetus, the anti-abortion lobby is making a powerful back door attack on abortion rights. The status of "civil personhood" would have established the concept of fetal rights more firmly in law than ever before. Opponents of abortion would have seized on the contradiction between concern over embryos and the continuing legal termination of pregnancies at a much later stage. The door to abolishing abortion rights would have swung wide open.

There has been a welter of statutes and court cases concerning the rights of fetuses. The law in Britain continues to uphold the view that a fetus is not a person in law.[6] The notion of rights for the fetus, however, both as a patient and as an entity in court cases, profoundly if often subliminally influences the moral climate affecting how we view the autonomy of pregnant women to make decisions affecting their health and well-being (McLean 1994).

Fetalism: A New Punishment for Women?

Since 1980, in the United States, there has been an increasing number of criminal prosecutions of women charged with "prenatal child neglect" because of how they behaved during their pregnancies. Women have been imprisoned or committed to institutions. Courts, mostly in the United States, have allowed children to sue mothers for prenatal injury. There have also been cases of women tied down, forced to undergo Cesarean section deliveries in the interests of "fetal patients." In medical journals, doctors are describing women as the "maternal environment"—more or less passive spectators in their own pregnancies. A medical textbook on fetal medicine confirms doctors' loss of interest in the pregnant woman: "obstetricians, *having resolved most of the problems of the mother,* turned their attention to the fetus" (Beard and Nathanielsz 1976, quoted in Franklin 1991, p. 201; my emphasis).

The main target for the statutes has been women who use illegal drugs or alcohol, but other behavior has come under scrutiny. Children have even been taken into care because a mother "ate what she liked" during pregnancy without considering whether the foods "were good for the unborn child." Treating the womb as a dangerous environment and women as the major threat, punishes the person most vital to the fetus's well-being and deters women from seeking antenatal care for fear of ending up in jail. When women avoid antenatal clinics for fear of criminal charges that too is cited, as further evidence of fetal neglect.

No one acknowledges the women's circumstances and lack of choices—the inadequate provision of drug and alcohol treatment programs, to cite just one factor. Individual women are to take the blame—for their poverty, and their poor health (Johnsen 1987). Most of the cases have been taken out against poor Black and Hispanic women. Women who can pay for their medical care are much less likely to be ordered about in this fashion. And this approach to fetal health says nothing about men's behavior—the impact of tobacco, alcohol or drug use on their sperm.[7]

Can women really be turned into ideal fetal containers by laws and health policies? According to one enthusiast, they can and should:

> parents have a duty to receive genetic counselling and carrier testing, to use contraceptives, to be sterilised, to reveal a genetic risk to a spouse or relative, to protect their gonads against adverse affects, and to consider whether they have a "right" to knowingly pass on deleterious genes.
>
> (QUOTED IN JOHNSEN 1992, p. 267)

In 1979 in West Virginia, the Cyanamid company gave five female employees the choice of being sterilized or being fired from a factory where the work entailed risks to pregnant women (Faludi 1992, pp. 477–91). The company said that it wanted to protect unborn children. Several companies in the steel, chemical and rubber industries have developed "fetal protection" policies as an excuse not to hire any women of childbearing age, although the Supreme Court decided in 1991 that the Cyanamid company had acted unlawfully (Hubbard 1994). The sperm is at least as vulnerable to toxic substances, but ideological obsession with the fetus is what underlies these policies, not protection of workers. The U.S. anti-abortion movement has keenly supported such cases. They know that gaining legal rights for the fetus and controlling pregnant women's behavior is a useful foundation for curbing access to abortion. It works both ways: curbing access to abortion and gaining legal rights for the fetus is also a foundation for controlling pregnant women's behavior, and maybe the behavior of women in general. The cases have mostly been against women who are relatively weak targets (Rosoff 1989). It is not difficult to persuade judges and the public that "society" should intervene to protect the offspring of women who are alcoholic or who use drugs, and defending them is an unpopular cause.

But hard cases make bad law. Paradoxically, the new laws may actually increase abortions, as women end their pregnancies in order not to be sent to jail. What is more, fetuses seem to be accumulating more rights than 2-year-old citizens enjoy; there is little "pro-life" interest in the fact that children die in infancy because of poverty, unequal access to health care and decent housing. The risk of dying in childhood is higher in New York than it is even in Mexico City. The cultural message beamed out by these policies is that women are selfish, and neglectful, and thoroughly to blame. They lack maternal devotion and self-sacrifice. Further down the road, women lose custody of their children for similar reasons.

The Battle for Time Limits

In British parliamentary battles to achieve legal abortion or to defend existing legislation, the time limit has always been a highly susceptible target for the anti-abortion lobby. Anti-abortion MP David Alton said that the advances in intensive care for premature babies made it immoral to perform abortions after eighteen weeks.

Feminist campaigners for abortion have never satisfactorily sorted out a clear public view on the morality of late abortion. Most defenders point out that the number of abortions being sought after eighteen weeks is very small, and yet are often the most urgently needed of all—whether the grounds are social or medical. In 1992, around 11 per cent of abortions in Britain were performed after thirteen weeks and less than 2 per cent after twenty weeks. There were sixty abortions beyond twenty-four weeks.

It is often the very youngest women who need late abortions the most. A study of women having abortions between twenty and twenty-four weeks found that almost half of them were under 16 years old (Brewer 1978). In other research, almost a third of the women *and* their doctors had failed to recognize the pregnancy until very late.[8] Some severe abnormalities can only be reliably detected after eighteen weeks, and with some, waiting a few weeks to see if suspicions harden into certainty can avoid unnecessary abortion (Mason 1989; Hall 1990).

What is more, Britain's abortion law, which permits abortion for serious fetal handicap after twenty-four weeks, poses agonizing dilemmas for doctors and patients alike. Some detectable conditions are so painfully lethal that, if born, a child will survive only a short time and may suffer a great deal. Others, while incurable, need not prevent a happy and satisfying life.

Because of a lack of clarity in the law, many doctors, deeply uncertain of their ethical ground, are refusing to recommend abortion as late as the law allows, even for lethal abnormalities (J. Green 1993).

The outstanding objection to abortions later in pregnancy is that, if in one part of the hospital, doctors are using all their skill and expensive technology to help increasingly tiny and premature babies survive, it is wrong for doctors in another part of a hospital to be carrying out abortions. Whatever the law permits, there are some doctors who now argue that after viability, there can be no ethically defensible abortions, even for fetal abnormality, unless the woman's life is in danger or the abnormalities are the sort which entail certain early death (Chervenak 1995). The medical profession is deeply divided about the ethics of aggressive neonatal care, which some see as a "razzmatazz of macho medicine" and some feel is a profoundly worthwhile effort. Nevertheless the ethical questions created by neonatal medicine impinge heavily on abortion morality and demand an answer.

The current limit of viability is determined by the development of the lungs. Before twenty or twenty-one weeks there is no way of keeping the infant breathing at all. At present, the medical consensus is that the age of viability is around twenty-four weeks, although weight and the presence of medical expertise and technology may affect this (Greaves 1992). Whether or not the threshold ever shifts back still further, it is highly debatable whether this should automatically dictate the time limits for abortion. Would women be refused abortions after twelve weeks? Ten weeks? Eight weeks? If women can only have abortions up to the point of viability, could this become an argument for denying abortion altogether (Fost et al. 1980)?

It is partly the methods used in late abortion which make it so distressing.[9] Late abortions represent a wafer-thin line between the tolerable and the intolerable, the merely disturbing and the truly revolting. There is no militant lobby in favor of late abortions and yet, and yet. East London gynecologist Wendy Savage describes twelve women who requested late terminations of pregnancy in her health district and the seven whose requests were carried out (Savage 1985). All had severe social or psychological problems. A 12-year-old girl, for example, was found to be twenty-six weeks pregnant after her teacher noticed her stomach and sent her to a doctor. The girl's mother, whose husband was in prison and who was preoccupied with other children, said she'd considered the weight gain to be "puppy fat." The girl said she had been raped in the lift of her block of apartments. And it later transpired that the alleged rapist was sexually involved with the mother. An abortion was authorized on the grounds of the child's mental health and immaturity. To reduce the time limits to say eighteen weeks, as proposed in 1988, would severely impinge on the already distressed lives of such vulnerable girls and women.

On four occasions, LIFE, one of the biggest anti-abortion pressure groups in Britain, has referred cases to the director of public prosecutions, alleging that fetuses born alive following abortion have been deliberately left to die. "Mindful of the distress of the mother," the public prosecutor has taken no action.[10] There is seldom as much furor about late miscarriage—the preciousness of human life is only selectively valued, amidst a great deal of hypocrisy. All too often, women who miscarry late in pregnancy are dismissively told by doctors to "run off home and try again." They receive scant support. Nor is there any vocal opposition from the fetalist lobby about the effects of environmental poisons such as dioxin, which are not only causing birth defects but also miscarriages.

MP David Alton attempted to reduce time limit on abortion, in the name of the sanctity of human life. An eighteen-week limit could in fact lead to more abortions, not fewer, as women who suspected fetal abnormalities, but could not be sure until after eighteen weeks, might seek abortions of healthy fetuses. It might also pressure women in difficulty about deciding what was best for them to rush into a decision, and have a hasty abortion, for fear of being beaten by the looming deadline. When Alton's bill was being debated, the *British Medical Journal* pointed out that making abortion available on demand before twelve weeks of pregnancy would have a greater impact on reducing later abortions than an eighteen-week time limit (Smith 1988).

The bill was a thinly disguised attempt to scapegoat women and restrict their rights but it was certainly cleverly framed. Implicitly, defenders of abortion conceded that there was indeed a moral difference between a late abortion and one performed early in pregnancy. The defense of late abortion was argued in terms of the limitations of prenatal diagnostic technology and the need to prevent disability, and not in terms of what it would mean to force women to carry pregnancies to term. Women's need for abortion on "social grounds" was scarcely raised (Franklin, Lury and Stacey 1991a). In order to protect abortion services overall they conceded ground on "late abortion," and the term was picked up by the media, which dwelt on "child destruction," shifting public perception of abortion away further still from women's needs and reasons (Steinberg 1991).

Although late abortions require more heart-searching than those performed early in pregnancy, offering late abortion does not automatically imply a unstoppable slither into moral recklessness.[11] There are cogent reasons for saying that the later a woman applies for an abortion, the more she needs it, but this begs the question for the anti-abortion camp. To them, a woman never "needs" an abortion, any more than someone "needs" to commit murder. It is only by changing the frame of the argument—away from the "fetal personhood" perspective, and away also from the public-health defense of abortion—that late abortion can be defended on women's terms: by acknowledging the integrity of their decision-making and not setting them up as perverse adversaries of the fetus. For that is the drive behind anti-abortion morality. Insisting on abortion as an integral part of women's reproductive lives, and seeing women as active agents in their pregnancies instead of as "maternal environments," paves the way for a far more unified approach to all aspects of pregnancy, childbirth and child-rearing. The fetters of concepts such as "fetal personhood," and even of "women's rights," contribute little to this unity.

5

From Mortal Combat to Feminist Morality

THE ABORTION DEBATE can never be a purely philosophical disquisition. Too many competing interests—perspectives on the self and the world, biological and psychological data, ideas about gender, moral and religious theories—all confront each other in the maze beneath the debate on abortion (Callahan 1986). What is more, the argument could never be confined to narrow philosophical reasoning. What is going on in the moral philosophy of abortion is that each side finds the other's basic tenet fundamentally unreasonable. Much of the moral argument against abortion is founded on the premise that the fetus is a person and therefore its moral status carries as much weight as the moral status of an adult woman. That is an ideological statement as much as a moral one, yet the moral argument is often conducted as if there were no underlying contest of conflicting ideological values.

Nevertheless, even in its own terms, the philosophical framework shapes our thinking profoundly and sometimes without our even knowing it. The slogan "Abortion—A Woman's Right to Choose," for instance, is underpinned by a framework of moral rights, and counterposing it are the rights of the fetus. These clashing viewpoints are united by a concept so familiar to us that we hardly notice its presence—*rights*. Our whole way of thinking, in the West in particular, is deeply imbued with rights—to vote, to free speech, for minorities; United Nations' Declarations; consumer rights; and so on.

The question of "rights" comes up all the time in the morality of abortion. If the fetus has "a right to life," this affects a woman's sexual and reproductive rights. It might even mean she must incubate an embryo and bear a child against her will. But can a woman's decision "outrank" the rights of the fetus? Unavoidably the whole issue becomes a trial of strength, pitting rights against one another in a kind of moral arm-wrestling.

Suppose, hypothetically the fetus is a person? In a famous article exploring the moral implications of such a proposition, philosopher Judith Jarvis Thomson poses the startling dilemma of a woman who wakes up to find that she has become connected by tubes to a world-famous violinist with a grave kidney disorder (Thomson 1971). Unless he remains attached to her circulatory system, for at least eight months, he will not survive. After that he will be OK.

Meanwhile what? He is unquestionably a person: thus he has a right to life. Ingeniously Thomson argues that despite the fact that he will surely die if disconnected prematurely, the woman has no moral obligations to remain umbilically attached to the violinist. It is too great a sacrifice. She draws a parallel with a woman denied the right to decide whether to end a pregnancy. Thomson says she too is being asked to make an unjustified sacrifice, not merely to refrain from killing another person. In other words, *even if the fetus is a person,* as the anti-abortion lobby believes, this does not resolve the issue of a woman's autonomy nor define when she has a right to decide to have an abortion.

The idea of individuals having moral rights and an equal right to be treated as human beings is a relatively new western idea. It was a powerful engine for campaigns such as the anti-slavery movement and for the early women's movement too. In current debates about population growth, the concept of women's reproductive rights is both stronger and more contested than ever, as, for instance, at the 1994 United Nations Conference on Population and Development (see Chapter 9). Basic moral rights include the rights to life, liberty, self-determination—the ideas are part of everyday speech.

In 1995 a six-months pregnant 19-year-old Florida woman, Kawana Ashley, was facing a possible murder charge for shooting "herself" in the stomach. The bullet had missed the vital organs of the fetus she was carrying, but hit its wrist. After an emergency Cesarean operation, the child survived for two weeks. Her defense lawyers pleaded that she could not be charged with murder, for shooting a body which was her own (Hunt 1995). Likewise, Thomson's woman, attached to the sick violinist, may well have prior claim to her body —it's hers and no one else's—but pregnancy is special and the fetus is not simply an extension of the woman's property, over which she has "property rights." And after all I do not merely own my body, like a computer or a houseplant—I am my body. So perhaps the woman has no moral right to exercise her property rights in a narrow legalistic sense, if the result is someone's death.

Property rights apart, an absolute ban on abortion would clearly infringe a woman's moral rights. The risks of childbirth or of an illegal abortion would expose her to harm, even to death itself. Forcing her to undergo pregnancy and childbirth is an infringement of her moral rights to liberty and self-determination.

It is clear from twenty years of philosophical debate and legal argument that, as long as we stick with an orthodox framework of rights, the pregnant woman's interests will be forever challenged, and pitted against those of the fetus. "It is impossible in practice to grant equal moral rights to fetuses without denying those same rights to women" (Warren 1991, p. 311). There are several other difficulties arising out of the rights perspective. First, the Thomson illustration assumes that pregnancy is unplanned and unwanted, originating perhaps in rape. Many countries have laws which acknowledge that coerced sex is a legitimate basis for abortion even when the same law regards the fetus as a person from the moment of conception. Such overrides may be nonsense, morally and logically, but that is law. Even in Ireland, with the harshest laws of fetal protection, the law now concedes that under certain conditions its citizens are free to travel abroad for the destruction of fetal "persons."

Conceding the right to destroy fetuses conceived through crimes such as rape or incest, or fetuses suffering from severe handicap, seems to imply that abortion can be tolerated, and fetal rights overridden, as long as the woman is not somehow responsible. But if a fertile woman has apparently chosen to have sexual intercourse, even using contraception which she knows might have the smallest chance of failure, she knowingly runs the risk of pregnancy, say the anti-abortion zealots. The unwanted pregnancy or the child that must be given up for adoption becomes the woman's punishment—for having desires of her own, or for being "feckless." "Because I had had sex, someone thought I deserved to die," reflects a woman who had an illegal abortion in the 1960s (Cerullo 1990, p. 89). It is wildly discriminatory, proscribes all thoughts of sex for pleasure, and takes no heed of the fact that, for many women, heterosexual penetrative intercourse is more or less compulsory in their relationships.

Secondly, a right is a hollow abstraction. United States law frames abortion as a private, individual choice, but the "right to choose" can seem more like a bad joke when the government has no duty to supply any facilities for the exercise of those rights and choices. Many U.S. states refuse to spend public money on sustaining their citizens" rights to abortion. When eight out of ten U.S. counties have no abortion provision, the right to choose exists in name only.

Thirdly, "it's my right" is an individualist stance, relying on autonomy, privacy and bodily integrity to defy any outside scrutiny or comment.[1] So when defenders of abortion wear badges declaring, "Get your laws off our bodies," they may inadvertently bolster the pernicious portrayal of women who have abortions as doing so for no more reason than their own feckless whim and shallow "convenience."[2] Such images of selfishness and wanton cruelty by women are nothing new in the masculine imagination: the ancient Greeks created Medea, who ripped her children limb from limb and strewed the bits over the sea out of peevish rage towards their father, Jason.

Which brings us to fathers. The fetus is as much part of the man who conceived it as of the woman, genetically speaking. People are increasingly questioning women's access to abortion with the argument that putative fathers have a moral stake in this decision too.

Fathers' Voices

It is only women who get pregnant and bear children. Historically, it has been women who have raised and cared for them too. That is why feminists argue that women's control over their reproduction is a condition of women's equality and freedom, so that women can choose whether or not to take up the responsibility of childcare. But in recent years men have been claiming a stake in the abortion decision, on the basis of their genetic relationship to the fetus. Blood ties are momentously important in our society. It is the yearning for blood ties which makes so many infertile people perceive adoption as a poor second to having a baby of "their own" by means of assisted conception.

Abortion law in Britain does not recognize rights for fathers or for anyone else. It is doctors who decide whether a pregnant woman's physical and mental health will be at risk if she continues her pregnancy. But in the courts of the United States the question of spousal consent to abortion has rumbled around for a considerable time, and a number of states have tried to make spousal consent or notification part of their abortion law. Hollywood, that barometer of public opinion, has produced a spate of films reflecting popular fears about fathers" rights and the loss of patriarchal control, such as *Kramer vs Kramer, Three Men and a Baby* and *Bye Bye Love* (McNeil 1991).

In 1987, the European Court of Human Rights heard the case of a Norwegian couple who had planned to marry, but decided to have a child first. Once pregnant, the woman changed her mind—about everything—and sought an abortion. The man, Robert Hercz, said he would care for the child. "All you've got to do is go through the pregnancy and the birth," he told the woman as he tried unsuccessfully to prevent the abortion.

The claims of twentieth-century men for paternal rights have unmistakable echoes of the law of the Romans, which punished a woman who sought abortion because she had deprived her husband of his *property*. But being a parent—mother or father—is not a raw biological state of being, it is a social role: that is what adoption is all about. When people get confused about who should be considered the "real parents" as a result of artificial insemination by donor, egg donation and even surrogacy, they are trying to distinguish between the social and the biological relationship. When it comes to abortion, or contested "ownership" of embryos conceived through in vitro fertilization (IVF), a man's only claim is his genetic link to the fetus. It is, however, the social role of fatherhood which counts, not the biology.

We should not brush aside the distress caused by abortion to men who would willingly support and care for a baby and feel a close relationship to a partner's pregnancy and a commitment to her as well. Scant research has been done to explore men's feelings about their partner's abortions. This is a thorny question for feminists campaigning for women to be the sole deciders about abortion, and not having to justify their decision to anyone. How can women insist that this is their exclusive right, if at the same time they call on men to exercise greater responsibility and care in the processes of reproduction?

The anti-abortion lobby has leapt to expose this vulnerable spot in feminist politics. On Father's Day, a crowd regularly pickets a Toronto hospital, with banners declaring that raising children "is not women's work, it is humanity's work." When men have gone to court, with the clamorous backing of the pro-life pressure groups, citing their paternal rights and their willingness to raise the child, they have presented themselves as protectors of the fetus, against the would-be destroyer, the woman. (Vengeful Medea is not far away.) Because the primary responsibility for raising and supporting children still remains women's burden, such men are seen as heroic and exceptional.

Rights for fathers are nonetheless grist to the mill for the anti-abortion strategy of attrition on pregnant women's rights as long as those fathers want to *thwart* abortion. No one has suggested men should be able to pressure a woman towards an abortion, although there is some evidence that if a man favors abortion, this can have an enormous influence (Ooms 1984; Kenny 1983). More reflective people in psychology and social work have advocated that fathers or spouses should perhaps be consulted before an abortion and that this could become part of the counselling process. I do not see women's control over the abortion decision as incompatible with asking men to take more responsibility for raising children (and for contraception, too), but women will always have a greater stake in the reproductive process. The corollary of outlawing abortion is not after all, forced "fatherhood," it is forced childbearing—an event whose significance in a woman's life is seriously and curiously disparaged in the anti-abortion polemic, as Robert Hercz's "all you've got to do . . ." remark shows so plainly.

Contending rights—for fetuses, women, putative fathers—spawn and multiply. The result is a bear pit, which compels the protagonists to stress their differences and frame their claims only in detriment to their rivals. Nonetheless, rights are an international common language and it is incredibly hard to discuss abortion in any other way, especially when faced with a microphone and demands for a "soundbite." The case for the right to abortion as one of the fundamental elements of women's equality and sexual freedom is powerful, even if it derives from the male-dominated western tradition of individualism and property rights. Thus it is, with all its faults, the borrowed language of feminism. Tactically, rights have proved a most successful way of obtaining access to legal abortion.

Shared Respect for Life

The issue of whether the fetus is a person and the contest of maternal/ fetal rights have pushed the abortion debate into a shouting match of accusation and calumny. Philosopher Ronald Dworkin, observing that there is no militant lobby in favor of abortion on demand in the third trimester, concludes that people on both sides of the abortion argument *share* a commitment to the intrinsic sacredness and inviolability of human life. Where they differ is in their belief as to what life's values should be (Dworkin 1993, Chapter 3).

The idea that an abortion should only be undertaken "reluctantly and with a strong sense of tragedy," is almost universally expressed among defenders of abortion rights (Callahan 1976). A few feminists, however, have pointed out that it reinforces women's sense of shame and failure to foster an image of abortion-seekers as always desperate, always traumatized, never *wanting* to have an abortion. As one recalls:

> When I was young and unwillingly pregnant and afraid I wouldn't find an illegal abortion in time, *that* was traumatic. Finally arranging for an abortion and having one produced a great relief, the end of my trauma. My desperation consisted of not wanting to be a mother in 1968.
>
> (CERULLO 1990, p. 90)

The case against abortion derives much of its momentum from its advocacy on behalf of the fetus—an innocent human being, wantonly destroyed. We are invited to see the fetus as a creature in isolation, quite separate from its mother, poignantly pitting its moral strength against hers. But as writer and poet Adrienne Rich says: "The child that I carry for nine months can be defined *neither* as me nor as not-me" (Rich 1976). The medical journals which refer to pregnant women as a "maternal environment" and Rich's succinct aphorism are worlds apart. Rich is saying that pregnancy is far more complex, and to reduce it to raw biology, without taking account of the social relationships, is to reduce pregnant women to mere vessels.

It is not easy to explore the serious implications of life and death, without appearing to compromise the integrity of women's moral judgments about abortion. In Holland, the policy for staff at abortion clinics is simply to satisfy themselves that the woman has come to her own decision to have an abortion and is not under any pressure, from family or partner. If she shows ambivalence, she can have as much time as she likes to talk about her feelings, can go away and come again; no one will lose patience with her for being uncertain. But it is considered paternalistic to probe into the reasons given by women who seem sure of themselves.[3]

Perhaps the counselling process does need to be thought through again, so that women can feel sure that all their feelings have been thoroughly explored, and doubts do not rear up years later in the form of self-recrimination at moments of crisis. This is a far cry from calling for mandatory counselling or setting down protocols. Both will debase the counselling process, as has happened now in Germany. In the United States too, informed consent and counselling have been devalued and now rarely mean more than women being forced to see or hear mischievous propaganda such as that "Abortion is major surgery" or "Do you know that fetuses have fingernails?" Perhaps counselors should be encouraged to give women the *option* of knowing more about the development of embryo and fetus: as an option, it could give a richer meaning to the notion of informed consent. More positively, good counselling can do much to help a woman see an abortion as an act of self-affirmation:

> If, in a moment of psychological vulnerability such as that caused by unwanted or ill-timed pregnancy and abortion, women reflect adequately on the event and receive counseling, the result may be to help them grow, enhance their ability to choose other behavior voluntarily, and to begin to acquire greater confidence in their own decisions.
>
> (LONDONO 1989 p. 173)

However, it is hard to see how the ideals of sensitive and gentle counselling can be achieved, when abortion services are beleaguered, literally in some cases. What remains certain is that the case for fetal personhood and the arid conflict of rights do not get us very far. That's why some feminists have been searching for another way of looking at the morality of abortion.

Philosophy Is Sexist

The clash over abortion has prompted a great deal of research, in psychology and philosophy as well as in medicine. One particularly fruitful study, by Professor Carol Gilligan of Harvard University, has fundamentally challenged the relevance of conventional moral philosophy, which tries to clarify abstract moral principles, and specifies the moral duties upon us which flow from those principles.

Gilligan interviewed twenty-nine women considering abortion. It was a difficult decision for many, not because they believed the fetus to be a person, but because of the conflicting *responsibilities* they were facing—to themselves, to their families, to the fetus. When they worried about their ability to shoulder their responsibilities to "the child," they meant the future child, not the present fetus. Gilligan concluded that women think about uncertain moral issues in a different way from men: what matters to them is their sense of responsibility to care and nurture others and not to injure or cause pain. She called it an "ethic of care," rooted in the concerns of daily life rather than in abstract universal axioms. Gilligan warned against the "blind willingness to sacrifice people to truth," a danger inherent in the conventional search for abstract moral principles (Gilligan 1982). Interviews with fifty women in Romania, who against all odds, managed to obtain illegal abortions during the brutal Ceausescu era, are a poignant example of Gilligan's argument:

> Almost every woman considered abortion as a way to protect and secure her existing family. As they perceived their sacrifice as a form of devotion, the women took upon themselves all possible risks to their health, freedom and wellbeing . . . "I did what I did for my family, to bring up my children. I was confident God would understand."
>
> (BABAN AND DAVID 1994)

Gilligan's conclusion is also echoed by a very different study of 1,900 women in the United States and their reasons for wanting (legal) abortion. Many said they were too poor to care for a child properly; many framed their reasons in terms of their personal immaturity or the impact of one more child on existing children or personal relationships—in other words, in terms of their responsibilities to others. How ironic, say the authors, that women seeking abortions are dubbed selfish, when

> Their abortion decisions reflect their desire to optimize the quality of their marital and child-bearing experiences, and to reduce the risk of physical, psychological, social and economic disadvantages for themselves and for their existing children.
>
> (RUSSO, HORN AND SCHWARZ 1992, p. 202)

When women ponder abortion, they do not act out a law court in their heads, assessing elegantly argued cases in a cerebral balance of conflicting moral rights. Their moral reasoning takes place within a framework of interpersonal relations and their responsibilities towards themselves and others. One has to be careful not to overload Gilligan's case with a mischievous chromosomal inference. The study does not "prove," as some U.S. right-to-lifers have suggested, that women's moral reasoning derives from their essentially nurturing natures. What it shows is the incompleteness and aridity of the quest for universal truth and moral duties. A framework such as

Gilligan's, however, does not deny the value of the fetus, nor the intrinsic value of life; it says something altogether different. The conventional moral philosophy approach is gender-biased in its failure to take the reality of women's ethics into account.

Good and Bad Reasons?

Supposing a woman says, "I do not want to be pregnant, I do not want to have this baby." Some would say that she is simply exercising her moral right to determine her own future and that absolutely no one—lover, church, state, doctor—is entitled to require any justification or to pass comment on any reasons she might give.

Yet assertions as trenchant as this provoke unease. There is an aggressive insularity about rights, implying that no one else can scrutinize, comment or need even understand. There is also the smack of consumerism lurking in the vicinity of a "right to choose," as if an abortion was an item to be selected according to personal, even whimsical, preference. That may be what led a feminist doctor to describe in the *British Medical Journal* how she balked when she encountered a well-heeled woman in her consulting room, confidently asking for an abortion. The patient explained that she wanted a fourth child, but not just yet, as the family had booked a skiing holiday and it would be inconvenient to be pregnant before the spring (Greenhalgh 1992).

This doctor places herself among the staunchest defenders of abortion but she deplores women seeking doctors' authority for abortions which merely suit their own "convenience." There is a seldom-questioned assumption that abortion must never be for a "trivial" reason, or else somehow the moral force of the woman's decision will be diminished. But as Dutch sociologist Evert Ketting remarks, "I'd hate to be the baby who had to be born to parents who said they'd rather spend their money on a new car than on bringing up a child, and were told their reason was trivial and they could not have an abortion." "Convenience," of course, is a dirty word when we are discussing motherhood, the supremely self-sacrificing state of being. What may be desperately harsh life circumstances to a pregnant woman, such as poverty, poor health, single parenthood, may be cruelly dismissed as convenience or capriciousness by critics of her abortion.

Dividing reasons for abortion into "good" and "bad" is a treacherous moral enterprise. Contraceptives used but did not work—good; contraceptive remained in the bathroom cabinet—bad. Will be thrown out of school or family if pregnancy is discovered—good; pregnancy will mess up holiday plans—bad. Abortion as a tragic, desperate measure—good; abortion as calculated means of fertility control after a decision to use condoms and not the Pill—bad. How can anyone make such moral judgments? The whole business is riddled with assumptions about our social behavior. It assumes that we make rational, informed consumerist choices, and are never muddled or ambivalent about our relationships and our lives when in fact most of us are for much of the time. It also assumes that fertility ought to be 100 per cent controllable.

The fact that individuals do not determine their social circumstances does not invalidate their choices or their capacity to make them. It may suggest that, rather than focusing on "good" and "bad" choices, we have to strive to change the social background against which we choose, work and reproduce.

There are, in particular, some opportunities for seeking abortion which scarcely existed when the 1967 Abortion Act was passed or when the United States 1973 *Roe v. Wade* decision was handed down. First, prenatal genetic screening offers women the chance to seek abortion on the grounds that the fetus is to some degree abnormal. Most detectable genetic diseases are as yet untreatable prenatally, so access to abortion is central to the provision of prenatal diagnosis. Secondly, the same technology also makes possible sex-selective abortion, if the fetus is found not to be of the preferred sex. Both these kinds of abortion have been held to account for whether they are "good" or "bad" abortions.

Prenatal diagnosis offers parents-to-be extraordinary scope to discover an ever-increasing amount of information about possible fetal defects, in pregnancies which start out, it is fair to assume, as welcome. These new technologies pivot on the availability of abortion—the only "remedy" at present for nearly all detectable abnormalities. Doctors have queued up to approve this method of reducing the prevalence of disability, seeing prenatal diagnosis as a powerful technique of preventive medicine.

Feminist attitudes have been divided. Some have been highly critical of the implications of prenatal diagnosis and, indeed, much of the new reproductive technology. They have warned women not to be dazzled by the gadgetry and duped by doctors into acting as accomplices in a plot to create a perfect society in which women's wombs are treated as little more than animated pots in which to grow "designer babies."

The technology does offer a double-edged sword. Barbara Katz Rothman, who has extensively explored its implications for women, argues that in gaining the choice to abort less than perfect fetuses, women are at the same time losing the choice simply to accept babies in whatever condition they come (Rothman 1984, p. 30). Yet to say that because the potential is there to abuse the technology, women must therefore reject it and the choices it offers, wholesale, is to endow the technology itself with a kind of magic, instead of recognizing that the pressures come from the politics of medicine and motherhood, which determine how the technology is applied.

Whatever women choose, they are vilified from one direction or another. If they refuse tests or abortion they are seen as irresponsible, especially by doctors. A woman choosing abortion for reasons of a fetal abnormality gets attacked from other quarters. She is accused of selfishness for her willful refusal to sacrifice herself to care of a baby with disabilities, even "where the abortion decision is as much about the foetus's chance of a reasonable life as the mother's willingness to care for it" (Himmelweit 1988, p. 49). Locating abortion in a framework of individual moral rights serves to bolster the willful aspects of a woman's abortion decision. (There is more about prenatal diagnosis in Chapter 7.)

Sex-selective abortion of healthy fetuses seems to pose an impossible dilemma for feminist defenders of abortion. It is surely as outrageous to abort a female fetus, following prenatal diagnosis, as to practice female infanticide. The quest for sons, which totally devalues women—unless they manage to grasp a few shreds of social esteem by bearing sons—seems to be nothing more than the "original sexist sin" (Powledge 1981, p. 196). But outlawing abortion or the use of diagnostic technology for purposes of sex-selection is a small step from proscribing further reasons for abortion. While no one would militantly defend abortion in order to encourage sex-selective abortion—whether to get boys or girls—the women who undergo late abortions in such dire circumstances need compassion, not denunciation of their "sexist acts." (Sex-selective abortion is discussed further in Chapter 6.)

A Feminist Morality of Abortion?

A moral framework which pits the rights of a pregnant woman against the rights of a fetus, each with mutually exclusive interests, offers nothing towards making the world a more caring, collectively responsible place. But, "the polemical power of rights language as an expression of aspirations for justice across widely differing cultures and political-economic definitions cannot easily be dismissed" (Correa and Petchesky 1994, p. 110). Women who have searched for a feminist ethic of abortion have explored different aspects of the *context* in which women make choices—asking how a decision about abortion is made and, above all, questioning the nature and meaning of the woman's relationship to the fetus.

Is it merely the patriarchal system of sex-role conditioning which creates a woman's relationship to the fetus or makes some women feel ambivalent about abortion? Several feminists have written about their own pregnancies, acknowledging that whatever the eventual outcome—abortion or birth— they did not feel that the growing fetus was a mere "blob of tissue" or "clump of cells."

If a fetus is more than a blob of tissue, by the same token a pregnant woman is more than a passive vessel in which the developing fetus does its own thing, as the anti-abortion lobby tends to depict the scene. Nor does a pregnant woman's feeling of a relationship with the fetus merely betray how deeply she has been brainwashed by patriarchy, as some feminist radicals have alleged. She is in fact an "active agent" who (willingly, or unwillingly) nurtures the fetus as it grows within her. Before birth, no one but she can do that: after birth, such nurturing becomes a social role—others can become the baby's mother.

Stressing the woman's *relationship with* the fetus helps us to think in a different way about the vexed question of personhood, or self. Rosalind Petchesky, who has made a major contribution to a feminist morality of abortion, points out that "personhood," whether defined in terms of a God-given soul or as a genetic package, renders the mother a bystander in the development of the pregnancy and leaves out any *social* conception of humanness (Petchesky 1984, p. 345). And a relationship is not just about wanting or valuing something or somebody. To say that the fetus merits respect or has moral significance solely *because it is valued by others* would open the door to the destruction of unwanted newborns.

Petchesky argues that it is not the biological continuity from fertilization to newborn which is the basis of the mother-fetus relationship. What counts, she says, drawing on the studies of writers such as Lacan, Balint and Piaget, is the formation of a concept of self in the infant. And that "*can only occur* in an interactive and social context" (her emphasis) (Petchesky 1984, p. 345). A sense of "me" cannot possibly be an in-born characteristic, and since it is focused on a constructed, social relational concept of personhood, it allows the possibility of including the late fetus and the newborn within the moral framework. The awareness of the relationship may at first be one-sided—only the woman has it, of course—but it is a feature which is irreducible and indispensable.

This complex argument strikes simple chords in everyday life. It acknowledges the pregnant woman's nurturing efforts and sense of relationship to the fetus that makes many women hesitate about late abortion: our habits of language reflect the practice of abortion, that is, the preference for early abortion. An early spontaneous abortion, we call a miscarriage. Later on people say, "She lost her baby." By focusing on the significance of both the process and the relationship, it is possible to see that at the very least after quickening, a woman begins to become intimate with the "personality" within her and with its relationship to her. What makes giving up to adoption so traumatic is the existence of the developing relationship. There is no way of eliminating the pregnant woman as the active agent in the humanization of the fetus. She must nurture and she must be aware. And because of all this, it is the woman whose decision is most likely to be morally informed. To judge abortion morality by reference to holy writ is to discredit women's moral judgment.

Forcing her to participate unwillingly in this process by denying an abortion is a failure to recognize what good nurturing entails and how impossible it is for it to be properly carried out by those who are unwilling. It is as cruel to an unwanted fetus as to an unwanted child "to force it upon an unwilling mother, and it is a singularly cruel punishment to impose upon the woman" (Himmelweit 1988, p. 50). This approach makes it possible for the grounds for abortion to shift—to become humanitarian, rather than rights-based.

More Than "A Woman's Right to Choose"

Despite the allure of "a woman's right to choose" as a political slogan, for many women it has a hollow ring. Their economic and social circumstances are such that they hardly experience the decision to seek an abortion as a matter of "choice," an affirmation of their power and right to determine their own destiny. Opting for an abortion often exposes mercilessly how limited and illusory the "choices" really are.

What is more, in isolation, asserting that women have the right to choose is only half the story. Abortion is a symptom of the social relations and sexual divisions which assign liability for pregnancy and child-rearing to women. Perhaps, in the absence of other forms of progress towards women's equality, access to abortion lets men, and a male-dominated society, off the hook. Radical feminist lawyer Catherine Mackinnon—who sees male domination as "everywhere and relatively invariant"—believes that current laws on abortion are designed to permit men to evade the consequences of sexual intercourse. She is not an opponent of abortion but women have abortions, she says, so that men can control them and have access to their bodies. She brackets abortion alongside forced sterilization, something men do to their victims, women (Mackinnon 1991). Mackinnon's reductionism and her portrayal of women as dupes and victims are mirrored exactly by the anti-abortion lobby, in its bid for the feminist vote. Why else, they observe, should Hugh Hefner's Playboy Foundation give such big donations to the United States pro-choice lobby, if not to pursue men's selfish, sexual exploitation of women? They argue that in a "just society" women would not be driven to abortion. In one jump the anti-abortion lobby then makes this a reason for preventing women getting abortions in the here and now. Even in a perfect society this takes no account of women who want to shape their own lives, to remain childless, to have sexual pleasure without pregnancy or birth, and whose contraceptives fail. Mackinnon is conspicuously silent on these points.

It is not only the anti-abortion lobby which looks forward to the dawn of a perfect society, evasively arguing that it is purely the economic and social pressures of a society marked by poverty, racism, poor housing, and personal and institutional injustice and oppression towards women which lead to abortion. Marxists also have ventured to suggest that when "the whole community assumes responsibility for the welfare of mothers and children, [then] the community as a whole should now have a share in judging whether a particular abortion should be performed" (Jaggar 1976, p. 358). How easy it is to lose sight of the outrage that forced motherhood represents and to discredit the moral judgments which women make.

In the post-war period some eastern bloc European countries relied on abortion as the main form of birth control, and beyond their rhetoric posed very little meaningful challenge to the gender divisions of society. Perhaps this did condone male irresponsibility. Ironically, when the abortion rates rose, social commentators condemned women for their selfishness, not men for their irresponsibility.

Of course Mackinnon and the anti-abortion lobby have a good point: women can never have free choice in a male-supremacist society. Many women have indeed had abortions which they would not have had if there had been alternatives, including a supportive partner. Many would not have had sex in the first place if they had not been under pressure to do so. But admitting this does not constitute a reasonable case for forcing women to bear children that they do not want. Denying abortion to women is a perverse and cruel way of dealing with the problem that men get away "scot-free."

A "humanitarian" perspective puts no time limit on abortion and allows it on request. "Humanitarian" is a far from ideal term, with its do-gooding overtones, but it takes abortion out of the context of an individual claim and makes it possible to consider it as an aspect of pregnancy, childbirth and reproductive health care. It enables it to be placed in the context of decent access to health care, rather than being pursued as an abstract legal right for women. Access to abortion becomes something you want to be available "just in case" but you hope you never need, much akin to decent health care for breast cancer. In such a context it might even become possible to explore the wider reasons and the circumstances of women's choices. In her important 1988 essay in *Feminist Review,* Susan Himmelweit calls for a public debate, to challenge the loneliness and privatised nature of the decision-making which is implied by "a woman's right to choose," especially with later abortions. It might also help to create an atmosphere in which there would be greater "public responsibility for what are now seen as private matters." As Mackinnon observes in an uncharacteristically delicate moment:

> While most women who abort did not choose to conceive, many women who keep their pregnancies did not choose to conceive either. The priority women make of their offspring may be more true in the abortion context than it seems. Many women have abortions as a desperate act of love for their unborn children.
>
> (MACKINNON 1991, p. 1318)

The public debate could ease some of the pain and guilt of the decision: a woman would know that her actions were supported by at least some sections of public opinion acknowledging the difficulty of her circumstances.

There is no single "feminist" position on abortion morality, but there is a remarkably consistent emphasis on the relationship between the pregnant woman and the fetus. Because of the loss of that relationship and what it stands for, women may grieve after an abortion. Grief, however, should not be conflated with regret, which is a different matter.

Likewise, we should not confuse the *political* question raised by abortion—who should decide?—with the moral question about whether an abortion is right or wrong in a given instance. The *law* emerging from a humanitarian framework might be indistinguishable from a law based on a "woman's right to choose" and the politics must be crystal clear: women have the power to decide, not medical, legal or religious authorities. Giving women the power to decide, in whatever circumstances seem to them compelling, does not remove from us the moral capacity to scrutinize the reasons for their decisions. We may condemn sex-selection, we may feel ambivalent about the pressures towards abortion after diagnosis of fetal abnormality. This does not imply putting individual cases into the dock or, as now, requiring women to make a plausible case. Rather there should be an ongoing debate, similar perhaps to the debate about the acceptable limits of in vitro fertilization and other infertility technology.

Choice does not exist as an abstract freedom and it cannot be disconnected from the realities of power and powerlessness. An unwanted pregnancy is an unjust dilemma in a world in which most women have so little power to choose anything at all, to control any aspect of their lives. And, even in an ideal world, since biology dictates women's special relationship to reproduction, women must always have the option to end an unwanted pregnancy and should not be coerced into pregnancy and childbirth. We have to acknowledge that people do not determine or control the social framework in which they have to make hard choices and respect their dignity and their moral capacity to decide.

What counts is to "focus less on 'choice' and more on how to transform the social conditions of choosing, working and reproducing" (Petchesky 1984, p. 11). A morality of abortion is a process of recognizing the injustice of the very dilemma of abortion and bringing the politics and the morals closer together.

6

A Woman's Right to Refuse:
India, China and Britain

"A WOMAN'S RIGHT TO CHOOSE," probably the best-known feminist slogan of all, demands the most fundamental freedom for women—that they should be able to decide when and if to have children—and it arose directly out of the struggle to legalize abortion twenty-five years ago. At that time the technology of prenatal diagnosis was scarcely on the horizon and the techniques of sex-selection, both embryo-sorting and sperm-separation, were still the stuff of science fiction. Now these technologies are accessible—some quite widely—and are being used in ways which pose troubling challenges to the ideology of medicine, of birth control, and of feminism.

Sex-selective abortion has become a political issue, above all in India and China, where there are women seeking abortion not out of a desire to avoid pregnancy itself, but to avoid the birth of a baby who is female. Defenders of sex-selection, whether by abortion or sperm-sorting, say that choosing the sex of a child is a logical extension of family planning, and that it is inexcusably paternalistic to deny this new opportunity to would-be parents. Feminists and their allies say sex-selection is "one of the most stupendously sexist acts in which it is possible to engage" (Powledge 1981, p. 196).

The technology being used is making the issue of sex-selection much more visible that it was in the past, but the principle of favoring boy babies is itself not new. Female infanticide is as old as the human race. What is different today is that sex-selection, mainly by means of *legal abortion*, is raising new questions about women's freedom to seek abortion.

Both China and India have permissive abortion laws: but it would be a travesty to say that all Chinese and Indian women undergoing legal abortions are exercising "a woman's right to choose" in the intended sense of that slogan. Prenatal sex-selection by abortion is practiced in India by families trying to avoid the burden of bearing and raising daughters. China's stringent one-family-one-child policy has led to an appalling catalogue of abuses of women, including forced abortions, as well as selective abortions of female fetuses by couples trying to ensure that the single child they are permitted to have is a boy.

Abuse of legal abortion of a different kind has been taking place in Britain too. Notably, the British military establishment for twelve years illegally ordered pregnant women in the armed services to have abortions or leave the services. Secondly, some of the original campaigners for legalizing abortion advocated it as a potential tool for maintaining the social order. To put it bluntly, they urged society to adopt such measures, not for the sake of women themselves but, crudely, to curb births among women in the "underclass" of babies who seemed likely to become tomorrow's delinquents and criminals. Not surprisingly there are times when doctors or social workers, in the belief that they know what's best, push such women towards abortion.

Today there are thousands of women undergoing legal abortions they themselves would not choose to have, to comply with state orders, or family bullying, or the pressures of socially discriminatory officialdom.

India: A Fierce New Twist to Old Traditions

Women in India are pressured to undergo abortions which, although they are legal, represent a travesty of any desires to avoid pregnancy itself. The source of the pressure is the intractable and constricting strands of tradition and discrimination against India's girls and women, combined with the matchless allure of the ultrasound scanner, the amniocentesis test and its logical result—sex-selective abortion.

"Boy or girl? We tell you with 100 per cent accuracy," proclaims a roadside poster outside Ludhiana, in the northern state of Punjab. "Save 50,000 rupees later by spending 500 rupees now." All over India, there are clinics performing amniocentesis and ultrasound scans, even in districts too poor to afford supplies of clean drinking water. Every day an estimated 3,000 female fetuses are aborted. And there are doctors making a mint.

A woman has just had an abortion: the fetus was female. She is 25 years old and her husband is a businessman in Ahmedabad, northern India. She has three daughters. Her husband wants a son, she explains,

> and I am his wife so I have to give him a son. How can it continue? Maybe I will never have a son? Maybe it is my fault? Only God knows. But what do I have to do? I am so afraid, afraid that my husband will divorce me and take a new wife who will give him sons.
>
> (ROGGENCAMP 1984, p. 272)

The woman says she would have the test again in future pregnancies and if necessary more abortions, "if only my body can take it," she says.

> He is the man. He has a right to a son. You just don't know what I been going through in these last seven years because all I gave birth to were girls! Again and again it is a girl. I carry her for nine months. The family prays to God, the priest pays a visit, the family undertakes *puja* (a religious ceremony). Then the day arrives, the labour starts. Then finally, the birth. And again—nothing. After my second and third delivery all they did was to send my little brother-in-law to see me at the hospital. It would be so much easier for me with a son. My husband and his family would respect me much more.

Boys are such precious jewels compared to girls, it is no surprise to find that India is short of 50 million women and there are on average 93 females to every 100 males. (The norm is 105 females for every 100 males.)

Watering a Neighbor's Plant

The arrival of a girl baby holds no promise, only the certainty of expensive rituals, the greatest of which is her wedding dowry. When a daughter belongs to the family only until her marriage, and her departure may cost the entire family life savings, avoidably bringing girls into the world indeed looks reckless. As the Indian saying goes, bringing up a girl is like watering a neighbor's plant.

The gynecologists involved in prenatal diagnosis of sex say that by helping couples to be sure they will have a son they are helping their patients—alleviating the anguish that women would suffer by giving birth to girls.

Preventing the birth of unwanted girls is a humanitarian act in itself, the doctors say. There will be no need for women to have extra girls in misfired attempts to achieve their goal, and prenatal diagnosis and sex-selective abortion is a boon, say the doctors, to curbing India's birth rates.

It is bride-wealth or dowry which underlies these abortions. Despite a multitude of laws against it, the dowry system is nothing less than an open, get-rich-quick, extortion racket. Jewels, fridges, cars, scooters, new clothes, and cash are demanded by the bridegroom's family upon marriage. The bride's family must pay up if they are to avoid the shame of an unmarried daughter—the greatest possible stigma.

Bride-burning is dowry's sinister partner. Every year young brides are doused in kerosene or cooking oil and burned to death because their dowry is deemed too small and their impoverished parents can provide no more. Next comes fresh wife, fresh dowry. Sometimes the husband's family, including his mother, conspire with him in this terrible crime. Official figures record that in 1991 alone, almost 2,500 women died this way. Everyone knows the real total is far higher. Better, surely, to kill a female before birth to avoid that expensive burden of living misery, or death as a human torch.

Of course, sex-selection in India did not arrive with the first prenatal test. Infanticide is its ancestor and still goes on today, probably accounting for more female deaths than sex-selective abortion. Baby girls are still starved, poisoned, or fed with scalding fluid within hours of their birth. But since 1971, abortion—up to twenty weeks—has been legal in India. In 1975, the All India Institute of Medical Sciences began to perform amniocentesis tests for fetal abnormality. The word—that daughters need never be born—spread like wildfire. The main centers for sex-selection test and abortions were Delhi and Bombay, India's financial capital, but in quite small towns across north and west India, as well as in Tamil Nadu in the south, it became possible to buy the test and the abortion. Between 1978 and 1982 in Bombay, there were around 10,000 sex-selective abortions and almost every obstetrician in the city was performing the test (Wertz and Fletcher 1989).

The dowry system is at its strongest among Hindu communities, although it is now widely practiced by other groups. It is among Hindus that son-preference finds strongest favor. Sons are desired to continue the family name, to care for parents in their old age, to light the funeral pyre and nurture the parents' souls. Like the dowry, the preference for sons has extended beyond the Hindu community and sex-diagnosis tests are being requested by Muslim and Sikh families as well as Hindus. A closer look at the sex ratios in different areas sheds light on other causes of the preference for sons. For instance, in the rice-growing areas of India—mainly the east and the south—the dowry system is not so inflated, female children are regarded as less of a burden and suffer less disadvantage because their labor is traditionally needed in the fields. Enhancing the opportunities for women to work and earn in India is not just a principle of gender equality in a country where 90 per cent of women are illiterate; it may eventually save the lives of female fetuses and little girls in many rural households (Bardhan 1988).

Indian feminists have not witnessed this booming nation-wide business in genteel silence. They have organized a massive campaign to outlaw the testing and change attitudes: "Daughters are not for slaughter" is their slogan. In 1983, testing for sex was banned in government-run hospitals, but to no avail (Balakrishnan 1994). Private clinics sprang up all over India, and the ban simply invited doctors to hike up their private fees for providing this precious information. In 1986, the state of Maharashtra prohibited pre-natal sex tests outright, with dire penalties for law-breakers. It is a law which is being blatantly ignored: doctors have stopped keeping records and have put the fees up yet again. In 1994 India's Parliament outlawed sex determination again, with similarly stiff penalties, not only against doctors, but also against their women patients if it can be proved that they were not under family pressure. It is not difficult to imagine a family which has browbeaten a woman into undergoing such an abortion, further browbeating her to tell a court that she "was not under pressure." Yet another case of victimizing the victims. Only four states—Maharashtra, Rajasthan, Punjab and Haryana—have implemented the act; the tests continue. For middle-class Indians the chance of escaping the financially crippling dowry is as powerfully tempting as ever. "Doctors, social workers, they all come for the test," explained one doctor.

Feminist groupings such as the Forum Against Sex Determination and Sex Preselection know that laws are not enough to stem the tide. There have been laws against dowry for years, after all. But their work has made sure that, although the tests are widely known about, people also know that there are laws against it and that it is wrong.

The irony is that, despite this abuse of legal abortion, illegal abortion far exceeds legal abortion in India. Women who simply want to end a pregnancy cannot get the safe, legal, medical help they need because there are too few doctors and too few facilities. There are still 4 to 6 million illegal abortions every year, with the accompanying death, injury and disease.

China: A Mockery of Women's Rights

More than twenty-five years ago, the Chinese government accepted predictions that its economy and education system would be unable to support the population unless its rate of growth was slowed. Unchecked, the number of people in China would increase by a staggering two-thirds in the next fifteen years. In the 1970s, official campaigns began to persuade people to marry later, to use birth control and to have their children "late, sparse and few."

In 1979, policies of encouragement gave way to compulsion. The Chinese target was to reduce population growth rate to zero by the year 2000. They announced that "women who give birth to one child only will be publicly praised; those who give birth to three or more will suffer economic sanctions." The 1980 Marriage Law states that it is the duty of all married couples to practice birth control (Li et al. 1990). The western idea of "family planning" had a quite different meaning in China, where birth planning meant that the state planned births "to bring the production of human beings in line with the production of material goods" (Greenhalgh 1994).

Couples who sign a one-child pledge can jump the queue for scarce housing, subsidized health care, and priority places for their children—in schools and even in jobs. Peasants can get extra land allotted to them. The penalty for having too many children includes fines amounting to between 5 and 10 per cent of salaries, plus the entire burden of health care and school expenses for the excess child.

The official rubric is that people can opt to participate. But in such matters there is only the flimsiest line between persuasion and brutalization. The language of official utterances is all coercion. Government employees responsible for population control are urged to "take all measures which are favourable to population control." Tactics such as ordering women to attend study classes and forbidding them to leave until they agree to have abortions, or cutting off water supplies to non-compliant families, may be officially denounced as "mistakes" and overzealous officials admonished, but the message is clear: do not resist (Aird 1990, p. 83).

Only Romania's efforts to *prevent* women controlling their fertility come close to the intrusiveness of the one-child campaign. Homes in China are visited regularly by village family planning workers, often neighbors, who are the backbone of the whole surveillance system. They are expected to know who is using contraception, which methods are being used and who is eligible to get pregnant. Women found pregnant without authorization are expected to have an abortion and some are told to get sterilized (never men).[1] Birth control officials are expected to meet Draconian quotas for villages or factories, and if they fail to meet their targets, they are penalized.

The temptation to abuse "non-compliant" women is, for some, irresistible (Davin 1985). In 1991, for example, according to Amnesty International, in southern China's Guandong province, officials surrounded a village one September night, "searched all the houses and forced pregnant women into trucks. They were driven to the hospital for forced abortions; one woman gave birth on the journey, but a doctor killed her baby with an injection." Amnesty knows of no case where sanctions have been taken against perpetrators of such abuse (Amnesty International 1995).

Across the country, implementation of the one-child campaign has been left to local officials. Killing excess babies, often crushing their skulls at the moment of birth, was described as a "remedial measure"—the euphemism for abortions inspired by this policy. Pregnant women hid in caves and woods to give birth, rather than face abortions at seven, eight, nine months of pregnancy. Despite vigorous attempts to deny such stories and discredit their sources, reports—of late-term abortions, lethal injections at birth, infanticide and secret births—seep steadily out of China year by year.

Chi An, for instance, had had one child and had terminated a second pregnancy. For almost five years, until 1985, she was director of the family planning clinic in a truck factory in Shenyang, northern China. If she kept the number of births in her factory below the quota, she received a cash bonus. If she failed, she faced a fine and an official rebuke. Chi An herself spoke to women with unauthorized pregnancies, cajoling them to undergo "remedial measures." If they refused they were threatened. If they still refused they were locked in a warehouse until they relented.

Then Chi An discovered that a close friend had been pregnant without authorization for five months, and she could not persuade her to have an abortion. She ordered her friend to the warehouse. The woman fled, but was tracked down and given her abortion and later sterilized. Chi An met her quota. It was a turning point.

Chi An could no longer bear what she had done to her friend and many others. In 1985 she went to join her husband who was studying in the United States. Unexpectedly, in 1987 she became pregnant. Planning in due course to return to China, Chi An requested permission for a second child. In reply the factory director ordered her to take "remedial measures." Refusal, she was warned, would mean collective punishment for her family and co-workers: "you would be condemned by all the staff and line employees of the factory. How could you bear the losses you would cause and suffer?" (Mosher 1994).

Chi An sought political asylum, which the United States government readily granted in its anxiety to appease the powerful U.S. anti-abortion lobby and be seen to take a firm stance against China's birth control policies. In 1992 the U.S. President, George Bush, defined a new category of asylum-seeking persons—reproductive refugees—people fearing persecution because of their country's "policy of forced abortion or coercive sterilisation."

Resistance to the one-child policy has been rife in China itself, especially in rural areas, where 80 per cent of China's population lives. It has been fundamentally undermined by the enduring traditional preference for sons. There are frequent reports of birth control officials getting beaten up. In one county in western China, it was found that 70 per cent of women who had IUDs fitted had succeeded in extracting them in order to get pregnant, despite the fact that Chinese-made IUDs were designed to be tamper-proof. They had no string. In the face of sustained popular resistance to intimidation and failure to meet the quotas, concessions have had to be made.

The Return of Eugenics

The logical development of a policy driven by the premise that there are "too many people" is only a few steps away from deciding that certain types of people, for instance with disabilities or other special needs, impose an even greater burden on the state's resources. China has now identified certain types of people as targets for eugenic control, publicly blaming them for producing children of "inferior quality." The pressure to save public costs in this way is familiar in the West and it is one of the most troubling elements of the trend towards screening increasing numbers of pregnant women for abnormalities in the fetus (see Chapter 7 for more on prenatal screening and testing). In China barefaced eugenic policies are being advocated to save state resources.

Chinese premier Li Peng announced in 1991 that a eugenics law would be drafted for the whole of China: "mentally retarded people give birth to idiots," he said. "They can't take care of themselves, they and their parents suffer and they will be detrimental to our aim of raising the quality of the population." A number of Chinese provinces, such as Gansu, had already set the pace, ordering the sterilization of any mentally handicapped people planning to marry, and abortion for any mentally handicapped woman found to be pregnant.

The new Maternal and Child Health Care Law was passed in 1994 (Rich 1994). It requires all couples proposing to marry to obtain a certificate of good health, following a check-up. If their health is found to be unsatisfactory they will either have to postpone marriage or agree to be sterilized. Pregnant women diagnosed as having certain infectious diseases or an abnormal fetus will be "advised" to have an abortion. People forbidden to marry include those with hepatitis, venereal disease and so-called "hereditary" mental illness.

Unveiling the law, China's public health minister, Chen Minzhang, said that China's population included more than 10 million disabled people, "who could have been prevented with better controls." His announcement, not surprisingly, drew a sharp volley of censure from outside China. Human rights organizations were in uproar; doctors and scientists accused the Chinese politicians of scientific ignorance. "A weird choice of diseases," said the scientific journal *Nature* (6 January 1994). There are, for instance, some parts of China, including eugenics pace-setter Gansu province, where people suffer from a remarkably high rate of cretinism, which is caused by lack of iodine in the local diet. The simple answer is the provision of cheap iodized salt, not a eugenics law which violates people's human rights and reproductive organs.

But why has such a policy been proposed in the first place? Reducing the nation's bill for the care of people with physical and mental disabilities is the answer of course, but there's more to it. The one-child campaign has not only been deeply unpopular, it is not reaching the targets which were set for it. The original goal was for China to reach AD 2000 with a population not exceeding 1.2 billion. That figure was reached in 1995 and the target is a lost cause. Throughout the 1980s, despite a tide of propaganda, the incentives were not a powerful enough magnet for young Chinese newlyweds. The average rural family has two or three children and only a small percentage of couples have signed up for one child. Too many forces are pulling Chinese families in the opposite direction.

Part of the pull comes from deliberate state policies, designed to turn the Chinese economy away from central planning and into a market economy.

In 1980, the collective commune system of agriculture was disbanded, and land was allocated to households, to be worked privately. This has severely undercut the logic of the one-child family. Children's labor is a precious asset when families must run their farms unaided. Without commune welfare to help the old and infirm, children seem an even more vital investment. By 1984 the government was compelled to relax the one-child restrictions for people living in rural areas, specifying that if the first-born child has disabilities, *or is a daughter,* a second pregnancy can be sanctioned. An additional countervailing pressure to the one-child policy came from lowering the age of marriage.

Bitter Rejection of Daughters

If the first-born child is a daughter . . . this telling concession reveals the enormous social pressure from traditional Chinese values, which the government has been forced to acknowledge. The preference among Chinese families for sons has, more than any other single factor, undermined the chances of success for the one-child policy.

There is an ancient Chinese proverb: "The most gifted and beautiful girl is not as desirable as a deformed boy." Such bitter rejection of daughters is deeply rooted. In pre-revolutionary China it was a man's most sacred filial duty to provide a son in order to continue his line and failure caused the gravest offense to the ancestors. Boy babies made sound financial sense too. With no state security in old age, parents looked to their sons to care for them when old age and infirmity came along. Daughters disappeared upon marriage, their duties owing entirely to their husband's family (Hillier 1988, p. 104).

In pre-revolutionary China, abandonment or killing of female babies was common. After 1949, the practice seems to have disappeared, and in the 1960s and 1970s the sex ratios at birth were close to the norm " roughly 105 boys born for every 100 girls. But soon after the one-child campaign got under way, a group of women from Anhui province wrote a letter to the Communist Party paper, the *People's Daily,* complaining of being persecuted for giving birth to girl children. With such pressures, they wrote, "we will never give up trying to have a boy . . . and we would rather die than be content with a girl." Son-preference renewed its meaning with the need for sons' labor in the family fields. Infanticide surfaced again, dramatically and unmistakably.

A map in the 1994 *National Economic Atlas of China* shows the distribution in 1990 of sex ratios—the number of males per 100 females. The map follows the familiar nursery convention—pink patches for girls, blue for boys—to show where males or females are predominant. It is intensely and overwhelmingly blue: the patches of pink are quite isolated and pale by comparison with the swathes of deep blue. Also there are far fewer pink patches than there were in a similar map illustrating the ratios in 1981. The average sex ratio in China, at birth, rose from 107 in 1982 to 118 in 1992. The disparity between girls and boys born third or fourth in a family is nothing short of sensational: 25 boys for every 100 girls (Greenhalgh and Li 1993, p. 5). There are frequent reports of villages with five boy children for every girl.

Where are the missing girls? As many as 1.7 million a year have "disappeared" from the birth statistics. In 1983, the *People's Daily* did not pull its punches. "At present the phenomenon of butchering, drowning and leaving female infants to die is very serious." There are recurring reports in Chinese newspapers of newborn baby girls being greeted by death. A bucket of water waits by the bedside during labor. In a single Chinese village, forty baby girls were drowned in one year alone. Sometimes girls have been secretly given up for adoption, and neither the birth family nor the adopting family reports the birth. China's orphanages report that their numbers increase whenever birth control campaigns are stepped up in their area. Nearly all the babies left on the orphanage doorstep are girls (Johnson 1993). Well over 2,000 babies each year, 99 per cent of whom are girls, are being adopted by couples from the United States. They pay US$3,000 for each child.

Ensuring Sons the Modern Way

Before 1949, infanticide, abandonment or adoptions of girls were the only available sex-selection methods. Now ultrasound technology opens the door to a much simpler solution—sex-selective abortion. China manufactured its very first ultrasound scanner in 1979 and it now turns out 10,000 a year, as well as importing machines from abroad. The possibility of prenatal sex-selection has proved irresistible. There are around 100,000 machines throughout the country and business is booming in rural areas where the preference for sons is strongest.

The disparity in the sex ratios may mean that more than one in ten of all female fetuses are being aborted. The government has repeatedly banned such use of ultrasound technology, but bribes at the back door of the clinic are a risk well worth taking for couples with one daughter who are "trying again." The news can be given during a routine examination, nothing need be recorded or words even uttered—a prearranged smile or frown can say it all. If the fetus is of the wrong sex, an abortion can be legally obtained—it's all far less risky than infanticide.

Until recently, only the conglomeration of statistics has yielded the evidence of thousands of stealthy deaths. People in villages have worked hard to hide their secret killings, abandonments and adoptions from prying eyes. But access to scanners demands far more public acts of sex-selection. Pregnancies are visible well before the time when a scanner can detect sex with any reasonable degree of certainty and abortions require the connivance of medical personnel. Death by sex discrimination must have become a matter of public discourse, if, as is happening in some provinces, there is a resulting sex ratio of 164 newborn boys for every 100 girls.

Bias towards males is underwritten by the state. By 1988, two-thirds of Chinese provinces had adopted one-child policies which distinguished between a first boy child and a first girl child, saying that the birth of a girl would be disregarded, and a couple could try again.

Newborn daughters whose birth is concealed, for instance by unofficial adoption, face a lifetime of discrimination. These shadow children cannot receive any schooling, or even medical care. It is hardly surprising to find that it is girls born later in the birth order who suffer most: poor nutrition, lack of medical care—they get far less than if they had been the long-awaited sons. And mothers of girl babies may also face violence and abuse, especially if a second child is a second daughter. The government efforts to ban prenatal tests for sex determination have led to a sharp rise in divorce among couples with daughters. One woman's divorce citation read: "The man is not happy with girl baby. He beats woman and does not provide enough to support daughter."

Slowly, a paradox has emerged. Women are becoming a commodity in short supply and as elsewhere in the newly fledged Chinese market economy, scarcity equals value. People are waking up to the implications of having a growing surplus of men with absolutely no hope of marriage. By the year 2020, one million men reaching marriageable age each year will be unable to find a wife. Females, despised for themselves, valued for their potential scarcity in the marriage market: that is the paradox.

Does this mean that in future the cry "It's a girl" will evoke less disappointment than it does today?[2] Will the workings of demand and supply put an end to buckets of water waiting at the bedside, or backhanders in the antenatal clinic? It is impossible to assume that sheer scarcity value will improve the lot of China's little girls. A return to the ancient Chinese practices of bride-buying and infant betrothals cannot be seen as enhancing women's status and self-determination: recent reports of trafficking in newborn girls and abductions of young city women, delivered at a price to single peasant men, underline feminist foreboding.

The one-child campaign, with its abuses and violations of human rights, has led to spectacular state-sanctioned gender discrimination. Without an ethical bottom line, population policies are all susceptible to punitive implementation. The Chinese state is especially deeply implicated in the abuse of women's bodies in China, whether it is through abortion imposed from above, or sought by couples who want to prevent the birth of a daughter.

Must Sex-selection Be Tolerated?

India and China are not the only places giving credence to proverbs such as "Having a son is like having two eyes. Having a daughter is like having only one eye." Becoming the mother of sons is for many women their only hope of status whatsoever, and of exercising any power within the family. When a prince is born into the British royal family, the event is greeted with a twenty-one gun salute; a princess merits no more than ten guns. In countries as disparate as Mexico and Indonesia, sons are favored, the most marked preferences being in Pakistan, Nepal, Bangladesh, South Korea, Syria and Jordan, although many of those countries have laws which outlaw or severely restrict abortion (World Health Organization 1992, p. 17). In South Korea, abortion is strictly outlawed, but widely practiced, and the marked trend toward dramatically smaller families has given a sharp twist to the traditional preference for sons. Korean doctors have spoken out about the misuse of prenatal diagnosis, but the profession is deeply divided and hardly any doctors have faced the professional sanctions which have been put in place to curb doctors' participation in sex-selection by screening and abortion (Hye-Jin 1996). A survey of geneticists in nineteen countries suggested that doctors may be willing to perform tests for sex-selection, in the belief that patients are entitled to whatever services they can pay for (Wertz and Fletcher 1993).

Prenatal sex diagnosis is predicated on the availability of abortion. There are prenatal tests, such as chorionic villus sampling, which can establish fetal sex as early as nine or ten weeks into a pregnancy (see Chapter 7). Are such early abortions, however repugnant the motive behind them, a lesser evil than infanticide or abandonment of newborn female babies? If so, should the fact that the trauma and messiness of sex-selective abortion is already being made obsolete by sex-selection techniques which can be employed much earlier in the pregnancy be reluctantly welcomed, because they can be undertaken at an even earlier "moral moment"?

The problem is not after all with the techniques in themselves. The process of sorting out embryos which have been fertilized in the laboratory and only implanting those of a chosen sex was developed originally to reduce the passing on of sex-linked diseases such as Duchenne's muscular dystrophy. For couples who know they are carriers of such diseases, and perhaps already have one affected child, the technology offers an extraordinary prospect of having a healthy child. But this method can also be used for sex-selection that is motivated solely by son-preference, as can the technique of sperm-separation.

As yet, sperm-separation is a far from reliable technique, but it is now being offered by firms such as the London Gender Clinic, established in 1993.[3] Already the clinic has opened another office in Hong Kong and a doctor in Holland is also offering the technique, amid hostile reactions from the medical profession and the Ministry of Health. For around £1,000, the male-producing sperm, carrying a Y chromosome, can be separated and artificially inseminated. Selection precedes pregnancy, so there are no messy abortions and, for all but the strictest Muslims or Roman Catholics, no pangs of moral anxiety. Although at present, sperm-sorting is hardly an improvement on other methods such as trying to time fertilization, it seems certain that a reliable technique will soon be on its way.

The rapidly advancing technology is now on offer only to the elite who can pay but such "choices" are the tip of an ethical iceberg. For what exactly is the problem with sex-selection? There is none, say some:

> If the pregnant woman is willing to undergo and pay for prenatal diagnosis, then society, if it is to grant her full autonomy in choice of reproductive outcome, cannot deny her the right to information about the sex of the fetus and the right to terminate her pregnancy.
>
> (HOOK 1994)

Are doctors who refuse to put their skills at the service of patients who want sex-selection being paternalistic? Feminists have been railing for years against "doctor-knows-best" policies. But is consumerism to be the only regulator, in the name of women's autonomy? Does feminist advocacy of abortion rights mean condoning this ultimate act of sexism, given that the practice of sex-selection overwhelmingly favors sons?

A society which tolerates female infanticide or abortion of female fetuses holds women in contempt, whatever status women may achieve as mothers of sons. Feminists in India have campaigned tirelessly against prenatal sex-selection. They argue that:

> To believe that it is better to kill a female fetus than to give birth to an unwanted female child is not only shortsighted but fatalistic. By this logic it is better to kill poor people or Third World masses rather than to let them suffer in poverty and deprivation! This logic also presumes that social evils such as the dowry system are God-given and we can't do anything about them, hence victimise the victims!
>
> (PATEL 1989, p. 7)

India and China may be extreme examples of son-preference, but surveys in western countries suggest it is present there too, in a more convoluted way. People say they want girls, but they want their *first-born* to be boys. If couples could reliably select the sex of their next child, how would this psychologically affect girls growing up in the knowledge that their parents chose them to be second? Also, sex-selection dramatically reinforces outmoded sex-role stereotypes. It's a fair bet that parents wanting a male are unlikely to have in mind a young man whose ambition is to make his mark in floristry, catering or dance. And finally, when parents go to such lengths and things go wrong, how will they feel towards the baby who turns out to be the wrong sort? Not all will be lovingly reconciled.

Advocates of consumer choice say sex-selection is a logical extension of family planning. After all, many people are already using contraception to determine how many children to have and at what intervals, and it would be wrong to deny couples the tools to plan for boys or girls. Far from devaluing women, they say, the gradual imbalance in the sex ratio will increase the value of females and so cure itself. The emerging scarcity of girls in China offers little comfort, however, and defenders of sex-selection are conspicuously few.

Outlawing prenatal sex-selection has symbolic value. At least people know that what they are doing is against the law. But the deeper problem is that such bans drive a wedge into the abortion laws, providing scope for everyone to pass judgments on "good" and "bad" reasons to have an abortion. Once you say that sex-selective abortions are bad abortions and ban them, it is only a small, logical step to finding fault with other non-medical reasons—poverty, poor housing, too many children already. Are they "bad" abortions too?

However flawed and ineffective bans may be, letting matters drift unchecked could bring prenatal diagnosis into disrepute, undermining its original medical justification, which was to prevent serious and untreatable genetic disease. Some doctors are worried that anti-abortion groups will use sex-selection as an excuse to curtail the use of amniocentesis and abortion for fetal abnormality. Picking their way between charges of knowingly withholding information and the notion that the "customer is always right," doctors have suggested that details of fetal sex, determined by amniocentesis or chorionic villus sampling, should be held in the test-processing laboratory. If a patient asks about fetal sex the doctors can honestly say, "I don't know," and ethical requirements can thus be met.

While no one would campaign for abortion rights in order to make sex-selection abortion available, it would be wrong to invoke feminism in order to censure women who undergo such abortions. Few women lightly undertake an abortion, especially a later abortion, for anything but the most pressing reasons, and a woman who goes through an abortion to avoid giving birth to an unwanted daughter should evoke only compassion. Denunciation is cruel.

The pace of technology is so fast: will there still be a place in ten years' time for debating the implications of sex-selection in a book about *abortion?* Yes; the technology of sperm-separation and sorting of embryos fertilized in vitro is unlikely to replace current methods on offer, at least not on a scale that could meet the vast demand from India and China within that timetable. Many pregnant women will continue to be threatened by their husbands to have a prenatal test and to "choose" between abortion and violence or desertion. Not to take account of this, when calling for abortion rights for women, is a failure of feminist principles.

The horror of China's forced abortions is quite widely known, if not the reasons behind them; likewise the fate of female fetuses in India. Not so widely known is the abuse of legal abortion in Britain.

Britain: Your Baby or Your Career

Until 1990, women in the British army, navy or air force were forced to choose between pregnancy and a career. Pregnant? Leave or have an abortion. It was an order by the U.K. Ministry of Defence, which perpetrated its abuse of legal abortion for twelve years.

The rule was justified on the grounds that military personnel had to be prepared to go anywhere at twenty-four hours' notice. The no-pregnancies policy was there, it was said, to prevent children being orphaned. The government ignored the fact that most women in the armed services work in clerical or nursing jobs, and that in many other countries servicewomen are allowed to combine their duties with motherhood.

The Queen's Regulations stated that no one could remain in the British armed services after the sixteenth week of pregnancy. Thousands of women who decided to continue their pregnancies were discharged. Many of them have now sued the Ministry of Defence (MoD) for unfair dismissal, because for twelve years the armed services' "military efficiency" policy was in clear breach of a 1978 European Community law outlawing sexual discrimination. The government has been forced to pay out £55 million already, to more than 5,000 women who opted to continue their pregnancies and were wrongly discharged. There are around 100 claims of various kinds still waiting to be heard.[4]

The choice was your baby or your job. Choosing pregnancy often meant giving up a steady job with reasonable prospects, even an excellent career, and for what? The answer for many women, especially those with few qualifications, was an uncertain labor market in place of the security of the armed services. As if the pressures of that alternative were not enough, many servicewomen found themselves roughly jostled into agreeing to abortions.

"They gave me a weekend to think about it," says a telephonist in the Women's Royal Navy Service, whose childhood ambition had been to be in the armed forces. "It was like I was going to the dentist to have a tooth out. There was no compassion and no counselling . . . My boyfriend didn't want to know. I had no choice."[5] "There was a culture of abortion," says one of the lawyers in the Armed Forces Pregnancy Dismissal Group, which is helping to represent the aggrieved women: "If you went to the medical officer, you got told how quickly an abortion could be arranged and that the military hospital was lined up ready to do the operation. It was common knowledge."

In the first case of its kind to come before an industrial tribunal, Alison Mutton, a former lance-corporal in the Women's Royal Army Corps, sought compensation for the abortion she was forced to undergo as the price of keeping her career. When she became pregnant for a second time, she could not face another abortion and was discharged by the army.[6] But at the time of the first pregnancy no counselling was offered, apart from a brief warning of a possible risk of infertility after abortion. In February 1995, the tribunal decided that the MoD policy was a "blatant and prolonged misuse of power," awarding nearly £100,000 compensation, including £12,000 for hurt feelings, suffered on account of the abortion under duress.

The services' policy not only broke European law on equal treatment, but because it was outside the law, the abortions themselves were legally precarious. The "good faith" of the service doctors authorizing them might be open to question: how could they have judged that continuing the pregnancy was a greater risk to the woman's physical or mental health than terminating the pregnancy? Likewise, the women gave their "consent" to the operations, but only because they had been deceived into thinking that the army regulation was lawful, when in fact it was a misrepresentation of the law.

Many of the women who left the services to continue their pregnancies are now coming forward to reveal that earlier in their careers, like Alison Mutton, they too had unwanted abortions to avoid being thrown out. The former servicewomen all share an enormous sense of anger at finding that the institution to which they had given such loyal service had ignored its obligations to treat them fairly. If they had known that the Ministry of Defence was breaking the law, how many would have acted as they did—having abortions to save their jobs, or sacrificing their careers in order to have children?

The armed services' bullying and sex discrimination were practiced quite openly; the abuse was sanctioned by military regulations and did not hinge in any way on personal or social judgments about the women. Every pregnant servicewoman, from the highest to the lowest rank, was subject to the pressure of choosing an abortion or civilian life.

Abortion as Social Control

Such blind, rule-bound pressure is very different from the much subtler social pressures which some women face when they become pregnant, especially if officialdom—in the form of doctors or social workers—judges their pregnancies to be problematic or assesses them as in some way unsuitable to become mothers. There is no denying that such judgments cause some women to find themselves hassled with unseemly haste towards abortion on social grounds. What's more, the idea of using social grounds for abortion to prevent the birth of babies who might later on prove to be a "burden on society" was a powerful stimulus for many of the 1960s' abortion law reformers. They set little store by notions such as a woman's *right* to choose when and if to have children.

A pregnant 19-year-old girl goes to the antenatal clinic for a check-up. The nurse asks her how she will cope, since she has no job. "And she said I should have an abortion," recalls the girl. "I was really annoyed. I just cried. I didn't answer her" (Phoenix 1991, p. 92).

Hard and precise evidence of women being coerced into abortions in Britain is hard to come by, but there is a persistent undercurrent of accounts of women regarded as potentially unsuitable mothers, or belonging to a social "underclass" being aggressively persuaded that they should take this course. Doctors agree more readily to sanction an abortion for a single woman than for a married one. They assume that a single woman is bound to be unhappy at finding herself pregnant, whereas a married woman should welcome pregnancy.

It is not only doctors who hold views about which women make the most suitable mothers. The public is deluged with articles, television programs, and statistics about the rising tide of teenage motherhood, pregnancy, abortion and sexuality—as a "major social problem." The government's *Health of the Nation* policy makes it a national priority to halve the pregnancy rate among under-sixteens by the year 2000.

How this is to be achieved depends on your point of view. The moral right speaks admiringly of the current wave of Christian fundamentalist True Love Waits sex education, now in vogue in the United States, in which teenagers sign Virginity Pledges and learn the dangers of AIDS and pregnancy (and hellfire). Family planning organizations deplore such fear-based teaching and point to the teenage pregnancy rate in Holland, at least seven times lower that the rate in Britain, which they attribute to no-nonsense Dutch sex education and accessible contraceptive services.[7]

The complex links between sex education, contraception and abortion are explored further in Chapter 9. The point here is that liberals and conservatives alike regard teenage pregnancy as a social problem of epidemic proportions. Among medical professionals and social workers, teenagers are perhaps more likely to encounter people with more liberal views about abortion, and to find themselves on the defensive if they are determined to continue their pregnancies. Underlying the strictures on teenage pregnancy and "problem mothers," there are deep-seated values shared by conservatives and liberals alike—about maternal instincts as part of the personality of a "sensible, normal" woman. The public worriers about teenage pregnancy scarcely challenge the fairy-tale view of motherhood, as something which ideally takes place within marriage, where reproduction is an individual choice—a private product of personal desires. Pregnant women whose cultures or circumstances do not fit that cozy (and certainly anachronistic) picture are disapproved of as candidates for motherhood. Tacit disapproval sometimes becomes vocal—urging the woman towards abortion and, if she insists on keeping the pregnancy, castigating her for her "irrational" selfishness. When motherhood is conventionally portrayed as an act of selflessness, a supreme expression of self-sacrifice, and abortion as the self-indulgent antithesis, it is a curious twist to find a woman who declines to abort and insists on her right to be a mother as selfish, because she has been judged unfit for the role.

In 1966 and 1967, Parliament, public opinion and the medical profession in Britain passionately debated abortion, and in particular the proposals to legislate for abortion on so-called social grounds. One of the first bills to reach Parliament proposed to allow doctors to approve abortion if they deemed the patient "unsuitable to assume the legal and moral responsibility for caring for a child." The phrase gapes with opportunities for doctors to give vent to their personal prejudices about "inadequate mothers" (Greenwood and Young 1976, p. 22). Not only would such a "social clause" improve family life, according to this thread of argument, but it would be cost-effective. The cost of unplanned pregnancy to the taxpayer has always been a major plank in the family planning establishment's pitch to politicians and policy-makers: penny-wise, pound-foolish, they declare.[8]

In 1968, just after the passage of the Abortion Act, the Family Planning Association (FPA) held a special conference as part of its campaign to get contraception publicly subsidized. The FPA's director, Caspar Brook, mapped out the future for unwanted babies. "Many of these, sooner or later," said Brook, "tend to become misfits and rejects, needing care and special attention as delinquents, criminals, indigents and deviants." Other pro-choice campaigners have used this theme to win public support for abortion, without which, they say, the unwanted babies of today are at risk of turning into gun-toting hoodlums and teenage mothers of tomorrow.[9]

Many reformers saw legal abortion as helping to maintain the family; relieve poverty, overcrowding and deprivation; and to limit future demands on state spending, "As if having fewer children could create more jobs, higher wages, better schools, etc." (Davis 1990, p. 17). Some, however, were alert to the dangers of allowing doctors free rein to sit in judgment over women. Barbara Wootton, veteran campaigner for social issues, warned against putting such powers in doctors' hands: "I have known too many Tory doctors who really think that the 'lower classes' ought not to be allowed to reproduce themselves, though of course they would not put it like that," she said (Greenwood and Young 1976, p. 24).

Underlying the debate on the "social clause" lay not only concern about the taxpayers' bill, but also the dishonorable E-word, eugenics. The birth control movement has never freed itself from the taint of this since the days in which the pioneer Marie Stopes began campaigning for contraception under the banner of her organization, the Marie Stopes Society for Constructive Birth Control and Racial Progress. The slogan coined by her contemporary, the U.S. birth control pioneer Margaret Sanger, was "More children from the fit, less from the unfit": that is eugenics in a nutshell. In the 1990s, the eugenic idea, policies which will foster the creation of a healthy nation and ensure quality and fitness at birth, is alive and well. And in the United States, with the rise of the extreme right, overt racial eugenics is once again becoming a respectable part of establishment discourse.

Sometimes eugenic policy—the science of the well-born—is fairly innocuous, even benign, such as encouraging pregnant women to attend antenatal clinics. But the idea that to have "too many" children is anti-social takes a more threatening form, especially as it instantly boosts the stereotype that black women in particular have "too many" babies. Thus it is disproportionately black women who find themselves referred to abortion clinics after their first antenatal visit, and who are persistently offered sterilizations, or long-acting contraceptives such as the implants which prevent ovulation for five years and cannot be removed, except by a doctor (Phoenix 1990).

Black teenagers, in particular, are singled out by the medical and social work professions as "problem parents." They are undeniably young, often poor and may have children already. While white teenagers are also seen as problems, it is the myth of black (and Asian) fecundity which makes black women a special target for discriminatory treatment. In fact, both black and white women of all ages have fewer children than they did fifteen years ago, but still it is leaflets on contraception that have been translated into Asian languages more often than leaflets on any other health education issue in Britain.

Outright coercion or bullying is hard to prove, but undoubtedly young mothers, poor mothers and, above all, poor young black mothers are being hustled towards abortion with no respect for their "right to choose." They may already feel oppressed and constrained by the realities of poverty—lack of housing, poor job prospects, lack of child-care facilities—so opting for an abortion hardly seems like a "choice." But making a decision for oneself, faced with that stark reality, is not the same as being pressured by prejudiced doctors or social workers who consider that pregnancy among "unsuitable mothers" or black women in general must be curbed, and talk their young clients into abortion.[10]

No one denies that there are real concerns about teenage motherhood, "children having children," particularly about pregnancy complications when a woman's body is not fully mature. And of course the family planning lobby's job is to put forward arguments which will persuade decision-makers, in order to make contraception and abortion services accessible to *all* women. But the moral panic feeds on fear of teenagers' sexuality, and on seeing motherhood among young girls as a form of delinquency, akin to criminality among teenage boys.

The received wisdom about teenage mothers is being increasingly questioned. First, it is not an epidemic: birth rates among women under 20 are actually falling. And, if their circumstances are compared, not with teenagers without children, but with single women over 20 who have babies, it is clear that the babies themselves do no worse than the babies of older mothers, when factors such as race, class, smoking and numbers of other children are taken into account. Studies show that it is not teenage motherhood which plunges young women and their babies into poverty and disadvantage. It was usually there before (Macintyre and Cunningham-Burley 1993).

Nevertheless, despite such cool-headed studies, it is unlikely that the spice will go out of public concerns, fuelled by politicians and the moral dogmatists. The ultimate ingredient in the sour cocktail of moral outrage and social rejection is pregnant women who have HIV/AIDS. They symbolize the most lurid image in the demonisers' paintbox—sexuality, contagion, death. Many are being told that they must have abortions. (See Chapter 7 for more on HIV/AIDS.)

Often, in accounts of coerced abortion in India and China or tales of forced sterilization in the Third World generally, the significance of abortion abuse is belittled. We are asked to believe implicitly that the price of lives is cheaper among the "teeming millions," where infants who survive childhood are regarded as exceptionally lucky, and where women's sensibilities are supposedly less finely wrought and their wrongs less acutely felt than in the West. For that reason, the experiences of the British servicewomen are especially important. Their accounts expose that baseless superiority for what it is.

7

New Controversies:
The Abortion Pill,
Genetics and HIV/AIDS

THE 1967 ABORTION ACT IN BRITAIN, which set the ball rolling for reform in Europe and the United States, was framed at a time when just
about the only safe method of abortion was sharp curettage abortion, when
detecting genetic abnormalities before birth was a rare, experimental technique and when HIV/AIDS was many years in the future. Such factors did
not have to be weighed in the balance in the battles to make abortion legal.
But today there are alternative methods of abortion which, along with the
other new factors, bring new political challenges and opportunities to the
politics of abortion, for opponents and defenders alike. First and foremost is
the "abortion pill."

RU 486: The Drug That Became a Hostage

"With this 'miracle', anyone can become an abortionist," thundered an anti-
abortion opinion column in *USA Today* (Zagano 1994). The author also
dredged up a Nazi scare—informing readers that Hoechst AG, the German
drug company owning the patent for RU 486 (the "abortion pill") was once
part of the company which produced the chemical used by the Nazis to murder millions in the gas chambers.

RU 486, developed in the early 1980s by the French drug manufacturer
Roussel-Uclaf—hence RU—makes possible *medical* abortion. It works by
blocking the activity of progesterone, a hormone which a woman needs for

a fertilized egg to develop after conception. It induces menstrual bleeding and the fertilized egg is sloughed off at the same time as the lining of the womb. RU 486 has had more advance publicity than any new pharmaceutical product ever. Its short history is spiced with anti-abortion threats of boycotts and corporate terrorism against the drug companies involved with RU 486; politicking by governments; and bitter rifts among feminists over its safety. It's a heady political concoction, and a story almost too convoluted for a spy novel.

On 23 September 1988, the French government approved the marketing of RU 486. The drug, together with Roussel-Uclaf, was instantly taken hostage to the abortion debate. After just one month of anonymous threats to wives and children of Roussel employees and warnings of commercial boycotts, as well as intense pressure from Roussel's parent company, Hoechst, Roussel canceled its plans to distribute RU 486. Two days later, the French health minister, Claude Evin, ordered Roussel to resume its marketing plans. RU 486, he declared, was the "moral property of women."

Eight years later, the row is as hot as ever. Under official pressure, Roussel, the maker of RU 486, and Hoechst, the German company which confusingly owns Roussel and the drug's patent, have agreed to sell RU 486 in just three European countries—France, Britain and Sweden. (China has made its own version, without commercial permission.) The story of RU 486 in the United States, or mifepristone as it is now called by Americans, is not surprisingly more fraught than anywhere else in the world. Until Democratic President Clinton was elected in 1993, the United States government was officially against any extension of choice in abortion. When Clinton arrived in the White House, one of his first steps was to order his pharmaceutical safety agency, the Food and Drug Administration, to test RU 486. But the flak directed at Hoechst and Roussel by anti-abortion groups in France was mere pea-shooting compared to the damage being threatened by the U.S. anti-abortion crusaders towards the company's sales and reputation. Threatened boycotts of Hoechst's other money-spinners in the United States, such as agro-chemicals and drugs for diabetes and hypertension, sent Hoechst running scared for its profits.[1]

To avoid a repeat of the French fiasco, Hoechst drew up tight conditions for giving any country its pill: a watertight law for legal abortion; "strictly controlled distribution" (to keep it off the black market); an invitation from the government; and above all, a public that manifestly tolerates abortion.

So far only Sweden and Britain have been able to overcome the Hoechst policy hurdles. Wolfgang Hilger, Hoechst company chairman till 1994, was a devout Roman Catholic who opposed Hoechst marketing anything which "eases" abortion and he had a strict veto over all Hoechst policy, so RU 486 was even opposed from within the company which made it.

Despite Hilger's retirement, company policy has not wavered. In 1994, Hoechst said that because Germany's abortion laws had not been sorted out in the wake of east-west unification, it would not get the drug. Hoechst/Roussel did nothing to apply for a U.S. product license, although the abortion rights lobby, weary of guarding clinics and escorting frightened women, sees the method of abortion as an extremely attractive alternative. Lawrence Lader, a veteran U.S. abortion rights activist, eulogizes RU 486 as "the pill that could end the abortion wars," whose "crowning achievement is that it could give women the option of more privacy in their childbearing decisions" (Lader 1991, p. 18). Even the *American Journal of Public Health,* not an organ given to such dizzy hype as Lader, urged the U.S. government to support RU 486. It pointed out that if women could get RU 486 from their private physicians, "they could bypass the anti-abortion protestors that obstruct so many clinics and be spared the ensuing emotional trauma" (Rosenfield 1992, p. 1325). Diffusing the targets for anti-abortion protest is one of the main advantages of RU 486 in the United States and it is anti-abortion protest which has also shaped Hoechst's obstructive policy.

Hoechst and Roussel's intransigence is dictating not only where the drug is available, but the way in which it is used. Roussel insists that women need to make at least three visits to the doctor, for the drug's use to be safe and properly monitored. In France meanwhile, by 1995, more than 150,000 women had opted for "medical abortions," and roughly a quarter of French women requesting an abortion ask for the pill. Four clinic visits are required, first to confirm the pregnancy and discuss choice of method and suitability for RU 486 (as with the contraceptive pill there are some women for whom it is not safe); next to take RU 486; and forty-eight hours later to take the hormone which accompanies RU 486. A final visit, a few days later, involves an ultrasound scan to check that the abortion is complete. A similar program of visits is required in Britain. In France, RU 486 is available up to forty-nine days after the last menstrual period; in Britain women can choose it until sixty-three days—after that it is an option only rarely (Birth Control Trust 1994b).[2]

Is RU 486 a Better Method?

After some early research, it was discovered that if RU 486 was followed up by a dose of synthetic hormone—prostaglandin—about forty-eight hours later, there were far fewer incomplete abortions. The prostaglandin, usually delivered in the form of a vaginal pessary, causes the uterus to contract and expel the embryo (Moore 1990). The timing and the dosage of RU 486 have been adjusted after a number of research trials. After the prostaglandin is given, the embryo is expelled between four and twenty-four hours later but the bleeding can continue for about twelve days.

Champions of RU 486 point out that it can be administered earlier in pregnancy than a surgical abortion and it avoids any risk of injury to cervix or uterus from suction or scraping. Because it is not invasive there is no risk of infection, and because no anesthetic is required, it eliminates the small risk from that. Many women who have experienced RU 486/prostaglandin feel more in control and say that it seems more like a miscarriage, in other words, more "natural" (Holmgren 1992). Given a choice, two-thirds of the women opting for RU 486 do so because they want to avoid a surgical procedure. (Other methods of abortion and their safety are described in Chapter 3.)

On the minus side, women have to visit the doctor more often than for a surgical abortion. To some extent this reduces the much vaunted "privacy" of RU 486. Also they may lose more blood than after a surgical abortion. They certainly bleed for much longer and for women who may be underweight, undernourished and anemic this could be a serious disadvantage.

But research has shown that the dose of RU 486 initially recommended by Roussel can be greatly reduced, and also that different kinds of prostaglandin can cut down the chances of immediate side-effects, such as pain—which can be quite severe—or vomiting or diarrhea.

Hoechst's burdensome demands for marketing the drug and Roussel's elaborate protocols for its use have rallied family planning organizations, abortion rights groups and many women's health activists into an alliance aiming to make the drug more accessible. In 1992, a powerful international conference in Frankfurt castigated Hoechst and Roussel for using the U.S. abortion impasse as an excuse for holding out on the rest of the world. International Planned Parenthood Federation chief Dr. Halfdan Mahler said that if Hoechst was so embarrassed by holding the patent for RU 486, it should give it away, perhaps to a non-governmental organization (Furedi 1993, pp. 26–9).

Women's Health Activists Divided

Among the women's health organizations which have backed the call for RU 486 are the Boston Women's Health Book Collective, the Federation of Feminist Women's Health Centers, and the National Women's Health Network. But other important groups in the women's health movement have voiced significant reservations and even downright hostility to RU 486. For instance, women from FINRRAGE, the Feminist International Network of Resistance to Reproductive and Genetic Engineering, have lambasted the abortion pill, calling the RU 486/prostaglandin combination a "drug cocktail." They accuse the advocates of RU 486 of exaggerating the risks of early surgical abortion, and of dismissing the bleeding and pain which RU 486 can cause. They say that far from making an RU 486 abortion a woman-controlled affair, the repeated visits enable doctors to retain all their traditional control over the process. Secondly, there is always a danger that women will not make the return visits and this will put them at risk of incomplete abortions. In all, surgical abortion is much safer, says FINRRAGE (Klein, Raymond and Dumble 1991).

The influential international feminist health organization, the Women's Global Network for Reproductive Rights (WGNRR) has also voiced concern. The Network points out that abortion techniques have to be assessed in the context in which abortion services are delivered. In Holland, where women can easily obtain a free, early abortion, performed by well-trained and sympathetic doctors, surgical abortion has an exemplary safety record. Indeed many people involved in abortion services in Holland doubt whether women there would see any advantage in RU 486 (Furedi 1993, p. 45). But in the United States, where abortion is embattled and threatened, the drug is certainly a far more attractive proposition.

Because RU 486 is new, little is known about its long-term health effects (Holt 1992). FINRRAGE highlights contradictory reports in medical literature about possible dangers. If an RU 486 abortion does not work, it is clearly risky to continue the pregnancy, in case the drugs have damaged the embryo, and there is already some evidence of this possibility (Pons et al. 1991). FINRRAGE makes much of the death of a French woman, soon after the drug came into use. The woman who died was a heavy smoker, had eleven children and was probably not in good health. She should not have been prescribed RU 486. FINRRAGE has been accused of misinterpreting data and exaggerating the dangers. It is precisely because RU 486 is not safe for everyone and patients need to be screened that the treatment cannot become a do-it-yourself method.[3]

It is hard to raise critical questions without playing into the hands of the anti-abortion opposition. Any hint of a downside for RU 486 is seized on and rapidly embellished. LIFE, the leading anti-abortion pressure group in Britain, contested the introduction of RU 486 by "every legal means in the book." Its harassment has resulted in elaborate Department of Health red tape for medical abortion in Britain. Only five out of a hundred abortions performed in England and Wales uses RU 486 (compared to one in four in France).[4] Not only must women live within one hour's travelling time of the clinic or hospital, but also a bed must be kept ready for them, which drives up the cost of providing the abortion (Baird 1994). All this comes on top of the notorious delays in getting appointments in the National Health Service. By the time many women get to hospital the normal nine-week time limit for a medical abortion has passed.

Initial euphoria about "magic bullets" and "popping a pill for an abortion" obscured the real issues posed by RU 486. But although the drug "has not turned out to be the private, women-controlled procedure that many early advocates had hoped, it still holds out promise for greater privacy and autonomy as its administration is refined," argues the Latin American and Caribbean Women's Health Network.[5]

Many women who have used RU 486 like the fact that as a method it demands more participation and responsibility (Holmgren 1992). An RU 486/prostaglandin abortion takes longer and can be painful. It is the pregnant woman who must swallow pills and it is she who must be the first to check whether or not the abortion has taken place. A number of women will see the embryo or fetus they have expelled and for some this is very positive. A surgical abortion is a largely passive affair, especially if it involves a general anesthetic as it does in Britain. Women who choose it say they do not want to be aware of what is happening to them.

Carry on Politicking

Whether or not women will get any choice in what kind of abortion they have is anyone's guess. The anti-abortion lobby talks of "chemical warfare against unborn children" and predicts that a license for RU 486 will put abortion on easy street, as if it will sweep before it all the political and practical difficulties women face now when they seek an abortion. There has been no significant increase in the abortion rate in France since 1988. The next falsehood is that a black market in RU 486 will enable women to self-abort. Although RU 486 might not be difficult to duplicate, Roussel logs and controls the purchase and consumption of every single pill. It would be very hard for a black market to thrive or for the drug to get into untrained hands, once abortion itself was legal.

Deaths, disease and injury are caused by illegal abortion, especially in developing countries. The prospect of another abortion method which could safeguard women's lives and health would seem worth energetically pursuing. On the other hand, it may well be that possible complications of the drug—anemia, risk of incomplete abortion—and its cumbersome protocol, requiring many visits, make it wholly unsuitable and even downright dangerous for use in countries where visiting a health care facility can mean a day's journey or more. In any case, Roussel and Hoechst, or *Hoechst Marion Roussel,* as the company became known in 1995, is now clearly letting it be understood that it wishes to have nothing more to do with the business of abortion politics and would in fact prefer to be rid of its troublesome substance altogether. It does not intend to apply for any further product licenses. Even in countries where abortion is legal and safely provided, such as Holland, it has not applied for a marketing license.

In 1994 Hoechst finally sanctioned an agreement in the United States with the Population Council, a United States–based international agency committed to population growth control measures and contraceptive research, giving the Council the rights to the U.S. patent. Now trials are going ahead at several clinics in the United States and once the drug meets U.S. safety rules a manufacturer will be found. Seal of approval by the U.S. drug safety agency is a passport to the international pharmaceutical market and could be a key to unlocking other American population agency funding. Hoechst hopes its ruse will lift the threats of boycott. Following its successful offloading of the patent for the mifepristone onto the Population Council, the company is quietly but actively searching around for a similar organization to take on responsibility for manufacture and distribution outside the United States. In 1996, approaches were made to the Wellcome Trust, a British medical research–funding charity. Wellcome declined the challenge, but it is clear that RU 486 no longer fits into Hoechst Marion Roussel's commercial plans and it is prepared to turn its back on this burdensome drug. It is quite likely that when the Population Council has found a manufacturer in the United States, Roussel might stop making mifepristone altogether, the French, Swedish and British markets being so very insignificant.

But Roussel and Hoechst are not the only drug companies facing trouble with the anti-abortion movement in the United States. Next comes the problem of the prostaglandin that has to work together with RU 486. There is at present nothing suitable licensed in the United States. Doctors in Europe are increasingly combining RU 486 with a prostaglandin called misoprostol, which is principally a treatment for gastric ulcers. It is cheaper than the hormone previously in use, it seems to reduce the nasty side-effects, and is made by U.S. company, G. D. Searle under the brand name Cytotec. But the U.S. anti-abortion lobby has taken the precaution of threatening G. D. Searle with boycotts, even though G. D. Searle wants more than anything not to become embroiled in the U.S. abortion furor. Not surprisingly medical researchers in the United States have also been casting around for alternatives to RU 486 itself—doubtless hoping to avoid having to submit to the straitjacket of the Roussel/Hoechst company protocol. In 1995, a study reported the success of trials conducted in New York, obtaining safe medical abortion in pregnancies of less than sixty-three days with a combination of methotrexate—a drug usually used to treat cancer—and misoprostol. The authors point to the advantages of not having to follow Roussel's protocol, these drugs already being licensed for the U.S. market (Hausknecht 1995). Publication of the study in the *New England Journal of Medicine* aroused the predictable storm of protest and threats. The author is now wearing a bullet-proof vest.

Finally, there is increasingly promising evidence that RU 486 may be an effective alternative to the current "morning-after" pill. Using it in this way could greatly prevent the need for abortions, rather than actually causing them. (It is only Catholic doctrine which would include morning-after contraception in the same morally heinous category as abortion itself: medical practice, along with many abortion laws, defines the beginning of pregnancy as the process of implantation, which occurs around fourteen days after conception.) Some scientists are even hoping that RU 486 might become the contraceptive of the future, without the side-effects of the Pill. Much more research is needed.

Menstrual Regulation

Although it is RU 486 which has stolen the headlines, it is not the only new technique in abortion. There are others, such as menstrual regulation, which challenge the legal definitions and ethical considerations framing abortion. Politics, too, is never far away.

In the tiny state of Bangladesh, abortion is strictly against the law, except to save a woman's life. Many Bangladeshis are strict Muslims. But in 1979, the Bangladesh government looked squarely at the reality of abortion. Around 8,000 women were dying each year from illegal abortions and countless others were suffering injury and illness. Illegal abortion was occurring on a massive scale. The government sanctioned an "interim method of establishing non-pregnancy," to be known as "menstrual regulation." In Bengali this term is called "washing out the uterus" and it is now carried out roughly a quarter of a million times a year in Bangladesh. It takes five or ten minutes, needs no sophisticated equipment, is easy to perform, and no anesthesia is needed. Most Bangladeshis live in the countryside and the operation is well within the scope of a small country clinic (Dixon-Mueller 1988).

Abortion in Bangladesh is still illegal. But most menstrual regulation is carried out two to four weeks after a period has been missed, a legal grey area for establishing pregnancy. Conveniently, no one can know for sure whether a delayed period signifies a pregnancy. Menstrual regulation—which provokes some bleeding—builds on the strongly held cultural notions that a delayed period is harmful to a woman's health and that it is a good idea to "bring on a period." This is an idea common to many cultures.

Of course, "menstrual regulation," is a euphemism: indeed in Bangladesh it is used to "regulate" periods which have been delayed for up to twelve weeks. Elsewhere it is known as vacuum aspiration abortion and accounts for almost all the abortions performed in that most highly technological society, the United States. The technique was originally developed in China, but in the West the flexible suction tube is often known as the Karman cannula, after the Californian, Harvey Karman, who pioneered the use of the tube and the syringe in the 1960s. Nowadays under modern conditions, using a manual or electric pump, the contents of the uterus are slowly and gently sucked out through a flexible plastic tube. If it is done very early on after a missed period, there is no need to dilate the cervix and since it is dilatation which hurts most, the procedure is not too uncomfortable. It is safer than the traditional abortion technique, sharp curettage, in which the cervix is dilated and the womb is scraped.

As well as ending suspected pregnancies, the technique can also be used as a treatment for incomplete abortions which is how it is being introduced in several African countries, such as Zambia (Dixon-Mueller 1990). In the main hospital in Lusaka, adopting manual vacuum aspiration has had a dramatic impact. Previously, care for women who had unsafe, quack abortions was almost swamping the hospital service. Thirty to forty women queued each day for hours waiting for "D&C" operations, and only emergencies could be attended to. Now such women can receive vacuum aspiration, there is less waiting, fewer overnight stays or complications, and less costly anesthetics (Bradley et al. 1991).

This simple technique requires little technology: it does not even require sterile drapes or masks. When with brief training it could be so easily adopted, especially in rural areas, it is an irony that dilatation and curettage remains the main method of abortion throughout the developing world, and so many lives are lost. There are many countries like Bangladesh where the chances of liberalizing abortion by law are virtually nil because of the religious or political climate. Those who provide "menstrual regulation" up to twelve weeks after a missed period are technically breaking the law of Bangladesh, but no doctor has ever been prosecuted.

RU 486 and vacuum aspiration abortion are both medically accepted and respectable methods which have been developed since abortion was widely legalized. But alongside them have emerged less orthodox innovations which may offer some women access to abortion when the law puts conventional abortion out of reach. First, the American feminist collectives' experience of "menstrual extraction," developed before *Roe v. Wade,* provides a model to some feminist abortion campaigners of what the future might just look like if abortion is recriminalized. Secondly, Cytotec, the ulcer drug, is being used as an illegal abortion method by thousands of women in Brazil.

Menstrual Extraction
and Women's Liberation

"Menstrual extraction" arose directly out of the U.S. women's liberation movement and the campaign for abortion law reform in the late 1960s. A small group of women in Los Angeles, California, pioneered a simple, gentle method for removing the contents of the uterus by suction, on or around the first day of menstruation (Rothman 1978). They regularly used the technique to relieve themselves of all the symptoms and hassle of menstruation. They saw their self-help activity as a positive, affirming experience for women—a form of "woman-controlled medical research . . . a means of gaining and sharing with other women information about our bodies and our periods" (Punnett 1978, p. 49) The group practiced on one another, in their homes, and discovered that simple, sterile techniques were sufficient. They also devised a simple safe vacuum pump, a modified version of the Karman cannula, using a screwtop bottling jar, a large stopper, some aquarium tubing and a 50 cc syringe.

Predictably, medical reaction was hostile, ranging from trashing it, usually on grounds of safety, to redefining it or even co-opting it, and removing in the process its original meanings for women's autonomy. But its champions continued to write about it in the feminist press long after abortion was legalized. They stressed that it was not a do-it-yourself abortion technique, but something which a group of women would learn together, over months, even years—observing, experiencing and performing, until they thoroughly understood the process. "Without this body of knowledge, the isolated woman, who generally has little or no familiarity with her body, is risking the dangers commonly associated with self-abortion" (National Women's Health Network, 1989).

It did not take long after *Roe v. Wade* for it to become clear that accessible, legal abortion was a far from guaranteed affair. In 1992, Carol Downer, one of the menstrual extraction pioneers, co-wrote a book to promote menstrual extraction in a United States where outlawing abortion seems a very real possibility. She argued that the legal twilight, that is, the impossibility of knowing whether or not there is a pregnancy without a blood or urine test, puts menstrual extraction out of reach of prosecution as a "back-street abortion" and makes it quite different from "menstrual regulation" (Chalker and Downer 1992, ch. 8).

Cytotec: A New "Ladies' Remedy" in Brazil

While menstrual extraction and group self-help are being championed as the alternative for U.S. women, in Brazil, where abortion is strictly illegal—and one in five deaths of adolescent women is caused by illegal abortion—women have been using a drug called Cytotec, marketed for treatment of stomach ulcers, to obtain illegal abortions.[6]

It was only in 1986 that Cytotec, or misoprostol, was introduced to Brazil. It is a prostaglandin, whose effects include, in common with all prostaglandins, stimulation of the muscles of the uterus. The packaging clearly warns that the medication is unsuitable for pregnant women, but it is on sale in chemists' shops, as are many other "prescription only" drugs in Brazil and other Third World countries. The message of its "unsuitability" was as rapidly decoded by Brazilian women as by Victorian ladies reading between the lines of newspaper advertisements for "ladies' remedies for menstrual blockages." Women went in droves to pharmacies and by 1991 Cytotec was known as an abortifacient all over Brazil (Barabosa and Arilha 1993).

When asked for help with "unwanted pregnancy," eight out of ten pharmacists recommended Cytotec, available for five or six dollars, in comparison with an average monthly wage of around US$75 (Coelho 1991). Most recommended four tablets, two by mouth and two in the vagina; but some said more: up to forty-six tablets. Scarcely anyone warned of any side-effects. In July 1991, the Brazilian government clamped down on the pharmacy trade and sales of Cytotec slumped by 80 per cent. Critics of Brazil's harsh abortion laws are divided in their judgment of the drug. Some gynecologists see it as a lesser evil because it is a less risky form of illegal abortion than the usual methods, and hospitals have been seeing far fewer cases of women with infections caused by sharp instruments. It has also provided a passport to legal abortion: when bleeding started women could go to a public hospital and the pregnancy would be surgically terminated in relative safety. The police could not intervene in such a medical emergency.

But besides the danger of the bleeding, and some women may hemorrhage badly, there is another risk. Left to itself, the prostaglandin does not always work. Women whose abortions fail might resort to other, more dangerous methods. Others might resign themselves to the pregnancy, having exposed the embryo to a powerful drug. There are growing worries that Cytotec may be causing malformations, some of them very severe indeed, such as acute facial paralysis, as well as fused fingers, like those of children born after thalidomide. The malformations are very distinctive and some doctors believe that as many as one in ten pregnancies which continue after Cytotec are showing signs of malformation (Schonhofer 1991). Cytotec's multinational manufacturer, G. D. Searle, averts its gaze, saying there is no scientific data proving that Cytotec is responsible (Rocha 1995).

Brazil is the world's largest Roman Catholic country and the bishops preach unceasingly against the sins of abortion and contraception. But the Cytotec phenomenon has encouraged a public debate about abortion, which, until recently, would have been quite unthinkable—bills proposing a relaxation of the law have recently been submitted to Congress. What has really hit the headlines has been the plea for abortion law reform from a nun, Sister Ivone Gebara, who lives in the slums of Recife, in the north of Brazil. Sister Ivone's words are a curious echo of Catholic anti-abortion rhetoric: legalized abortion would "diminish violence against life," she says. Her outspoken attack on Catholic morality has landed her in trouble with the Vatican, which has ordered her to be silent, but letters of support for her have poured in.

No one has any idea why it was in Brazil in particular that Cytotec became so popular for abortion. The crackdown on open sales has created a flourishing black market with cocaine sellers dealing Cytotec as a side-line. Although the drug is being bought for illegal abortions in Venezuela, Mexico and some parts of the Caribbean, nothing compares with the Brazilian experience. It has certainly helped to prize the lid off the tightly controlled public debate about abortion and to hurl it into the political arena.

New Methods: More Choice

There may or not be a future for Cytotec in abortion. As for RU 486, it seems unlikely that it will ever be allowed to slip out of the tight control of the medical profession. But menstrual regulation does offer a real possibility of "demedicalizing" abortion, and challenging the monopoly of doctors to grant or refuse women the abortions they seek. Whilst the practical possibilities for doing this may actually be quite limited, especially in the case of RU 486, the *political* point remains valid.

The new methods challenge the iron grip which doctors have exercised over abortion, ever since the nineteenth century, when the rising young profession used abortion legislation as part of its campaign to assert the supremacy and mystique of "medical men." It is probably no accident that at the same time as they were establishing themselves as the only profession fit to perform abortion and decide when one was necessary, they were also taking control of childbirth and driving midwives into second place in the care of mothers and babies.

But the profession has always been deeply ambivalent about being involved in matters of contraception and abortion. Many doctors spurn abortion as a distasteful (and boring), even degrading aspect of their work, and yet have been reluctant to allow anyone else to participate in it, for fear of losing their pre-eminence as the ultimate health experts (Rothman 1987; see also Chapter 10). The experience of Bangladesh has shown how simple early abortions can be safely performed, in the absence of expensively trained doctors. It provides a practical demonstration that there could come a time when women do not have to plead with doctors for permission to have abortions, or at least can have abortions performed at a much simpler, local level.

Prenatal Tests: Blessings and Burdens

The availability of abortion has been central to the opening-up of the technology of prenatal testing: without it the battery of tests would be quite pointless. The first prenatal test began to be used in 1967, the year of the Abortion Act in Britain. There has been an explosion of genetic knowledge since then, both in the medical and scientific world and in the public arena: "Manic mood swings are all in the genes," say the headlines. In 1995, an attempt was made to introduce genetic evidence in a U.S. court to show that Stephen Mobley, a man convicted of a fatal shooting in a pizza parlor hold-up, could not help his actions because he came from a family genetically predisposed to abnormally aggressive and anti-social behavior. His fate was decided in the womb, said his lawyers. The "natural born killer" evidence was rejected, but the wide reporting of the case lent credence to the thinking behind it.

But identifying defective genes is only half the story. For all but a minute percentage of genetic abnormalities detected in the womb, the only answer—cure would not be the right word—is abortion. Indeed, the success of many screening and testing programs is measured precisely by the number of pregnancies terminated.

The medical world hailed the discovery of genetic screening and prenatal diagnosis as a major advance. To most doctors it was self-evident that the birth of a baby with disabilities was a tragedy which should be avoided. The new tests for abnormalities, conducted during pregnancy, offered people opportunities for information and the choice to avoid such births. Doctors saw no losers, only winners. There are now more than 4,000 genetic traits which have been catalogued, tests for at least 300 of them have been developed, and the experience of pregnancy has radically altered as prenatal testing becomes an accepted part of it for many women (Henifin, Hubbard, and Norsigian 1989).

In Sardinia, the community has been dogged for years by the hereditary blood disorder thalassemia, which is present in many communities around the Mediterranean region. It is an incurable wasting disease usually leading to heart failure. One in seven people in Sardinia is a carrier and each year there used to be around 100 babies born with thalassemia, condemned to a diseased life and an early death. Until 1974 that is, when the island began a massive screening program, offering abortions to women whose pregnancies were affected. Around 2,000 births have been prevented and now only

PRENATAL TESTS

Diagnostic Tests

Amniocentesis

This test involves testing the fetal cells from a small amount of the fluid surrounding the fetus. The fluid is withdrawn from the womb with a hollow needle and the test is carried out at around fifteen to seventeen weeks. A few weeks' wait is required for the laboratory results of any genetic abnormalities. So if an abortion is requested, it had to be done at a very late stage, which can be very distressing. Some hospitals are now offering amniocentesis as early as thirteen weeks, but there is a higher risk of miscarriage.

Chorionic Villus Sampling (CVS)

This test can be carried out before twelve weeks of pregnancy and looks at a small amount of placental tissue. It carries a greater risk of miscarriage than amniocentesis, and a small risk of giving the wrong diagnosis. It may also mean an unnecessary number of abortions, because some of the pregnancies would have miscarried naturally in the early stages, without the tests warning that anything was wrong. This is an important emotional cost, to be weighed against the possible advantage of earlier abortion than is practical with most amniocentesis. Recently, some studies have raised questions about an association between CVS and the risk of limb defects.

Screening Tests

Amniocentesis and CVS are *diagnostic* tests: they give a yes or no answer. Because there is a small risk attached to both tests, scientists have looked for *screening* tests, to pinpoint more closely women who should be offered the invasive diagnostic test and to identify those whose risk is much lower.

Alphafetoprotein (AFP)

Unusually high levels of this substance in the mother's blood may indicate that the fetus is developing with defects of the neural tube, that is, some form of spina bifida. The blood sample is taken and tested at around sixteen weeks.

The "Triple" Test

This is a simple blood test, performed at around fifteen weeks, which identifies three possible markers of risk of Down's Syndrome, spina bifida, and the lethal anencephaly (no brain). If the blood sample, together with the woman's age, indicates that there is a risk of these, the woman can decide whether or not to undergo a more definite, but invasive diagnostic test.

The advantage of the test is that it can be given to younger women, a small

continued

proportion of whom do give birth to Down's Syndrome children, but are not in them-selves a high-risk category for Down's. Its disadvantage is that it is not very accurate: It may miss some abnormalities and give other pregnant women needless hard deci-sions and anxiety.

Ultrasound Scans

These are used to help pinpoint the dates of the pregnancy and to check on fetal growth. They are also used to guide medical staff carrying out other tests, such as am-niocentesis. On its own, ultrasound cannot detect many abnormalities, but those it can spot are among the most serious, such as hydrocephaly—a condition often asso-ciated with spina bifida—or fluid in the kidneys.

New tests are being investigated all the time. There is some evidence that mea-suring the fetal neck (using ultrasound), at around eleven weeks, may be a good in-dication of certain chromosome abnormalities, such as Down's.

None of the tests can guarantee a normal baby. At most, 40 per cent of mental retardation is caused by genetic abnormality. Maternal infection, or lack of oxygen at birth, are among the other causes.

Sources: De Crespigny with Dredge 1990; Newburn 1993

---

four or five babies are born with thalassemia each year (Konner 1993). The Sardinian program was modelled on a similar scheme in the United States, to reduce the incidence of Tay-Sachs disease, which is almost only found in the small, tightly knit community of Ashkenazic Jews. Tay-Sachs causes se-vere mental retardation as well as blindness and is terminal in babyhood.

Doctors and politicians unite in their advocacy of screening and testing. Government support for prenatal testing is based on calculations that the cost of such programs will pay for themselves in as little as three years in the case of some disorders, such as spina bifida (Farrant 1985). Even anti-abortion MP David Alton, who in 1988 sponsored a bill to ban abortions in Britain after eighteen weeks of pregnancy, offered no opposition to abortions on the grounds of fetal handicap after that stage. A number of well-known anti-abortion MPs had also supported a call for a national prenatal screening pro-gram. Screening represents not only cost-effectiveness, but also an extraordi-nary expansion of private choice, argue the enthusiasts. It seems obvious to them that everyone should have a right to know that all is well in a pregnancy, and have the option to terminate the pregnancy if tests bring bad news.

Of course, the chance to undergo prenatal testing gives people who know they carry a genetic disease a real chance to give birth to healthy children. Many might otherwise never embark on pregnancy or would immediately opt for abortion if they accidentally became pregnant (see sidebar on prenatal tests). Tay-Sachs disease is an extreme example: the disease kills, usually within two years, and entails acute suffering. There are other painful, lethal conditions, such as the chromosomal disorder trisomy 18, which offer the prospect of only a few days or weeks of life, and it is not too difficult to make a strong case for abortion as an ethical way of avoiding physical suffering and deep emotional stress. One of the commonest uses of prenatal testing, however, is to detect Down's Syndrome. The risk of Down's Syndrome increases with the age of the mother and it has become public policy almost everywhere in Britain to screen pregnant women for Down's and to offer the chance of amniocentesis to women over the age of 34.[7]

But as more and more conditions become detectable in pregnancy, is there a line to be drawn? Potentially, there are a great many conditions which can be identified, long before there is any outward sign of them. Huntington's chorea is an incurable hereditary disease, which killed the great folk singer and song writer Woody Guthrie, but not until he was 55. Hardly anyone experiences Huntington symptoms before the age of 30. Other incurable genetic disorders, now detectable, include cystic fibrosis, hemophilia, and Duchenne's muscular dystrophy. The markers have been found for restricted growth (dwarfism), male baldness, color blindness and breast cancer. Researchers are now looking for diseases such as colon cancer and diabetes, as well as Alzheimer's disease, and even some forms of manic depression. The problem is that the presence of the marker gene may indicate an increased risk of the disease, but is not a guarantee of its development, which is triggered by a host of other, far less predictable factors.

What is more, a positive result only says the tell-tale gene is present. It reveals little or nothing about the severity of any future disabilities or when a disease might strike, if at all. In some disorders, notably Fragile X or Down's Syndrome, the range of disability can be considerable, and an abortion after a positive result may destroy what would have become a reasonably healthy person. Many girls with the Fragile X mutation simply carry the genetic material but will not be personally affected (although they may in turn pass the gene to their children). Parents are caught in a riptide of conflicting currents.

At an individual level, prenatal diagnosis personalizes the decision to abort. It is now a question of aborting a particular fetus "in the hope of coming up with a "better" one next time," as Harvard molecular biologist Ruth Hubbard puts it, rather than seeking an abortion out of a simple desire not to be pregnant (Hubbard 1984).

At a wider social level, such selective abortion—sorting the genetically perfect babies from the less than perfect, carries the ineradicable stain of Nazism, although it goes back further than that. In the first half of the twentieth century, *before* the Holocaust with its eugenic principles of "racial hygiene," eugenic policies such as social biology were utterly respectable. In many American states, for example, sterilization of "mental defectives" and others was carried out on a massive scale in the name of eugenics. Their programs may even have furnished the model for Hitler's program of "race hygiene." In recent years the government of China has taken steps to reduce the number of "inferior" births, encouraging and even requiring sterilization and abortion, or prohibiting marriage among people judged likely to pass on hereditary disabilities. The state aims to reduce the burden of caring for dependent people (see Chapter 6 for more on Chinese eugenics).

China is up front with its eugenic policy, but by default a covert eugenic system is becoming more and more pervasive in the West.[8] The social pressures and values are such that the sum of individual choices amounts to eugenics by any other name. The mere offer of the technology, plus the breakdown of the public welfare system and the increasing stress on shifting the cost of caring for disabled people back onto the individual family, makes it seem more and more "irresponsible" to refuse abortion and knowingly give birth to a child with disabilities. Even declining to be tested is frowned on. Disability is depicted as a purely negative concept—of suffering, lack of fulfillment and dependence.[9]

As spending on welfare services diminishes, health policy conservatives are saying that it is better to spend public money on genetic screening (and, implicitly, on selective abortion) than on research into, or treatment of, the diseases themselves. Further down the road the state might refuse help of any kind to a parent who could have chosen not to bear a disabled child. As one woman's doctor told her, "It's up to you what you do, but if you keep it you will live with the problem" (Farrant 1985, p. 117). Counselling is often biased towards abortion. When proponents of mass testing for Fragile X say that it costs US$200 to do the prenatal test and US$2 million for a lifetime's care for a severely affected person, it is easy to see which way the wind is blowing.

There is another disturbing spin-off from genetic screening and "cost-saving abortions." There can be nothing more stigmatizing than knowing that you live with a condition which society seeks to prevent by abortion. The existence of the tests changes the way disabled people are viewed by others. In the United States and in Germany there have already been cases of doctors being sued for "wrongful life" because their advice failed to prevent the birth of a baby born with disabilities.

Despite all this, only one out of five parents of children with cystic fibrosis said they would terminate a future pregnancy which was found to be carrying the cystic fibrosis gene. If this holds true, testing known carriers would achieve very little in the way of preventing births; its main effect would be to make such parents look "selfish." This may be the final irony: the ineffectiveness of genetic testing, by its own lights. "Routinely available prenatal tests . . . test for fewer than 50% of serious birth abnormalities" (Marteau, Plenicar and Kidd 1993, p. 8).

For some it all adds up to a cast-iron case for total opposition to genetic screening, prenatal testing and selective abortion. The anti-abortion lobby predicts trigger-happy obstetricians, hellishly bent on "search and destroy missions" against less than perfect fetuses. It would outlaw genetic research and prenatal diagnosis, precisely because of the link with abortion.[10]

Some feminists too, notably those under the banner of FINRRAGE, the Feminist International Network of Resistance to Reproductive and Genetic Engineering, believe it is women's moral and political duty to reject outright the entire panoply of this technology. They denounce women who use or support the techniques of the new reproductive technology, including infertility treatment, as manipulated victims of patriarchal power who have failed to consider the implications of their actions for women as a social group (Rowland 1985).

The Burden of Choice

The promise of extended choices is hollow sales talk. Few women faced with diagnosis of a fetal abnormality experience a sense of choice. According to Barbara Katz Rothman, author of a moving and compassionate study of women facing amniocentesis, "it seems that, in gaining the choice to control the quality of our children, we may be losing the choice *not* to control the quality, the choice of simply accepting them as they are."[11] The doctors make their "preventive medicine" agenda plainly understood: fetal abnormality is to be avoided, at all costs. Most women hope for reassurance from the experts, but that is not the medical priority. As result, far from being liberated by the possibilities of this kind of abortion, many women find the whole procedure of testing, being counselled and deciding what to do is more akin to duress.

In a 1980 U.K. survey, three out of four obstetricians said they required a woman to agree to an abortion, before she underwent a test. Any other option they regarded as a waste of time and money. More recently, only a third of obstetricians required such an undertaking, although it was still plain that doctors and patients approach the issue of testing with very different motives (Green 1995). In taped interviews of obstetricians counselling pregnant women about amniocentesis, the chance of miscarriage prompted by the test itself was either not mentioned or misleadingly underestimated (Marteau, Plenicar and Kidd 1993). So in effect women have very little "choice": what they have is responsibility and guilt. If they choose abortion, they are rejecting selfless motherhood or are naive victims of the male medico-scientific establishment. If they shun testing or knowingly decline abortion, and a handicapped child is born, society sentences them to a lifetime of coping as punishment for wanton disregard of the public balance-sheet. Genetic screening is feeding the public perception of disability as a

---

PREGNANT, POOR AND HIV-POSITIVE:
ONE WOMAN'S EXPERIENCE

A 38-year-old Haitian woman in New York City learned that she was HIV-positive during her antenatal care in a hospital with an excellent record for high-risk pregnancy care. She was advised not to tell anyone of her HIV status, that her chances of having a baby with AIDS were extremely high and that she should abort the foetus. She was also told to go home and write her will, because she was going to die. She was asymptomatic.

She chose to continue her pregnancy. When she went for her next routine checkup, she was taken to another building for a meeting with several high-ranking medical personnel. They told her having a child with AIDS was worse than having a child with spina bifida, which her older daughter has. They said such a child would be a burden to society, and that she would be wrong not to abort. She insisted that she wanted to have the baby and pleaded that they continue her care. They refused, stating that the hospital was not equipped to treat her.

She was referred to another hospital for a second-trimester abortion. This was performed without counselling or obtaining her signed consent. She was placed in a room marked "Isolation" during her induced labor and left alone screaming for help for 15 minutes after the foetus was expelled. When she haemorrhaged because the abortion was incomplete, she was made to walk down the hall to the operating room. In both hospitals as soon as they knew she was HIV-positive, she felt they wanted to get rid of her.

The Center for Constitutional Rights in New York filed a case against both hospitals for discrimination, inflicting emotional distress, negligence and failure to obtain consent for abortion in the second hospital.

Source: quoted from Berer with Ray 1993, p. 94

medical problem and a maternal responsibility, rather than as a matter of equity and justice, requiring social and political change. It is hardly surprising then, to learn that 92 per cent of prenatally diagnosed cases of Down's Syndrome end in termination (Alberman 1995).

But the fact that some people do want access to that problematic technology and to the limited choices it offers is not in itself reprehensible: why after all should we demand more of a sacrifice from those with a "nonstandard" fetus than we do of those whose tests are reassuring? It is hypocritical to preach at those who decide that they cannot take on the responsibility of raising a child with disabilities, when the rest of us do nothing to ensure that people with disabilities get the support and respect they are entitled to. Nancy Smithers, a white 36-year-old lawyer awaiting the results of her prenatal test, sums up the feelings of many women:

> I was hoping I'd never have to make this choice, to become responsible for choosing the kind of baby I'd get, the kind of baby we'd accept. But everyone, my doctors, my parents, my friends, everyone urged me to have amniocentesis. Now, I guess, I'm having a modern baby. And they all told me I'd feel more in control. But I guess I feel less in control. It's still my baby, but only if it's good enough to be our baby, if you see what I mean.
>
> (RAPP 1995)

Abortion and HIV/AIDS: A Story under Wraps

For several years now it has been women who have experienced the greatest proportionate increase in HIV/AIDS diagnosis (Kelly et al. 1994). Biologically, they are more susceptible than men to infection through heterosexual contact, and they are socially more vulnerable, too. Sexual oppression means that women having heterosexual sex are forced to rely on men for their protection from HIV, hoping that men are both faithful and use condoms. It is for most women a vain hope and by the year 2000, more than 13 million women world-wide will have acquired HIV—the human immunodeficiency virus—and 4 million will have died from AIDS-related diseases.

The main way in which children are infected with HIV/AIDS is through their mothers being HIV-positive. Throughout the world an estimated one million children born in 1990 acquired HIV-infection from their mothers.

It is no wonder that pregnant women who are HIV-positive are singled out by doctors and health care workers, preoccupied with reducing the number of babies and children with HIV.[12] In 1987, the American College of Obstetrics and Gynecology's official policy was that "infected women should be encouraged not to become pregnant and should be provided with appropriate family planning assistance" including, if need be, abortion.

But since 1987, knowledge of HIV/AIDS has advanced stupendously (and the college has moderated its advice, towards respecting women's choices). In those days it was thought that the chances of a child of a mother with HIV having the disease were much higher. It is now known that out of ten children born to mothers who are HIV-positive, between six and eight will be unaffected. Despite this, many pregnant women with HIV have experienced pressure, most often from doctors, to terminate their pregnancies (see sidebar above for one woman's experience in New York). Positively Women, the organization which provides practical and emotional support for women with HIV/AIDS in Britain, conducted a survey of women with HIV and AIDS and found that almost half of them had come under pressure to have abortions or not to become pregnant (Gorna 1994, Section 7).

Sometimes there has been blatant scaremongering, telling women they have no future and their babies will die. "I know the chances of the child being infected, I have all the information of how to look after myself and to lessen the chance of infecting the child. My GP tried to tell me that if I go ahead I will have a premature baby, and insisted I have an abortion." Sometimes the pressure is more subtle: repeatedly asking the women at each antenatal check-up to justify their decision to have a baby and implying that this is an irresponsible thing to do.

Transmission rates—passing the HIV-infection from mother to baby—vary widely and nobody knows exactly why. In Europe as a whole, roughly one in six babies born to HIV-positive mothers becomes infected. In New York the rate is about one in three; in Kenya it is almost half. Higher rates go hand-in-hand with baseline poor health and lack of prenatal care, so poverty plays a big part. In the United States the women hardest hit by HIV/AIDS are disproportionately from the Black and Latin communities, and the pressure to make them terminate their pregnancies is reminiscent of the sterilization campaigns of the 1970s which targeted Black and Hispanic women (Davis 1988, p. 30). In Britain, Positively Women found that it was far more often women of African origins who had been tested for HIV without their consent.

There is no certainty that the disease will pass to babies born to mothers who are HIV-positive, and there are many other threats to the lives of babies of poor women, which are more easily preventable. Little or nothing is done to prevent them, but HIV/AIDS is seen as a unique threat to the community. In order to avoid being pressured towards abortion, for instance by doctors exaggerating the risks of transmission, some HIV-positive women are deliberately steering clear of antenatal clinics until late in their pregnancies.

Dubious Medicine, Dubious Ethics

Women who discover they are HIV-positive only after they have become pregnant are particularly vulnerable to such pressure in the antenatal clinic. They are in shock at the news and, like most people who only know what they have read in the newspapers about HIV/AIDS, they believe that all babies born to HIV-infected mothers will automatically "have AIDS": "I'm ill, the baby will be ill, I'll die." Positively Women comes across many such women who have hastily agreed to abortion, assuming that death waits just around the corner. Later they find out more about the disease. They are devastated and very angry at what they have been hustled into and quite a few decide to become pregnant again, this time standing up to whatever pressures they encounter.

There are people who are carriers of the gene for Tay-Sachs disease, for example, who have a one in four chance that their baby will be affected by this lethal and painful condition. No one suggests they should be sterilized. The chances of having an HIV-infected child in New York are no worse and may be considerably better than that but, "because in the case of HIV it is poor, black and Hispanic women who are at risk for prenatal transmission, discussion of 'suitability' for natural parenthood is all the more ominous. Such thinking has a long and dishonourable pedigree—eugenics" (Bayer 1989, p. 993).

Forcing a woman to have an abortion solely on the grounds that she is HIV-positive is ethically indefensible, whether it is her health or the health of her future child which is under scrutiny. Pregnancy and childbirth itself have no harmful effect on the health of women who have no symptoms of HIV-related illness.[13] What is more, there is no prenatal test which can detect whether the fetus is infected or will become so.

No wonder HIV-infected pregnant women face difficult decisions. If the baby does prove to be infected, they will feel guilty; if they have an abortion, they will never know whether or not they would have had a child in perfect health. The risk of transmission can now be reduced considerably by giving the mother the prohibitively expensive anti-retroviral drug known as AZT, although this "treatment" brings its own ethical problems, and is not a realistic option for most women in developing countries (Conner et al. 1994; Bayer 1994). There are some signs that Cesarean delivery of the child can also reduce the risk, but Cesareans carry much greater risks—of wound infection, for example.[14]

Above all the impetus to test pregnant women, voluntarily or without their consent, often with a view to dissuading those found to be HIV-positive from continuing their pregnancy, shows scant respect for women's moral integrity and autonomy in making decisions about their lives. All too often women are urged to have the test "for the good of the baby." They rarely receive specialist counselling by properly trained staff about the implication of undergoing a test. Few will understand that the test is a useless predictor of the health of the future child. The whole rigmarole blatantly exploits women's concern for a healthy pregnancy.

The United States' Public Health Service now recommends routine counselling and voluntary testing for HIV in all pregnant women (Centers for Disease Control and Prevention 1995). The stated intention is to ensure that women found to be HIV-positive can begin treatment with AZT, a policy which in itself remains fiercely controversial. It is already policy in some states to recommend that HIV-positive women should avoid pregnancy, a very short step indeed from urging those already pregnant in the direction of the abortion clinic. Several states are also considering mandatory HIV testing of newborn babies—a test which in reality is testing of mothers.

Having a child may be the most positive decision an HIV-infected woman can make about her life, and the more desperate she perceives her circumstances, the more urgent it may be for her to become a mother. After all, the chances are that the child will be healthy, and that is a gamble that women can and should be permitted to take.

If an HIV-infected woman decides to seek an abortion, she may face difficulties, even where abortion is legal. A third of clinics in the United States either do not operate on HIV-positive women, or at the very least, increase their fees. Where abortion is available in a very restricted way, an HIV-infected woman may have to confide in a doctor and hope that she will get a termination on grounds of danger to her health. In some east African countries, there are clinics regularly doing abortions in this way, especially for women who have already had one HIV-infected child, but they are afraid to make this public, for fear of stirring up anti-abortion protest.[15]

Some countries have considered making HIV a specific indication for abortion, but this would require women to breach their confidentiality in order to end their pregnancies. The answer for HIV-positive women is to treat them in the same way as other women who seek to end pregnancies, that is, to make abortion available early and late, and not to make HIV itself a reason for legal abortion. It may be that HIV/AIDS will serve as a stalking horse for abortion law reformers in some countries, drawing attention to the need for safe legal abortion, but this strategy carries grave dangers, not the least of which is that it can degenerate into an alarmist argument which demonizes women with HIV/AIDS and their children.

Of course, with the anti-abortion camp poised to spring on the faintest hint of liberalizing abortion laws for any reason, health care activists and defenders of abortion rights are reluctant to open a public debate about the range of needs for pregnant women with HIV/AIDS. It is an issue which transgresses almost every possible taboo of the crusaders for sexual repression and patriarchal power.

8

Contrasting Scenes:
Russia, Holland and Britain

WITHOUT CHEAP, SAFE, PEOPLE-FRIENDLY CONTRACEPTION, as well as the legal and safe means to end unwanted pregnancy, "anatomy is destiny," and women's lives are still a gruesome game of health roulette. But would perfect contraception make abortion go away? Will there ever come a time when a woman never has to face the fact that she has conceived and does not want to be pregnant? One word gives the lie to that: rape. There are other life-events which also make it essential for women to be able to interrupt pregnancies which have become blighted and impossible, even if they were originally planned. The link between abortion and contraception, how people view them and use them, is undeniably complex: Russia, Holland and Britain offer strikingly different accounts of fertility control and women's reproductive and sexual health.

Russia, the first country to legalize abortion, is unique among the countries of Europe in that abortion is legal, cheap and is used as the main method of birth control—contraception is practically unavailable. Probably every fourth abortion in the world is performed in the countries of the former Soviet Union.[1] Things couldn't be more different in Holland, which has the lowest abortion rate in the world and has been described by one family planning expert as having "the perfect contraceptive population." At least abortion and contraception policies pull in the same direction in Holland. In Britain, attitudes and policies sometimes conflict with each other, probably because there is so much double-think about sex itself. It would be crass to claim a simplistic cause-effect relationship between providing birth control services and the demand for abortion—a change in contraceptive services cannot be crudely measured in the abortion statistics—but ambivalence about abortion and about contraception is evident in Britain.

Russia: A Parody of Choice

A woman in Russia has between five and seven abortions in her lifetime.

> You stand at the door of the operating room, seven or eight of you, waiting to be taken in. The clinic's staff is too busy to do anything but operate, so as each woman who finishes staggers out, you take turns getting out of line for a few moments, just to help her get to the resting room down the hall. Then it's your turn and you go into a room spattered with blood where two doctors are aborting seven or eight women at the same time; they're usually very rough and rude, shouting at you about keeping your legs wide open etc. . . . . If you're lucky they give a little sedative, mostly Valium. Then it's your turn to stagger out to the resting room.
>
> (DU PLESSIX-GRAY 1991)

These abortions are not expensive, but such appalling lack of care is typical, and there is a chronic shortage not only of trained staff, but also of instruments, disposable gloves, and drugs, including anesthetic. Sometimes an extra charge will secure a guarantee of pain-killer, but it is no wonder that women try to avoid such production-line savagery. They shun the official hospitals and clinics not only because of such humiliating and poor quality treatment, but also because of their waiting lists. The final insult is that the doctor must record "abortion" on the sickness certificate, broadcasting the episode to the woman's employer (Ryan 1987).

The abortion rate in Russia today far exceeds that of any other European country. There may be 118 abortions for every 100 births, perhaps more, and in some parts of the country abortions outnumber births sevenfold (Popov 1990). There are no precise figures; it is all guesswork. Indeed, from 1936 until 1956, the period when abortion was forbidden by Stalin in order to boost the birth rate, no figures were kept at all. And there is still no reliable information on deaths or complications from abortion. Cobbling together estimates of illegal abortion is even more speculative, but to say that there are as many illegal as legal abortions is probably a conservative guess. In a society which is still extremely circumspect about pregnancy outside marriage, many women have strong reasons for wanting to keep an abortion secret. Seven out of ten girls in towns and nine out of ten girls in country areas ended their first pregnancies with abortion. In rural areas, problems of access to abortion facilities may put a legal operation beyond the reach of a young woman who does not want her family to know (Ryan 1987).

The astounding estimates of abortion are matched only by the soaring costs of raising children in Russia and in the new nations which were once part of the Soviet Union. There are thousands upon thousands of women in Russia who want a child but have an abortion instead, faced with a break-down in maternity leave and benefits, in medical care, in pre-school care and with the snares of 1,000 per cent inflation. Raising a child costs around half a monthly salary.

In a BBC television program about life for ordinary Russians, a doctor about to perform an abortion berates her patient, a woman in her early thir-ties, who has one child and is pregnant again: "A beautiful young woman like you should be forced to have children: who will revive Russia if we have no children?" says the doctor. The woman says nothing. She and her hus-band and son already share their tiny Moscow apartment with another fam-ily with three children. The doctor sighs. "It's your decision," she says.[2] Scenes such as this are being repeated all over the former Soviet Union. Abortion is a parody of choice, when there is no contraception.

There are condoms, if you can find them. The Russians deride them as "galoshes." Problems with foreign currency make imports of oral contra-ceptives as well as stocks of latex for Russian-made condoms very unreliable. Men's attitude to condoms is all too often: why buy contraceptives when abortion is so cheap? In any case, contraceptive services are virtually non-ex-istent outside the big cities. Women can douche with lemon juice and jump off the top of the cupboard if their periods are late.

Up till now the lack of modern contraception in such an advanced in-dustrial nation has been almost total but it has been the Kremlin which is to blame, not the Vatican. In 1974, the Soviet Ministry of Health more or less prohibited the Pill as a mass contraceptive and was supported by Soviet doctors, who continually stressed the health risks and the "unnaturalness" of oral contraception, while they supplemented their very meager incomes from private abortion. (Many doctors earn less than drivers or babysitters.) In closing the door firmly against the Pill, the Soviet government set the seal on abortion as the main method of birth control (Popov 1994). Doctors in

Greece and in Japan put forward much the same arguments to protect the livelihood they make from abortion.

Only a tiny minority of Russian women say they would choose abortion in preference to contraception, but in reality there is no choice. There is virtually no sex education, either in schools or through the media. As recently as 1982, girls were simply exhorted to protect their "maidenly honour" and sex education was denounced as a capitalist (and, for good measure, Jewish) plot (David 1992). Until *glasnost* arrived, the press could not print words such as "condom," "menstruation" or "masturbation." It is a measure of the changes taking place in Russia, that Dr. Inna Alesina of the Russian Family Planning Association now holds a weekly phone-in surgery on Moscow's radio station for women, and counsels women to seek help for sexual health and contraceptive problems. "I tell them, it is not good to have an abortion every year," says Dr. Alesina.[3] Recent figures show that where women can get contraceptives and accurate information, the abortion rate has dramatically fallen, by as much as 50 per cent in three years.[4]

But when many women are having as many as eight abortions, and some are undergoing fifteen, it is no wonder that the proportion of women dying as a result of abortions is ten times higher than that of women in Western Europe and the death or ill-health of many babies is also attributable to complications arising from crudely performed abortions. Despite the advent of vacuum aspiration, most abortions in Russia are still performed with sharp curettage. Women have to resort to repeated abortions and run the risk time and again of post-abortion infections, which if untreated can cause infertility.

The future is bleak. Thanks to inflation a pair of shoes now costs what a car cost a few months ago, and families cannot afford to feed and clothe their children. For the foreseeable future there is little alternative to abortion, mostly undertaken in hospitals and clinics where standards of healthcare are so poor that anesthetic is a luxury item, and half the hospitals have no hot water. Meanwhile, the Orthodox Church, with help from the American anti-abortion organizations such as Human Life International (HLI) is beginning to mobilize public opinion against abortion. HLI has formed a "Conversion Corps for Mary," which enlists volunteers to serve in Russia for a year at a time, "to save babies in the womb." Britain's own version of Operation Rescue, Father James Morrow, has also visited Russia and is trying to raise money for anti-abortion campaigning. "The current rate of exchange is ridiculously in our favour," he told supporters in Britain. "Even modest donations are of great help." Already a bill recognizing a "child's right to life" has been floated in the Russian parliament. There is a strong current in Russian culture calling on women patriotically to bear and raise larger families. The neo-Fascist leader, Vladimir Zhirinovsky, believes that will help restore Russia's position as the most powerful nation on earth.

As the law stands at present, a Russian woman has every right to abortion: she need not plead her case or justify her request. But with hardly any contraception, no control over the brutalizing conditions under which the abortion is performed, and the punishing costs of child-rearing, opting for abortion is not a "choice." Janet Chance, one of the founders of the British abortion reform campaign, wrote in the 1930s, when contraception was scarcely available, the "women do not enjoy abortions—they snatch at them in despair" (Jenkins 1961). She could have been writing about Russia, more than half a century later.

Holland: Lowest Abortion Rate in the World

"Where is the easiest place in the world to get an abortion?" someone asked me on discovering that I was writing this book. The answer is probably Holland. The law is liberal; services are free, local, specialized and compassionate. Abortion is indeed easy.

And Holland has the lowest abortion rate in the world. Policy-makers and family planning experts troop into this tiny country, asking for the secret of the Dutch paradox. There is no secret, say the Dutch with pride. They patiently explain, over and over again, their methods, their policy and their values. I went to look for myself, visiting abortion clinics in Arnhem and Rotterdam.

In a tree-lined Arnhem street, in eastern Holland, stands a rambling old house, with a neat garden. It could be the home of a university professor. Inside there is a strong smell—it's coffee. The rooms are carpeted, with pot plants on the sills. In an interview room, one wall carries a huge display of every kind of contraceptive. The atmosphere is completely informal—no white coats here, not even any gynecologists. The doctors who staff the Arnhem abortion clinic are all part-time GPs, as they are in Holland's seventeen other abortion clinics. Arnhem is close to the border with Germany. When my taxi driver realized I was not Dutch, he began to speak German: almost 45 per cent of the clinic's patients travel from Germany, to take advantage of Holland's liberal abortion laws. Others come from Belgium, Switzerland, Spain, Portugal, Greece, Poland and even South Africa.

Dutch abortion law is cursory: it leaves a wide space for interpretation. In the opinion of one doctor, a woman must be in "a severe emergency situation," and that doctor must agree to perform the abortion. Abortion within the time limit is not refused: it is the woman herself who defines a "severe emergency" and the doctor usually only checks to make sure that she is acting on her own behalf and is not being pressured by family or partner. Between the time that the woman first requests the abortion and the abortion itself, a five-day waiting period must elapse. This is called "thinking-time" in Dutch and its presence irritates many abortion providers, who see it as paternalistic: "What should she think about?" they ask. But even the five-day waiting period can be dispensed with if menstruation is not more than sixteen days overdue, allowing the woman to have a "menstrual regulation." The law places the time limit for abortion at viability: this is interpreted as twenty-two weeks after conception, and apart from danger to the mother's life, there are no exceptions after that, not even for severe fetal handicap.

No one living in Holland is more than one hour's journey away from a licensed clinic, which is where almost all abortions are carried out. The service is free to all Dutch citizens (others have to pay around 500 Dutch guilders—about US$300). The usual procedure is vacuum aspiration, with local anesthesia: a woman can arrive at the clinic early in the morning and be home by early afternoon. Strict records are kept of all procedures but patients' anonymity is scrupulously protected. The complication rate is extremely low and everyone is counselled about avoiding future unplanned pregnancy.

Dutch abortion providers talk almost passionately about the advantages of their system of specialist clinics, which stand apart from the main health service and are run as independent, non-profit organizations. But whatever their merits, they owe their existence to an accident of history, rather than a grand design. Dr. Willem Boissevain, of the Arnhem clinic, explained to me that in the 1960s Dutch women seeking abortion had to plead their case before cumbersome hospital committees and the law was very restricted. Britain's abortion law reform in 1967 gave a great impetus to campaigners for reform in Holland.

In 1970, after visiting the British Pregnancy Advisory Service, Boissevain and some other Arnhem family doctors sent a questionnaire to local colleagues, asking their views on the need for an abortion service. (Dutch women were going in droves to Britain for abortions.) The gynecologists in Arnhem's hospitals said they would not perform abortions although local

GPs agreed overwhelmingly that an abortion service was needed. According to Boissevain, he and his GP colleagues said to each other, " 'OK, we'll do it.' We started the clinic in 1970 and within three weeks the public prosecutor sent an inspector, to ensure that we were sticking to the law. But then they left us alone."

With the authorities turning a blind eye, similar clinics were started all over Holland. They were buttressed by the support of the vociferous Dutch feminist movement—"We women demand"—which focused a great deal of political energy on the issue. Throughout the 1970s, abortion was a highly volatile element in the mercurial system of Dutch coalition politics and caused the downfall of several governments (Outshoorn 1986). It was not until 1984 that the reformed abortion law came into effect.

But the system of small clinics, which had earned respect for its exemplary standards of care, stayed. Even the Rotterdam clinic, which sees more patients than most, is small. I was welcomed there by the director, Dr. Henk Doppenberg. In his open-necked shirt, he could have been the janitor. His clinic employs eight GPs, all of whom work part-time, but whose specialized commitment to providing abortion has produced a sympathetic, high-quality service. Having part-time doctors who also have a stake in the wider health care system probably also helps keep the clinic in touch with mainstream health services. In the United States, by contrast, where abortion clinic doctors work full-time, they risk developing a kind of tunnel vision on patients' needs, and it is also much easier for the opposition to brand them as "abortionists." The Dutch doctors see women in all stages of their reproductive lives and, as many Dutch women have their babies at home, regularly attend births.

"Most women," says Doppenberg, "arrive in a state of some fear—of the pain: they also fear that we will lecture them for needing abortion. The actual experience is far less traumatic." In Arnhem, says Boissevain, "many of the German patients are astonished that we are not angry with them. They have met hostile doctors, and they expect punishment and pain. When we talk to them about contraception, many say this is the first time they have had a chance to discuss it with anyone, and the whole experience is a great relief." Contraception is discussed in all clinics *before* the abortion, so that if a woman chooses an IUD, it can be fitted directly after the abortion is over.

Veterans of the Dutch abortion movement, such as Willem Boissevain and his colleague, Paul Bekkering, are outraged at being portrayed as purveyors of evil in anti-abortion literature. Holland has its anti-abortion campaigners too.[5] "By advising women about contraception, I prevent more abortions than the Pope," says Bekkering, "and we work hard here to handle sorrow and human difficulty with respect and compassion."

Leave Nothing to Chance

Critics of abortion reform often predict that "easy" abortion will lead people to be less careful with contraception and to use abortion "as a form of contraception." Yet Holland has the lowest abortion rate and the lowest unplanned pregnancy rate world-wide. Above all, Dutch people want reliable contraception and to avoid unwanted births. They are, in family planning jargon, "well-motivated" users of birth control. The figures are concise and eloquent. Each year, for every 1,000 women of reproductive age who are Dutch citizens, no more than 6 will have an abortion. In Britain the comparable figure is almost 14, in the United States it is 28 and in Russia it is 111 (Henshaw 1990). The Dutch figure has remained steady since the abortion law came into effect in 1984.[6]

It is only relatively recently that contraception has been so highly rated in Dutch society, even though it was in Holland in 1882 that the world's first birth control clinic opened. Until the mid-1960s, contraception was a taboo subject and the Dutch birth rate was one of the highest in Western Europe. There is not space here to dwell on the social changes in Holland which began in the 1960s. But among its key features were an astonishing opening-up of discussion about sexuality in the mass media, amid a strong current of anxiety about the need to curb family size, and about global population growth.

Because abortion was in a legal twilight throughout the 1970s, everyone, including politicians, stressed the need to prevent pregnancy. "The Dutch have never felt relaxed about abortion," says sociologist Evert Ketting, deputy director of the National Institute of Social Sexological Research (NISSO) (Ketting and Visser 1994, p. 165). To underline the message that contraception was part of a citizen's duty, rather than a private matter, the government made the Pill available free of charge. Almost everyone uses contraception (or gets sterilized) in Holland today, and the Pill is the most popular choice.

But the figure which really has the world's family planning experts agog is that eight out of ten women aged between 15 and 25 use the Pill. Holland not only makes contraceptive services easily available to young men and women, its program of sex education is exemplary. It is open-minded and realistic. It does not lecture, it accepts teenage sexual experimentation and activity as one of the facts of life. Jany Rademakers, a research fellow at NISSO, believes that for most Dutch teenagers using contraception is as unemotional as brushing your teeth to avoid the dentist's drill. Most young women, when they decide that they are ready for sex, simply equip themselves with the means to avoid pregnancy. They trust their family doctors to respect their confidentiality. It's straightforward, like getting a driver's license before you begin to drive. The Dutch are convinced that if children feel able to talk about sex, they will have safer sex.[7] There is no debate about whether it is ethical to give the Pill to 15-year-old girls and to respect their confidence (Rademakers 1993).

The Dutch point to Britain and to the United States for the fruits of reticence and moralism. In the United States in 1990, 117 out of every 1,000 girls between the age of 15 and 19 became pregnant and many of those pregnancies were unintended. In the same age group in Britain, around 70 girls per 1,000 face the challenge of pregnancy each year. In Holland, out of every 1,000 teenage girls, no more than 10 become pregnant. Of course, in all three countries, many of all those pregnancies end in abortion.

It is not only Dutch *women* who are concerned with birth control; male sterilization rates are among the highest in the world. But it is mainly women who take on the responsibility of preventing pregnancy. They start young and they are successful: nearly every Dutch child is "planned." Explanations abound for Dutch people's assiduous determination to avoid unwanted pregnancy. Some point to overzealous promotion of the Pill by Dutch GPs, some to the cultural heritage of Calvinism (Ketting 1994).

A Panacea for Social Change

But Holland's emphasis on the undesirability of unplanned pregnancy and also of abortion has an unexpected price. It is a basic tenet of modern feminism that "women can never hope to be liberated in any sense if they are denied the right to control their own bodies" (Driscoll 1970). Without this control they are "slaves of reproduction." In other words contraception and abortion give women the same sexual freedom as men, to enjoy sexual pleasure and seek fulfilling lives without the threat of unwanted pregnancy as "punishment." From this perspective it seems curious at first to find that the Dutch experience, for all its broadmindedness about sexuality itself, has done little to challenge images of women's roles outside the bedroom, especially maternal responsibility.

Dual careers for women are difficult to negotiate in Holland—publicly funded childcare services which accommodate the needs of working mothers are scarce and the tax system penalizes double-income families. Despite some recent reforms, Dutch women have to choose between career and child-rearing, and their traditional roles are still greatly valued. Fewer women work outside the home in Holland than they do in Portugal or France. It is not feminist ideology that has driven Holland to become the "perfect contraceptive population"; it is a powerful moral doctrine about not undertaking child-rearing until family finances are sound.[8]

Secondly, the constant emphasis on "perfect contraception" at almost any price, has sometimes led doctors to make light of the health risks of the Pill, especially among older women. There are after all other criteria, besides reliability, for choosing a contraceptive method, including sharing responsibility, or safety. But the Dutch have invested almost exclusively in reliability, and this has implicitly reinforced the stigma of abortion. Most clients at Dutch abortion clinics have used contraception; their abortions are no "fault" of their own. "Despite the clinic staff telling women, 'don't blame yourself, this can happen to anyone', women feel stupid and ashamed," says Ketting. "And when eight out of ten sexually active teenage girls are taking the Pill, if you don't you are an outcast."

Beatrijs Stemerding of the Amsterdam-based Women's Global Network for Reproductive Rights points out that Dutch GPs know practically nothing about methods such as the diaphragm and no one ever suggests that using a barrier method, with early abortion as a back-up, might be a reasonable option for women's health. The health education message stakes everything on reliability and how unacceptable it is not to plan pregnancy. There is little public debate about the price this might exact. Abortion is also frowned on, not because it is evidence of having had sex, but because it is evidence of less than perfect contraception. No one gets an abortion without being quizzed about future contraception.

Contraception and abortion services may even have provided a panacea for other changes, such as decent childcare services and other more radical improvements, which would have lifted the burden of inequality from Dutch women. "It suits companies that they are not required to take account of the needs of women with children, because female employees have chosen to postpone motherhood and quit when they decide to have a child," observes Ketting.

No one would dispute the huge pay-offs for Dutch women, with ready access to contraception and high quality abortion services for which they do not have to wheedle and plead. At least, for the time being: in 1995 the minister of health, Els Borst-Eilers, announced plans to save on the nation's health bill by no longer allowing oral contraceptives to be provided free of charge to women over 18. She also announced an end to subsidies for many family planning and women's health clinics. Faced with a wave of protest and predictions that making women pay for the Pill would lead to a rise in abortions and was a false economy from every angle, the health minister retreated, but the episode alerted the Dutch public that they could not be complacent.

Tolerant sex education and an open-minded society have a lot to be said for them: consider the mirror-images of negativity—in repressive, religion-dominated regimes. In practice, abortion is "on demand" in Holland, yet it occurs less than in many countries where it is a criminal offense. Liberalizing the law does not open the floodgates to abortion.

Britain: Muddle and Hypocrisy

In Britain attitudes and policies towards contraception, abortion and sex education have been marked by muddle and self-contradiction. One step forward, two steps back. British doctors' distaste for providing contraceptive services goes back to the profession's efforts not to be tarred with the same brush as purveyors of "rubber goods." Many doctors also turned their backs on abortion, seeing it as a disreputable gynecological chore. When the abortion law was reformed in 1967, many gynecologists were hostile—they feared that legislating for abortion on "social grounds" would open the door to "abortion on demand." As a result, the National Health Service (NHS) was totally unable to meet the demand for abortion which made itself felt as soon as it became legal.

Private clinics sprang up all over England and Wales, some run by charitable organizations and some for profit. Unlike the Dutch clinics, which had been set up by pioneering doctors, anxious to see a change in the law, the British clinics were a simple response to market forces, demand for legal abortion outstripping supply. The charities believed that the need for their service would lessen once the NHS got itself organized.[9] But hospital policies were strongly influenced, in some cases even dictated, by the attitudes of the gynecologists practicing there. It was common knowledge, for example, that an abortion was almost impossible to obtain in Birmingham, on account of the presence of Professor Hugh McLaren, who went on television the day the 1967 Act became law to announce that, "Whatever the law says, we will never murder little children in Birmingham."[10] McLaren gathered about him a covey of doctors practicing throughout the hospitals of the West Midlands who, with God on their side, invoked the Act's conscience clause and refused to perform abortions. Although the professor has long retired, NHS provision in the West Midlands is still among the lowest in the country.

Throughout the 1970s and 1980s, about half of all abortions in Britain were performed outside the NHS. The earlier the abortion, the more likely it would be to find it had been provided in the private sector (Paintin 1985). The NHS is notorious for its waiting lists, which are caused not only by a shortfall in services—doctors, beds, operating theater time—but also by delays in giving appointments and other bureaucratic hurdles. Where gynecologists have taken it upon themselves to champion local NHS abortion services and get them reorganized, they have demonstrated that women can obtain early abortions with far less fuss and delay (Saha, Savage and George 1992; Glasier 1993).

What is often forgotten is that contraceptive clinics did not become fully part of the NHS until 1974. It was only then that the government, spurred on by protests about soaring abortion rates—feminist arguments about women's right to control their fertility cut no ice—was persuaded to bring contraception into the NHS. The Family Planning Association (FPA) handed over its network of clinics, and GPs were authorized to prescribe contraception. The doctors wrangled for months about how much they were to be paid to prescribe contraceptives and refused outright to prescribe condoms (Shapiro 1987, p. 22). Eventually, a deal was reached but, if a woman wanted to discuss a full range of contraceptive options, she usually needed to find a clinic. GPs rarely prescribed anything other than the Pill.

After the 1967 Act, in the mistaken belief that the battle for abortion was over and done with, the Abortion Law Reform Association had almost declared itself redundant and had passed the bulk of its money to an organization campaigning for contraception on the NHS. But throughout the 1970s and 1980s, the Abortion Act was attacked again and again by its influential and well-financed opponents with a steady procession of bills in Parliament. Some of the largest national demonstrations to pass through London's streets in the 1970s were held in the cause of abortion, as defenders and assailants took to the streets. In such a climate it was no wonder that abortion services in the NHS could not and did not expand and improve. The anti-abortion lobby capitalized on public concern about later abortions, and it was quite difficult to command as much media attention with the simple but rather colorless point that if services were better organized, many such abortions could be avoided. In Tower Hamlets, for instance, where a day-care abortion service was set up in the 1970s, abortions after sixteen weeks fell significantly—an improvement for women and a saving on the hard-pressed NHS balance sheet (Savage 1985).

By the 1980s, as NHS managers with shrinking budgets began to cast around for ways to make savings, family planning services looked like an easy target and ferocious cuts began. Throughout the 1980s NHS managers scythed through the clinics, cutting the hours in many, closing some altogether. If doctors were able to provide contraception, they argued, clinics were a wasteful duplication of services.[11] In some places, clinic provision was reduced by half. As abortions also increased in the late 1980s, experts clashed over the possible cause and effect. "We believe there is a direct link between cuts in family planning services and the abortion rate," said the Family Planning Association, which could do little but protest. In 1990 the government finally reined in the NHS administrators, and the spate of closures dwindled.

National policy on contraception took another lurch forward in 1991, when the government's strategy for public health—*The Health of the Nation*—set as one of its five key targets the goal of reducing by half the pregnancy rate among girls under 16 by the year 2000 (Department of Health 1991). This was prompted by alarm at the fact that England and Wales enjoyed the dubious honor of leading Western Europe in the league table for teenage fertility, and moral panic about family values. Not that *The Health of the Nation*'s target-setting led to any consistency in policies to reduce unwanted pregnancies. For whilst many health authorities indeed set about making their services less off-putting to adolescents, at the same time teachers were being warned—by the Ministry of Education—that they might be committing a criminal offense if they gave schoolchildren "individual advice about sex education without parental knowledge or consent." (The final version of the regulations drew back from threatening criminal action and simply recommended teachers to "encourage the pupil to seek advice from his or her parents.") Teenagers kept on telling anyone who asked them that they would not seek help from anyone—GP or teacher—unless they could be sure that their confidences would be respected. Many would risk pregnancy rather than seek contraceptive advice. The row surrounding the provisions for sex education in the 1993 Education Act glaringly highlighted the government's double-think, double-speak and totally chaotic position on adolescent sexuality.

When, for example, Nick Fisher, the advice columnist of *Just 17* magazine, was commissioned by the Health Education Authority to write a sex education guide for teenagers, the minister of health branded it as "smutty," mostly for using teenagers' own language of sex (chapter headings included "Wanking Is Good for You" and "Dick Dimensions") and ordered the book to be pulped. Meanwhile teenagers carried on having sex, some girls got pregnant—including 8,000 a year under 16 years old. In a Somerset village a 16-year-old girl came home from school with stomach pains, got into the bath, gave birth to a baby and smothered him with her jumper. Her mother said she had not known that her daughter was pregnant. "Posters about contraceptive services placed in Somerset libraries are repeatedly removed by indignant moralists," stated the news report (Grant 1993). Removing posters and pulping straight-talking books about sex are both actions which are informed, if that is the right word, by the notion that denying young people sex education is the best way to ensure that they don't get sexy.[12]

Although the government had halted the attrition of clinics, the deep cuts of the 1980s were never restored and an FPA survey found that scarcely more than half the clinics were open for more than a few hours a week. Choosing between a clinic or the GP was a rare luxury for most women. And the trend towards targeting contraceptive services at adolescents left a huge swathe of sexually active young women out in the cold—women between 20 and 30, but especially those under 25 years old. Roughly one in three pregnancies is unplanned or unwanted and one in five of all pregnancies ends in abortion. It is women in their early twenties who have the highest abortion rates (Office of Population Censuses and Surveys 1995).

Some trends are positive. As the new pattern of the NHS, set in train by the 1980s reforms, begins to emerge, the proportion of abortions funded by the NHS is beginning to increase. In 1994 more than two-thirds of abortions were paid for by the NHS, and the trend of recent years has been steadily upwards. Individual gynecologists' influence over services is waning. Some local managers as well as GP practices which now control their own budgets are arranging for women in their districts to obtain abortions either in the private sector or in other parts of the country where NHS doctors' attitudes present no barriers (Mihill 1994). But many women seeking NHS abortions still face long waiting lists, and many turn directly to specialist abortion services because they fear insensitive treatment at their local hospital (Pro-Choice Alliance 1993). What is more, as Wendy Savage has observed, "abortion is still the most frequently performed operation for which the patient must pay" (Savage 1995, p. 83).

The opposition still does its rancorous best to thwart all attempts to give women easier access to abortion, citing the old chestnut of "abortion on demand." The pettifogging regulations imposed on the prescription of the "abortion pill," RU 486, have made it so expensive that surgical termination is still the only option in many hospitals (Smith 1993).

Many abortions could be avoided altogether if post-coital contraception—the "morning-after pill"—was easier to obtain. Emergency contraception is effective if taken up to seventy-two hours after sex, and if women could buy it in pharmacies without a prescription, as many as eight out of ten abortions could be avoided altogether, according to some estimates.

The teenage pregnancy rate is beginning to fall but the broader picture for contraceptive services is bleak. There have been serious threats to remove all but a few brands of Pill from the range which GPs can prescribe, and whether there will still be free contraception in ten years' time is anyone's guess. If the exemplary Dutch can contemplate making contraception a consumer item once again, then it would seem that there is little to stop the government in Britain from doing so, riven as it is by ideological conflict over sex, contraception and abortion, and with healthcare budgets contracting year by year. In a survey in 1993, 93 per cent of women undergoing abortion in Leeds said they would have used emergency contraception if they had known about it (Bromham 1993b).

To women seeking an end to their pregnancies, Holland is without doubt a beacon of civilized compassion. The brutal nightmare of abortion for women in Russia mirrors the brutality and squalor which attends so many aspects of everyday life in contemporary Russia, and Britain along with any number of industrial countries, such as Germany or even Catholic Spain, exemplifies what can happen when the ideology of abortion is set adrift from contraception and deep social ambivalence about sexuality and women's reproductive rights is played out.

9

Weapons of War:
Sieges and Strategies

THE ACT OF PREVENTING PREGNANCY—literally *contraception*—is technically clearly distinguishable from the business of terminating a pregnancy.[1] But they are both fertility control and for many women, "the crucial distinction is not between using a method before or after conception, but between having or not having a surviving child" (Dixon-Mueller 1993, p. 15). Abortion is still the commonest method of fertility control in the world and has not always been so sharply divided from other birth control methods, nor under such a powerful taboo. Yet the cultural message of almost the entire family planning and "pro-choice" movement today is that while contraception and "planned parenthood" are achievable, desirable and responsible, abortion is always a tragic and outmoded activity "which signals a social failure" (Jacobson 1988).

The anti-abortion campaigners aim to stigmatize abortion as a uniquely cruel and squalid act. It is a simple and effective strategy. Their relentless attacks, on every front—physical, legislative, ideological, medical—have greatly skewed the framework and the language used by those who strive to defend abortion rights. To speak of siege mentality among defenders of abortion is no exaggeration. In 1994, for example, at the world population conference in Cairo the issue of abortion almost brought the meeting to deadlock. But the quarreling between the defenders of safe abortion and the anti-abortion wrecking pact of the Vatican and fundamentalist Islam was accompanied by a peculiar undertone of unanimity. The warring parties seemed in perfect agreement that abortion was always unfortunate and could never be a woman's most appropriate method of controlling her fertility. It has been left to a few feminists to raise a note of dissent to this taboo and to argue for a unified approach to contraception and abortion.

Isolating Abortion

Confrontation and violence, especially in the United States, have grabbed headlines. The absolutist anti-abortion strategy is patently to isolate and surround legal abortion, to portray it as a uniquely barbarous procedure, and to erode women's access to it in every possible way. Television and newspaper accounts of anti-abortion protest are dominated by images of hymn-singing men holding out tiny crosses as if to ward off witches, silent women holding up pink plastic models of fetuses at eight months of pregnancy; screaming, banners and frightened women being jostled as they are escorted into clinics besieged by pickets. And firebombs and shootings. The protesters' placards say, "Arrest That Murderer!" "Stop Killing Babies," "Adoption, Not Abortion," "Unborn Women Have Rights Too!" "Ten Weeks After Conception—A Tiny Perfect Human Person!" "It Could Have Been You!" and "We Shall Overcome!" But direct action is only one aspect of the campaign.

Much of the protest has been led by religious groups and organizations— Christians in Europe, the United States, Central and Latin America and sub-Saharan Africa, and Islamists in predominantly Muslim countries. But many Roman Catholics all over the world disagree with the pope's proclamations on the sinfulness of birth control, and it would be wrong to assume any unanimity either within the Roman Catholic Church or within Islam, or to assume that those who disagree with abortion are conservative on every other related issue.[2]

In the United States, where litigation is almost a national pastime, the *Roe v. Wade* abortion judgment of 1973 was destined to be challenged, again and again, as abortion's opponents probed and pushed at the vagaries of the Supreme Court's law. In 1989, a more conservative Supreme Court came within inches of trouncing *Roe v. Wade* utterly and made it possible for individual states to rival the harshness of Romania's anti-abortion laws in the restrictions they imposed.[3]

The first major blow, however, had been dealt in 1977, when Congress passed the Hyde amendment, signalling the anti-abortion movement's determination to make a sham of the rights awarded by Roe (Tribe 1992, pp.

151–9). No longer could Medicaid provide abortions, unless the woman's life or health were seriously endangered. As I described in Chapter 1, the anti-abortion lobby argued that abortions on Medicaid amounted to government encouragement of immorality and Congress debated at length "precisely how much suffering and danger a poor woman must face before Medicaid will pay for her to have an abortion." Throughout the 1980s a relentless onslaught of cumbersome state restrictions on abortion services were introduced, as described in Chapter 3. Views on abortion became a test for hiring (or firing) public officials, including judges. And at the same time, by getting anti-abortion candidates elected at every level of public life, opponents worked towards their longer-term aim—overthrowing the abortion law.

In Britain, the 1967 abortion law came under attack no less than twenty times from anti-abortion MPs seeking to weaken it to the point of meaninglessness. The most serious broadside came in 1988, from Roman Catholic Liberal MP David Alton. His shrewdly drafted bill called for a ban on abortion after eighteen weeks but was styled to set off a process of gradual erosion of legal abortion by creating a new criminal category of "late" abortion. (See Chapter 4 for more about the Alton Bill.) Britain's anti-abortion lobby, organized in Parliament into a powerful All-Party Pro-Life Group, also chipped away year after year at the minutiae of abortion regulations.

In 1982, for example, they managed to get the wording on the form signed by doctors authorizing abortion altered, eliminating "social grounds" as an indication. The law itself has not changed, but the form now only lists medical reasons. This may act as a brake on doctors who are not whole-heartedly "pro-choice" as well as inhibiting doctors who are not so familiar with the law. Organizing mass opposition to such a detail in an obscure NHS document was never realistic, but the alteration was nonetheless a significant political victory (South 1985). The anti-abortion pressure groups sedulously publicized the "conscience clause" in the 1967 Act, encouraging doctors and nurses to report "incidents," which they then whipped up into "scandals."[4]

It was with wholehearted backing from anti-abortion pressure groups that college student Robert Carver tried to prevent his girlfriend from "selfishly" having an abortion. Carver presented himself as a committed would-be father and by bringing a court case, inviting maximum media attention, attempted to force the woman to carry and give birth to a child she did not want (McNeil 1991). In 1988, as the parliamentary debate on David Alton's Bill was beginning, SPUC—the Society for Protection of the Unborn Child—fanned the flames with a series of reports of fetuses aborted but delivered alive. "Abortion Baby Took Three Hours to Die," said the headlines.

The allegations were used to stoke up public sympathy about the abortion of fetuses "capable of being born alive" and to blame women who "callously" sought later abortions (South 1985). More recently there have been questions about the incineration of fetal material, about the introduction of RU 486 and about the incidence of post-abortion syndrome, the last designed to talk this much disputed condition into existence on the parliamentary record.

In 1984, Enoch Powell MP sponsored an Unborn Children (Protection) Bill, which aimed to give the fetus full legal rights, from the moment of conception. It was defeated. If the embryo had been granted full status, potentially all abortions could have been banned, and that, for many, was the real thrust of the bill.[5] The attacks have certainly made the Department of Health extremely chary of pursuing anything which might make abortion easier to obtain. But on the whole, attempts to weaken the legislation itself have been unsuccessful, thanks to the equally energetic pressure groups which defend the 1967 Act. The Act itself has hardly been altered at all, except for its upper time limit.

But the relentless sniping gets talked about: it raises the profile of the fetus and its claims as a victimized "person." When the Alton Bill was under debate in Parliament, with Alton's supporters energetically inflating the myth that many, perhaps even most, abortions were being performed troublingly late, the media reported this as a fact. During the Alton Bill campaign, anti-abortion pressure groups circulated the famous Lars Nilsson photograph of the fetus, claiming it showed a living, eighteen-week-old fetus, in the womb. In fact in 1965, when Nilsson took the picture, such photography was impossible and Nilsson's subject was an aborted fetus in saline solution. It was also twenty weeks old, so looked more mature and "human" than the subjects of Alton's Bill.

Every time something relating to pregnancy or fetuses crops up, the anti-abortion lobby is ready to give it their predictable spin. The tactics switch nimbly from topic to topic. From premature babies "rescued" by the miracles of medicine, to use of fetal tissue to treat people with Parkinson's disease, to preserving injured, brain-dead pregnant women on life support for months, and so on, the strategy never wavers. The aim is to talk up the fetus. Besides doing that, serious public discussions of these vital and complex issues are poisoned and distorted by having them extraneously dragged into the shrill feud over abortion. And abortion is always talked of as "murder" or "killing"; later abortion as "gruesome" or "traumatic." As they say in Hollywood, accuracy is not the point; it is the atmosphere that counts.

Moving Images

Defenders of abortion never have anything to match the visual image of the fetus, the most emotive weapon of all. Anti-abortion supporters often wear a tiny gold-plated lapel pin, in the shape of two little feet. A leaflet from LIFE, one of Britain's main anti-abortion groups, shows the little feet, held between huge fingers. "An adult holds the feet of an aborted baby of about eleven weeks—these feet were made for walking," says the leaflet. Without such images—photos, films and ultrasound, often gruesome, always compelling—the anti-abortion lobby only has arguments about chromosomes or theological disquisitions about when human life begins. Not much to fan the flames of the "righteous fire" and grab the public's imagination (Petchesky 1987).

Films such as *The Silent Scream,* presented by the apostate U.S. abortionist Bernard Nathanson, purport to demonstrate what an abortion is like from a twelve-week-old "victim's vantage point." The only shot of the woman is of a pregnant woman on an operating table. As Susan Faludi comments, it is the woman who is the truly silent character in *The Silent Scream* (Faludi 1992, p. 459). As the suction cannula—"the lethal weapon"—approaches the fuzzy image of the fetus, Nathanson tells us it is about to "tear the child apart." At twelve weeks, however, the fetus has no cerebral cortex with which to sense pain, and its movements are reflexive and purposeless. The film was speeded up to make it look as if the fetus, shown on the screen twice the size of an actual twelve-week-old fetus, is frantically avoiding the reach of the cannula.

Defenders of abortion rights—with little other than the bloody coat-hanger image to remind us of the bad old days of illegal abortions—are utterly routed by the tiny feet or the manipulated trembling of the *Silent Scream* fetus. For people born after the 1950s, calls for "no return to the back-streets" have little appeal. They are conscious of high-technology medicine's capacity to sustain the lives of premature babies weighing no more than a bag of sugar, and have little or no memory of when contraception and legal abortion were practically unavailable. Ours is a culture of pictures. Seeing is believing. Every newspaper editor and television news producer knows that however powerful words may be—recalling the grisly squalor of illegal abortion and its links with every kind of racketeering—it is to pictures, and above all to images that move, that people respond. No words are needed to accompany pictures of little mangled legs, hacked arms, crushed skulls. Award-winning commercials director Tony Kaye shot graphic footage of fetuses for a feature film about abortion and commented: "When you see those fetuses, it is pretty much game set and match as far as I am concerned." So the anti-abortion lobby hopes it will be for the rest of us.

Above all ultrasound—a "window on the womb"—makes the fetus real in an entirely new way. With the gloss of science it has created what amounts almost to a cult of the fetus. In the screen's grainy blur the fetus floats alone, like an astronaut in space: the woman is invisible, truly she has become nothing more than outer space (Gallagher 1987). The sonogram has even become a torture weapon against women with unwanted pregnancies. In the anti-abortion state of Louisiana, women seeking abortions are required to look at their fetus on a sonogram before they can consent to the operation, to ensure that they are truly "informed." Of course, it is not the technology itself which is to be blamed. For many women happy to be pregnant, a sonogram may offer an elating, reassuring and almost miraculous promise of what is to come.

"Rescuing" and Other Anti-abortion Tactics

"Whatever force is legitimate to defend the life of a born child is legitimate to defend the life of an unborn child," says Rev. Michael Bray, who has served four years in U.S. prisons for bombing ten clinics. This simple idea has inspired thousands of anti-abortion militants in the United States to conduct what amounts to a low-intensity civil war against abortion clinics and women seeking abortion. Sinister groups, with links to the paranoid racist Right, styling themselves "Missionaries to the Pre-Born," have formed armed militias dedicated to an anti-abortion gospel of "direct action." Federal investigators of the 1995 Oklahoma City bombing of a U.S. government building (unconnected with abortion) might have been interested to learn of an anti-abortion terrorism manual, produced in the 1980s, which included an elaborate illustrated plan for a fertilizer bomb like the one used in Oklahoma City (Rich 1995).

Doctors performing abortions now are meeting difficulties for which no medical textbook has prepared them. They receive death threats, their cars are stalked, their children are followed to school. Normal life can become quite impossible: "How would you like to come out of a restaurant and find fifty people chained to your car?" as Joseph Scheidler, author of a handbook, *Closed: 99 Ways to Stop an Abortion Clinic,* put it. In states requiring two visits to a clinic, with a waiting period in between, patients' phone numbers

OPERATION RESCUE

Operation Rescue was founded in 1985 by Randall Terry, a former used-car salesman and hamburger flipper. By 1988 Operation Rescue was conducting mass blockades of abortion clinics in New York, in which more than 500 people were arrested, it had a mailing list of 35,000 and donations were pouring in. Terry urged his followers on with a new fire and brimstone anti-abortion "pro-life" gospel. "If you believe abortion is murder, then you must act like it is murder," he said, and that became Operation Rescue's motto. Along with abortion, he condemned birth control, homosexuality, and sex education in schools. Operation Rescue staged its most spectacular event in its "summer of mercy" in Wichita, Kansas. In 1991, Wichita was not only in the heartland of the evangelical Bible Belt, but was also the home of Dr. George Tiller, one of the handful of U.S. doctors who performed late abortions. Operation Rescue in Wichita involved 30,000 volunteers and almost 3,000 arrests. They blocked the clinic entrances, chanted at pregnant women, "Please don't kill your baby," and prayed rapturously as the police finally arrested them. Tiller was shot and seriously injured by an anti-abortion fanatic in 1993.

Terry's foot-soldiers learned the vocabulary of "rescue." A fetus was never a fetus, always a baby, even a "pre-born" or "unborn." The clinics were to be called "abortuaries" or "abortion mills"; the doctors "baby killers" or "godless human hyenas"; and abortion itself was "murder." Pregnant women were never women, but always "mothers"—sometimes nothing more than "wombs." Blockading a clinic was a "biblical act of obedience" and getting arrested was a way of obeying God's law and repenting for the sins of apathetic Christians who allow abortion to continue. The Missionaries of the Pre-Born routinely pray for the deaths of doctors who perform abortions. A typical Operation Rescue comment on the shooting of doctors: "The fact is that over a dozen babies would have died in his hands today." When abortion is "murder," killing a doctor becomes "justifiable homicide." From praying for death to taking action is not such a huge leap, once the language has been so debased that violence can be thus condoned.

are traced by means of car number plates outside the clinic. Women can arrive home to find clinic picketers at their door haranguing them, their families, their parents and their neighbors, with gory leaflets, accusations and predictions of hellfire.

Throughout the 1980s, clinics were firebombed and vandalized. It was a miracle no one was killed sooner.[6] Since shooting began in March 1993, with the death of Dr. David Gunn, killed outside his Florida clinic, at least five people have been killed and others wounded. Bullet-proof vests, bodyguards and handguns are the order of the day.

In paramilitary-style camps, anti-abortion volunteers can undergo a

US$600 twelve-week course in tactics of civil disobedience, intimidation, harassment and fear. They learn "sidewalk counselling"—intercepting women on their way into clinics to harass and humiliate them—and they learn how to jam phones, seal locks, chain themselves to furniture and cars and "outreach to the community." The camp recruits are "ambassadors of Christ," says Wendy Wright, full-time organizer for Operation Rescue, whose name comes from Proverbs 24, "rescue those who are unjustly sentenced to death" (Tisdall 1993). (See sidebar on Operation Rescue.)

Direct action can be devious as well as confrontational. Throughout the United States there may be as many as 2,000 establishments "counselling" woomen in bogus "pregnancy" clinics, listed in the phone books under "abortion service providers," offering "pregnancy option counselling." Of course, women with unplanned pregnancies take the bait and arrive seeking help at the clinics, only to be trapped into watching graphic videos of mutilated fetuses, while staff urge them, "Don't murder your baby," and warn that abortion leads to death, disease, insanity and sterility.

As the 1980s wore on, the U.S. anti-abortion lobby became increasingly aggressive. More moderate elements disowned the direct action, fearing that it undermined its quest for political power inside the Republican Party. But the militants, bent on "loving action to protect the unborn," do not give a fig for such oleaginous politicking. In their eyes the moderates are self-serving opportunists whose sense of urgency has been blunted.

Even if the shock-troops of Britain and other European countries seem much less sinister than their U.S. counterparts there is nonetheless a militant wing to Europe's anti-abortion movement. Britain's abortion clinics receive their share of harassment—bomb scares, acid thrown on doctors' cars, and hate mail sent to staff whose addresses have been traced from their car license plates. Some clinics are regularly staked out by a handful of protesters, who pray and sing hymns and "counsel" women entering the clinic. It can be very intimidating to find yourself hemmed in on all sides by people yelling at you not to "murder your baby" as they thrust gruesome photos and anti-abortion tracts into your face.

But plans to emulate the mass pickets and invasive tactics of the United States have never really amounted to much, despite the efforts of Rescue America, an organization similar to Operation Rescue, to train anti-abortion militants here for clinic blockades. For Britain, fifty protesters constitutes a "mass picket."[7] Despite the dogged efforts of Father James Morrow, an elderly Roman Catholic priest who champions American-style "rescuing" from a small village in Scotland and has been imprisoned for his part in "rescues" which included assaulting the pregnant manager of a clinic, only a handful of followers have trickled to his side. The mainstream British anti-abortion pressure groups have strenuously distanced themselves from Morrow and his allies and an editorial in the *Catholic Herald* cautioned its readers against the "vengeful Old Testament mentality" of "extremists who have hijacked the American pro-life movement." In March 1995, in language that left no room for doubt, the pope's eleventh encyclical, *Evangelium vitae* ("Gospel of life") warned Catholics that they were under a "grave and clear obligation" to join non-violent anti-abortion protest. The pope's message came within inches of endorsing anti-abortion militancy as a religious duty[8] and the mainstream lobbyists fretted that it would whip up the fanatics to further image-damaging antics.

British efforts at direct action have, nonetheless, forced clinics to take security seriously. Video cameras watch the gates and doors; some clinics have bolt-cutters on hand to free themselves of intruders who have occasionally chained themselves to equipment. But it has been enough in the main simply to ignore the taunts and the hindrance, and clinic providers, such as Ian Jones, director of the British Pregnancy Advisory Service, which runs seven clinics throughout England, are confident that their opponents pose no real threat to their work.

While violence in the United States has certainly given the anti-abortion movement an "image problem," especially since the shootings, the constant *threat* of it has seriously affected the clinics' ability to provide a decent service. To protect staff and the service, clinics are forced to employ guards, install electric fences and security cameras, take out injunctions against trespassers, and organize escorts for frightened women to pass through picket lines of screaming "pavement counselors." Who can blame young doctors contemplating a career for crossing off abortion work or even gynecology itself from the list of specialties? No one sends death threats to staff in dermatology clinics or harasses their children on the way to school. After every shooting, another batch of clinic staff pull out, fearing for their lives. There are roughly 200 violent incidents against clinics, each year, in which some are completely destroyed. The latest tactic is bogus malpractice cases against clinic doctors, aimed at driving insurance premiums to punitive levels.[9] Resources, human and financial, are stretched to breaking point.

And while the terrorism and harassment may alienate some public support in the United States, it has kept abortion in the public eye, as "the most divisive cultural issue since Prohibition." The fanatical fringe buttresses the public sense of unease and ambivalence, which the movement's respectable battalions exploit so well. *Their* frontline troops act as snipers—lawyers, lobbyists and politicians who set out to remove the meaning and potency of abortion rights. They have won restrictions on the right of minors to have abortions without their parents' knowledge; they say that abortion must not be paid for out of the public healthcare budget; they erode the upper time limits for abortion. These issues are presented as "compromises," necessary curbs on "easy" abortion. But to the poor, the young and the vulnerable they are often insuperable hurdles (Henshaw 1995b). By working for consensus on these sensitive marginal issues their aim is to "slowly work their way towards criminalizing the procedure as a whole."[10]

The marginal issues in Britain are different, but the strategy of constriction is the same. Abortion's opponents protest vehemently against almost all infertility research, especially if it involves experimentation with embryos. Mention prenatal diagnosis of fetal abnormality and the anti-abortion lobby flares up instantly with a tirade against the eugenic horrors of the Third Reich. In 1994 when the Human Fertilisation and Embryology Authority asked for public comment on the possible use of eggs donated by live women, or from aborted fetuses for infertility research and possible treatment, it received an astonishing 10,000 replies, most of which were not only very hostile but clearly orchestrated.

Just months later, Father Leo Chamberlain, Benedictine headmaster of Ampleforth boys' school, Yorkshire, became famous for fifteen minutes with a new obfuscation. He said Roman Catholics must refuse rubella vaccination for their children because the vaccine originated in a culture of cells from the lung tissue of a fetus—aborted more than twenty years ago. "If you murder someone twenty years ago it is still murder," argued Father Chamberlain, although his views were at odds with the joint Bio-ethics Committee of the Roman Catholic Bishops, who said that consenting to vaccination did not condone abortion. Before the fuss faded, a number of Catholic parents with rubella-affected children—deaf, blind and brain-damaged—challenged Father Chamberlain and urged Catholics not to hesitate. But the priest's maverick views were plainly intended to chill the atmosphere surrounding abortion.

In every arena, the anti-abortion strategy is to take abortion out of context and above all to take women out of the frame. Abortions, they say, cannot be paid for out of public health funds, because abortion is not about health—it is about killing babies. This ranks it somewhere beneath removal of warts or liposuction as a health priority, with the innuendo that a woman seeking abortion is feckless and selfish thrown in for good measure. Secondly, although many opponents of abortion hate contraception almost as much as abortion because it separates sexual pleasure from "responsibility," their public tactic is to drive a wedge *between* contraception and abortion, to isolate abortion as a uniquely cruel and repulsive act.

The Road to Cairo

Anyone watching television news in September 1994 could be forgiven for thinking that the International Conference on Population and Development in Cairo was simply the world summit on abortion. Every ten years the United Nations hosts a conference on world population. Since 1974, when the threat of the "population time-bomb" arrived on the world stage, these meetings have provided a platform for the abortion controversy to be played out in the glare of international media attention. In 1984 the conference was in Mexico City and in 1994 it was held in Cairo.

Both the Mexico City and Cairo meetings loom large in the politics of abortion and the struggle to increase women's access to reproductive choices. The anti-abortion movement has played its part to the hilt with results that resemble something between a farce and a tragedy.

In 1984 the Mexico City conference gave anti-abortion U.S. President Reagan and his allies the chance to force the nations of the world to make a pariah of abortion. Since the election of President Reagan in 1980 the United States had dramatically turned its back on its former Malthusian rhetoric about the evils of population growth, and now held that "population is neutral" and not a factor affecting economic growth. The U.S. delegation, led by New Right celebrity James Buckley, denounced abortion, saying it was "not an acceptable element of family planning programs." Buckley also made the most of the abuses and coercion in China's efforts to limit population growth (Finkle and Crane 1985). The final conference document spurned abortion. Only Sweden was willing to defend women's right to safe, legal abortion.

Back home in the United States in 1981, right-wing anti-abortion lobbyists had already succeeded in getting USAID, the U.S. overseas aid agency, to suspend all funding for research touching on abortion. Now they wanted to force other countries to adopt the narrow anti-abortion agenda that they were working to impose at home.

At the end of the Mexico conference, Buckley announced that the United States would no longer give any money from its aid budget to any abortion-related activities (M. Green 1993). The eventual ban—which became known as the "Mexico City policy"—covered international bodies such as the United Nations Fund for Population Activities (UNFPA) and U.S. nongovernmental organizations. One of the biggest international family planning agencies, International Planned Parenthood Federation (IPPF), decided to forgo millions of dollars from USAID, when the full implications of compliance became apparent. It would for example have meant buying no more books about abortion for IPPF's library. It would also have made IPPF a tool of U.S. policy, compelling it to impose similar anti-abortion restrictions on its member family planning associations throughout the world.

In many countries, however, such associations are the only providers and promoters of birth control. To receive IPPF money, indirectly from USAID, there would have to be no more advice and information about abortion services here to get one, when it might be an option—and certainly no more lobbying to preserve or expand access to legal abortion, *however legitimate that might be under the laws of the respective countries.* Already the screws had tightened, prompting funding organizations such as the Pathfinder Fund to withdraw in 1983 from its training program in Bangladesh, where it was paying for hundreds of doctors and paramedics to learn how to perform "menstrual regulation" abortions (see Chapter 7). USAID provided almost all of Pathfinder's money.

Scarcely anyone dared mention the A-word, let alone ask for money to research into the need for it. Self-censorship and fear of inadvertent violations reinforced the stranglehold of USAID censorship. For fear of losing international funding, a clinic in Pakistan decided not to buy equipment for treating women who needed abortions on medical grounds, sanctioned even under the stern laws of Pakistan. Elsewhere a publisher of thousands of recently out-of-print medical textbooks, worth US$75 a piece, offered them to an agency receiving aid from USAID. But the books mentioned termination of pregnancy, so they were refused and consigned to be destroyed. In country after country services were forced literally to disintegrate. Abortion was frozen out.

In fact the "Mexico City policy" was so legalistic that hardly anyone could interpret it. But it was a huge burden for agencies tracking each and every USAID dollar they received and making sure that none was used to "promote" abortion. The policy was a tremendous boost to the increasingly internationalized anti-abortion movement, helping it to step up its "monitoring," that is, harassment, of family planning organizations in developing countries. They were able to raise the level of political tension under which many local family planing agencies operated. The number of anti-abortion organizations in Latin America and the Caribbean, for instance, has mushroomed since 1984: the U.S. policy underwrote them and colleagues in the United States sent financial help.

Some of the population agencies and family planning organizations hoped that segregating abortion from contraceptive services would appease their attackers and reduce the vulnerability of family planning provision. But the 1984 success only whetted the appetite of U.S. anti-abortion militants and their New Right allies for abolishing U.S. overseas funding of contraceptive provision as well.

The run-up to the Cairo population conference in 1994 was different. With President Bill Clinton now in the White House, the Vatican had lost its mightiest ally. United States policy returned to the view that population growth is a fundamental cause of environmental degradation and a brake on economic growth and that was the conference's consensus. Also, one of Clinton's first actions on arriving at the White House in 1993 had been to cancel the so-called "Mexico City policy." Unfazed, the emissaries of the Holy See busied themselves with plans to derail the entire meeting, on the issue of abortion.

It is easy to be cynical about the linguistic shadow-boxing of international conferences and their densely printed policy documents. But set alongside the outcome of the Mexico City meeting, the final 1994 document represents a significant change and something substantially new for women. It was, for example, the first time that women's health and rights advocates had had any part in shaping the conference agenda (Richter and Keysers 1994). In 1974 and 1984 the terms had been set mainly by the United States, the Vatican and the lobby for Third World countries. As for abortion, which had taken such a hammering in 1984, the draft declaration for Cairo stressed the need to provide not just contraceptives, but a full range of "reproductive health services." "Full range" means including abortion, which turned out to be the sticking point of the entire ten-day meeting.

The Cairo conference was pure political theater: it could have been billed, "the Cairo Capers." The show got on the road in June 1994, in Rome, with an extraordinary *rapprochement* between representatives of the Holy See and some Islamist leaders. They resolved to convey to the faithful the essential ungodliness of the UN document and to blast it out of the water. The pope hoped that his new Islamist allies would back him not only in opposing abortion, but also in his crusade against artificial contraception. In this he was mistaken. The Islamic fundamentalists reserved their big guns for the parts of the document relating to adolescents: they were concerned about promiscuity and the spread of western immorality, but did not attack fertility control itself in the way that the Vatican would have liked.

Nevertheless the campaign grew increasingly apocalyptic as September approached. The Iranian prime minister described the Cairo arena as part of a "future war between the religious and the materialists." A chorus of Islamist voices protested that the UN was becoming the vehicle of an "American and Israeli attempt to dominate the Islamist world by the spreading of immorality." Four Arab countries, Saudi Arabia, Sudan, Lebanon and Iraq, announced that they would boycott the proceedings altogether.

Much of the lofty language of a summit document is agreed between government representatives months beforehand. What cannot be agreed appears in the final draft document with square brackets around it. The anti-abortion lobby had fought fiercely throughout the three-year run-up of pre-Cairo meetings, pouncing on every word or phrase which might imply endorsement of abortion. They contested "reproductive health," defined as women's right to "safe, effective, affordable and acceptable methods of fertility regulation of their choice." The Vatican said talk of "fertility regulation of their choice" amounted to the establishment of an international right to abortion. The Holy See's obstructiveness ensured that phrases such as "family planning," "safe motherhood" and "reproductive rights" all had the infamous brackets around them as the curtain rose for the Cairo showdown itself.

For four days in Cairo, the fundamentalist bloc stonewalled on abortion. The phrase "legal abortion" gave rise to especially heated exchanges—abortion could no more be legal than could robbery or rape, said the protesting Guatemala delegation. How could you talk about safe or unsafe abortion, argued the Holy See, when one person always died? The negotiators ducked and weaved to redraft the contentious paragraphs. The outcome of the conference hung in the balance.

Eventually the Vatican allowed the conference to proceed, saying it had succeeded in outlawing abortion as a form of family planning and in denying any suggestion that it should ever be legal. But whereas before the meeting the pope had the support of thirty or forty delegations, by the end, this had become a rump of no more than a handful of servile Catholic governments, such as Malta, Guatemala and Honduras. Even John Paul II's own nation, Poland, deserted his cause.

Finally the compromising and euphemistic finessing enabled everyone to claim the conference a triumph for their faction. "Safe motherhood" emerged from its brackets and survived, as did "family planning." In paragraph 8.25

INTERNATIONAL CONFERENCE ON POPULATION
AND DEVELOPMENT, CAIRO, 1994

Revised Text of Paragraph 8.25

In no case should abortion be promoted as a method of family planning. All governments and relevant intergovernmental and non-governmental organizations are urged to strengthen their commitment to women's health, to deal with the health impact of unsafe abortion* as a major public health concern and to reduce the recourse to abortion through expanded and improved family planning services. Prevention of unwanted pregnancies must always be given the highest priority and all attempts should be made to limit the need for abortion. Women who have unwanted pregnancies should have ready access to reliable information and compassionate counseling. Any measures or changes related to abortion within the health system can only be determined at the national or local level according to the national legislative process. In circumstances in which abortion is not against the law, such abortion should be safe. In all cases women should have access to quality services for the management of complications arising from abortion. Post-abortion counselling, education and family planning services should be offered promptly which will also help to avoid repeat abortions.

Source: Women's Health Journal (1994) 4/94, p. 41

* Unsafe abortion is defined as a procedure for terminating an unwanted pregnancy either by persons lacking the necessary skills or in an environment lacking the minimal medical standards or both (WHO).

---

of its final document, the conference recognized unsafe abortion as a preventable health problem.

The conference agreed on four main goals: reducing maternal, infant and child mortality; better education, especially for girls; universal access to reproductive health services, including family planning; and gender equality—with much stress on "empowerment" of women. There is no space here to assess the wider political significance beneath the well-intentioned froth. Is women's empowerment anything more than the flavor of the month with the population agencies? What does talk of women's reproductive choices mean, when in many cultures women's sexuality is so strictly controlled?[11]

The intransigent alliance of the Vatican and its Islamist allies provoked the creation of another alliance—that between the population agencies and women's health and rights organizations. It is not an easy alliance and there are plenty of voices warning against the risks of the feminist lobby being co-opted by the international family planning establishment.[12]

In her closing speech to delegates, Nafis Sadik, chief of the UNFPA, concluded that the declaration "fulfills the original intention of concentrating on unsafe abortion as a serious and preventable health problem. Abortion is not a means of family planning. There will be less abortions in future because there will be less need for abortion." She also underlined the fact that "nothing . . . limits the freedom of nations to act individually within the bounds of their own laws and cultures."[13] As if anyone needed reminding that none of what they had struggled for was binding in any way.

The jury is out on whether the textual wrangling at Cairo has led to progress on abortion. The assertion that "in no case" should it be promoted as "a method of family planning" is, to the untrained eye, little more than what was said ten years before in Mexico City. "The population lobby caved in to pressure . . . by conceding that abortion is not a family planning method," say feminist critics (Hartmann 1995). But emphasizing the important health aspect of unsafe/illegal abortion—treating the health impact of unsafe abortion as a preventable "disease" of epidemic proportions—may make it possible for women's health advocates in a great many countries to begin to debate the issue in public. The health perspective is seen by many as a more promising channel for calling for legal abortion than the argument based on human rights (Correa 1994). Politically, building alliances around "safe motherhood" looks more promising when the climate surrounding women's rights is frosty. (And so the pope is right to suspect what might go on under the cloak of "safe motherhood"!)

And the problem with fundamental rights for women is not only that they are individualized, but that talk of rights also immediately raises the hackles of the anti-abortion movement, which retaliates with fundamental rights for the fetus. But that may not be the only reason why the population lobby and the family planning organizations have taken refuge in the health perspective on abortion.

Would the declaration have been bolder, from women's point of view, if the Vatican and its allies had not been there to chase out any mention of legalizing abortion as an inextricable element in women's basic reproductive rights (Boschmann 1994)? I suspect not, because defining abortion as a health issue keeps the abortion decision firmly in the hands of doctors and evades the whole question of whether women should be entitled to decide for themselves.

At the mention of abortion, government delegates at international conferences tend to become extremely defensive and conservative, muttering about respect for national sovereignty. Among the government delegations in Cairo, Norway's prime minister, Gro Harlem Brundtland, was almost a lone voice in insisting that "decriminalizing abortion is a necessary means of protecting the life and health of women."

Perhaps it is unrealistic to ask for more in these ponderous international arenas. Even the Cairo acknowledgement that abortion is a crucial issue for women's health represents a defeat for anti-abortion campaigners. Nevertheless the context of the discussion does not seem to have moved forward very much in ten years. The Cairo paragraph on abortion (see sidebar) stresses that "Any measures or changes related to abortion within the health system can only be determined at the national or local level according to the national legislative process"—a more hands-off attitude to "women's empowerment" could hardly be imagined.

But if, as the United Nations now sees it, abortion is not a method of family planning, what is it? It is treated as little more than a malevolent and unfortunate mischief-maker which has to be tolerated by the family planning world, but which must always be stigmatized in order to appease the enemy at the gates.

Defending Abortion in a Culture of Shame

The family planning world's idea of defending abortion is to apologize for it. There is a culture of shame surrounding abortion, which is quite different from the way in which contraception is presented. Abortion is the oldest and most widely practiced of all forms of birth control and it is still widely used in that way today, beyond the reaches of medical orthodoxy. But the modern phenomenon of abortion is that it is something quite distinct from birth control. The early birth control pioneers took great pains to distance birth control from abortion, especially when their activities were conflated by their critics with those of abortionists.[14]

The terms they used for birth control, such as "sexual hygiene," were designed to distinguish them from the squalid, sinister world of the backstreet abortion. It worked well: birth control today equates with responsibility, family planning, even family values. Where does that leave abortion? When Nafis Sadik told the Cairo conference that in future there would be less need for abortion, she was feeding them the second fantasy promoted by the family planning establishment in its attempt to propitiate public opinion: more contraception—less abortion. Of course—think only of Russia where women have as many as five abortions because they have no other options. But the line is misleading—it implies not only that contraception is always preferable to abortion, but also that the development of a foolproof contraceptive is desirable, in order to hasten the day when abortion might be obsolete.

There is no such thing as a perfectly reliable contraceptive. Even if women all used the most "reliable" methods (regardless of whether these were suitable for their health), a third of abortions would probably still be necessary (Westoff 1981). A recent study of women requesting abortion in Britain found that seven out of ten had used contraception but it had not worked (Bromham 1993a). People who have chosen a reliable method, and are unluckily let down by it, are more likely to seek abortion, because unplanned pregnancy is so unacceptable to them and they believe it is their right to control their fertility. And a stress on the importance of preventing unplanned pregnancy, far from obviating the need for abortion, can actually increase the demand for it, especially if contraceptive hardware is difficult to obtain.[15]

The overwhelmingly defensive stance on abortion beams out the message that family planning is always preferable to abortion. In the new morality of contraception, abortion's connotations are of deviance, failure and irresponsibility. When their voices are heard, many women describe the way health professionals seize on the occasion of unplanned pregnancy as an opportunity for education as an unwanted, moralistic paternalism. They feel as if, as a condition of getting an abortion, they must "atone" in some way for their failure to contracept effectively and that they are being blamed and made to feel stupid. Unless they show remorse and promise greater care in the future they will not *deserve* the abortion. The deep-seated belief on the part of the medical authorities is that fertility is controllable by appropriate and conscientious methods. That is why women seeking repeat abortion are under such a cloud (Ryan, Ripper and Buttfield 1994).

But if failure and irresponsibility are to be avoided at all costs, women have to be persuaded to use a contraceptive which is, above all, reliable. Other possible criteria for choosing it, such as safety, acceptability to both partners and so on, must take second place. In Holland, which has been dubbed the "perfect contraceptive population," the low abortion rate is attributed to women's consistent use of the Pill and the IUD and the prevalence of male sterilization. Is this the only model to be emulated, or are there alternatives?

If, for instance, abortion is legal and can be performed early, a woman's health may be best served by using a simple barrier method of contraception, with abortion as a back-up for occasional failures. Comparisons of the safety of various methods show that this combination carries the lowest health risk for women.[16] At present, hormonal contraception is billed by the medical profession and the family planning establishment as effective, modern contraception, and many women use it, but with vague unease about risks to their health (Doyal 1995). Just how shaky women's confidence in the safety of the Pill can be, was dramatically shown in Britain in October 1995, when the government issued a warning that 1.5 million women taking a range of oral contraceptives were risking an increased possibility of deep vein thrombosis. Despite advice to continue their current course of tablets, many women stopped immediately and many became pregnant in the weeks that followed. Nearly five months after the announcement, 60 per cent of the women said they were anxious about the safety of the Pill.[17] Research is already going on into contraceptive vaccine and other reliable, long-term methods, easy to administer on a large scale. It is provoking bitter criticism from some feminist health advocates. For, as Betsy Hartmann points out, "If all women were guaranteed access to safe, cheap legal abortion, the profile of contraceptive use might well shift from riskier but more effective varieties" (Hartmann 1987, p. 242). Hartmann is thinking of the long-term dangers associated with use of the Pill and the IUD; risky, in family planning terms, exclusively means the risk of an unplanned pregnancy (Mintzes 1992).

Secondly, there may be times or circumstances in which women consider abortion a better option than contraception. Women can be afraid to use contraception in relationships where men have prohibited it and threatened violence. An abortion can sometimes be arranged without the sexual part-ner's knowledge. What is more, to some women "inducing a miscarriage" can seem more natural than taking a pill or having bits of metal inserted in the womb (Dixon-Mueller 1993). If a woman is uncertain about her part-ner's commitment to their relationship, she may use a pregnancy to test the solidity of their bond: the pregnancy may not be unwanted, unless he rejects it too (Browner 1979).

Why must so many defenders of abortion always present it in negative terms and never talk about how, for some women, the decision to have an abortion is a tremendously positive experience, even if an unplanned preg-nancy is not a prospect to be welcomed in itself? An unplanned pregnancy confronts a woman with a decision between alternative futures and for some women their crisis is the first time in their lives that they have weighed up their lives and their priorities. Supportive counselling offers a great deal in helping women clarify conflicting relationships and responsibilities, and the opportunity to reassess what really counts can be energizing and empower-ing (Lunneborg 1992, ch. 5). No one is saying, "Go and have an abortion because it is a great experience or opportunity," simply that the crisis can be put to good ends and is not invariably a tragedy.

The "pro-choice" organizations nonetheless obdurately maintain that abortion is an unfortunate fact of life and should never be a method of family planning. In the United States, where activists defending abortion have to use every means at their disposal to win the allegiance of the seemingly muddled, ambivalent and hugely ignorant public (or so the opinion polls represent them), they have chosen to embrace women's choice as a key plank in their appeal. The powerful cultural aura surrounding choice—whose antithesis is surely slavery—is a heavy counterweight to the pro-life lobby's own rhetorical champion, the sanctity of life. But "to be pro-choice is not to be pro-abortion," says their literature, primly rejecting any "zealous advocacy of abortion" and merely urging that people should be free to choose for themselves (National Abortion Rights Action League 1992). Women seeking abortions are depicted as unfortunates whose circumstances are so far from the ideals of motherhood that abortion must be their tragic option.

Most women, given the choice in theory, would prefer a contraceptive that worked *and* did not entail a risk of damage to their health, rather than face the prospect of an unplanned pregnancy and the stigma of abortion. Many settle for far less than that and take daily risks with their health, carrying IUDs or taking the Pill, or using long-term hormonal contraception, such as injectables or implants. Although abortion is under siege from a constituency claiming a monopoly on morality—defenders of the fetus, family values, and so on—it does not serve women well to defend abortion by excoriating it as "a necessary evil," the resort of the desperate, the unlucky and the merely "foolish" and never as a legitimate method of birth control.

The new puritans of the family planning establishment have made a modern sin out of unplanned pregnancy. By relegating abortion to the sidelines, they hope to safeguard family planning's hard-won respectability in the corridors of power and propitiate public hostility to abortion on demand. In their quest to satisfy the unmet need for contraception, they cite abortion, legal or illegal, as nothing more than tragic testimony to the need for effective family planning methods.[18] Family planning not only pre-empts the need for abortion, we are told, but costs the health budget far less.

But women seeking what are meant to be safe, legal abortions are having a hard enough time, passing through picket lines drenched in spit, or justifying their case to doctors who decide what they deserve. Must they feel guilty failures into the bargain? Perpetuating the culture of shame, by expediently isolating abortion from its historic context of women's traditional birth control, perpetuates the hangover from the days when abortion was criminal and only "bad" women had abortions.

10

The Pitfalls of the Law

IN BRITAIN ALL ABORTIONS ARE ILLEGAL, unless they are covered by the exceptions set out in the 1967 Abortion Act. Failing to observe the terms of the Act renders the abortion illegal and is a crime. The state does not lay down precise circumstances defining when other kinds of health care procedures can be offered—when, for instance, an organ transplant may be performed or how to treat someone with depression. But if a woman requests an abortion it is the doctor's duty to assess what can best be done for the patient within the terms laid down by the Abortion Act. Until 1990, when the Human Embryology and Fertilisation Act was passed, no other area of medical care was covered by law in such a manner.

If there must be a law governing abortion—and that is a question worth exploring because some countries do not regulate abortion in this way—is there a watertight and flexible framework? Are there some legal approaches which look plausible but have hidden pitfalls? What is a good law on abortion?

Laws may work in ways which cannot be predicted by those who first proposed them (Fox and Murphy 1992). In 1973, the historic ruling on *Roe v. Wade* swept away virtually all legal barriers in the United States to abortion in the first twelve weeks of pregnancy. But the judges of the Supreme Court did not envisage how the forces of conservatism would make a mockery of the "right to choose" in the years to come by exploiting the vagaries of their definitions.

Constitutional Quicksands

Part of the problem for the United States is that abortion is a *constitutional* issue rather than a simple health care requirement. For the court had defined abortion as an element of women's right to privacy, which it said was protected by the constitution. This sounds rock-solid, but has proved an extremely vulnerable perspective. A country's constitution is loaded with national emotion and placing a woman's right to an abortion in such elevated company as the right to free speech, and so on, presented the opposition with an irresistible challenge to get it thrown out. After one such constitutional testing, the ruling on *Casey* (see Chapter 1), almost twenty years after *Roe,* the main principle of the battered *Roe* judgment was confirmed, but as the Supreme Court's Chief Justice Rehnquist observed, "*Roe* continues to exist, but only in a way a storefront on a western movie set exists: a mere facade to give the illusion of reality" (Benshoof 1993, p. 168).

For more than twenty years, the court has umpired abortion battles and, whenever a judge retired, both sides in the feud have held their breath to see whether the successor chosen by the president will be for or against abortion. Republican presidents—Reagan and Bush—consistently appointed judges who were against abortion, not just in the Supreme Court, but throughout the court system. Judge Blackmun, who shared in making the original *Roe* decision, and who was an outspoken liberal on abortion, clung to Supreme Court office until he was 85 and the election of President Clinton had ensured that his replacement would not contribute to the demise of *Roe.* Blackmun knew, as did anyone who could count up to nine, that a woman's right to choose in the United States was up for grabs.

Ireland also discovered the bitterness of mixing the abortion controversy with constitutional politics and leaving judges to sort out the muddle which ensues. The 1980s witnessed a series of courtroom wrangles, with legal experts expensively attempting to pin down the meaning of the bitterly fought 1983 Pro-life Amendment, which with its "flabby, imprecise and dangerous wording" had guaranteed the fetus rights under the constitution (Solomons 1992). Even after the traumatic "X" case in 1992, Irish politicians are still loath to grasp the nettle and legislate for a rational abortion policy.

Both the United States' and Ireland's constitutional approaches to abortion vested the pregnant woman and the fetus with "rights." Predictably, the claim for rights sparks rival claims, and both countries have witnessed bitter legal and political disputes pitting the pregnant woman against the fetus.

Doctor Knows Best: A Tactic of Expedience?

In most of Europe, the framework of abortion law has conceded little to the notion of rights. It has framed abortion as a public health issue, leaving it to doctors to be the arbiters of necessity. The 1967 Abortion Act in Britain, for example, stands forever in the shadow of the 1938 trial of Dr. Aleck Bourne, which established that the opinion of a doctor, given in "good faith," is a legitimate defense against the charge of illegal abortion (see Chapter 3). The 1967 Act says that *two* doctors must "in good faith" believe that a woman's case fits within the prescribed categories of legal abortion. Unless the procedure is authorized in this manner, it remains illegal. At the time the law was being debated, reformers were adamant that it was essen-

---

MAKING A CASE THAT FITS THE LAW

"It must be the law in South Australia that you have to be deemed to be, I'm not sure what the term is now, but as though I wasn't mentally stable enough to have the child. And I was saying, 'But that's not the point at all!' and she (the counselor) said 'Look, we have to write that'. I felt like that shouldn't be down on my health records that I am not mentally fit. Because I am mentally fit, I am mentally fit to decide, to make an intelligent decision, and they are trying to tell me that I am a bit loopy! Yes, so that really quite upset me a lot. But it was a non-negotiable point on behalf of the doctor and I guess she does that all the time and couldn't really see why I was getting so upset . . . But when you see that written on your form I think it is a bit distressing really. Especially if you feel that you have made a really hard decision. You have been sensible about it, not negligent or something like that.

"Also the long-term consequences of it really upset me. Well, just stressed me out more than anything. Becuase I thought, like I don't know how long your medical records last. But if something happened to me and they went back into my records and they said, 'well she has had a bout of mental instability . . .' I mean, maybe that is being a bit paranoid, but it is still just a thing that is inaccurate, an inaccurate record about yourself."

Gabriella Cartez, aged eighteen, no children

Source: quoted from Ryan, Ripper and Buttfield 1994, p. 113

---

tial to avoid a law which would permit "abortion on demand," by having doctors as the keepers of the gate.

Other European countries and many of their former colonies have similar laws, which state that an abortion is illegal *unless* . . . The indications for legal abortion vary, and women twist or stretch the truth, or even lie, in order to overcome the hurdles to their abortions. A study of European abortion policies in the mid-1980s, for instance, found that the stated reasons for most abortions in Britain are medical, in Switzerland they are psychiatric, and in the then West Germany most were on social grounds. In the three countries abortion rates were similar; women's lives are not starkly different. The explanation is simply that women and their doctors are saying what the law requires them to say (Ketting and Praag 1986). "Seemingly transparent hypocrisy can be enshrined in law and practised daily with a straight face," says Marge Berer, reproductive rights activist and editor of *Reproductive Health Matters,* asking why a woman cannot be allowed to say with simple honesty, "I just don't want this baby at this time." Berer points out that it is only the youngest and the most vulnerable who don't know how to twist the truth and frame their needs to fit their country's law (Berer 1993a, p. 35).

Pleading a case can be humiliating, especially when the requirement for a legal abortion is a diagnosis of mental instability or incompetence. (See sidebar on making a case that fits the law.) To many women it feels as if the price they have to pay for an abortion is to persuade a medical expert that they are in some way unfortunate, inadequate, unlucky or generally "deserving," and above all that they "won't do it again" (Ryan, Ripper and Buttfield 1994).

Women's access to an abortion can seem like a lottery of inequality, depending on the sympathy of the individual doctor. What is more, the scope of the so-called "social" indications is a constant source of political trouble, with anti-abortion pressure groups complaining that it permits women to have abortions for "convenience." In deeply Catholic anti-abortion Bavaria, in southern Germany, in 1989, a doctor in Memmingen who had performed abortions for low-income women under West Germany's "social hardship" indication was convicted of carrying out illegal abortions. The police commandeered his medical records, which went back twenty years and contained the names of 500 former patients. Many women were ordered to testify in court against the doctor. Not only were their names published—many were practicing Catholics—but 200 of them were convicted of having illegal abortions and fined or sent to prison for one month. The judge found that they had no real grounds for claiming social hardship (Clements 1994). In

Spain and in other European countries similar trials and threats of action have been instigated to intimidate sympathetic doctors, and women who might need abortions. In Belgium, however, where abortion was strictly illegal until 1990, but where for at least fifteen years some doctors had risked the law and had been performing abortions, "show trials" helped to fuel the campaign to bring the law into line with practice.[1]

Many liberal doctors are ill at ease with their role as moral entrepreneurs, though few are so candid as this Scottish gynecologist about the capriciousness of the process:

> I've found it so difficult in discussing the problem with the individual patient to come to a decision, and I realise only too well that one's opinion might be influenced by your mood that day, perhaps even affected by the weather, perhaps by the number of people you have seen that day. And I also realise that patients—some patients—are good at putting their case, some shed tears more readily and yet may not feel the problem any more than somebody who seems more stoical. And I have known suicides occur in patients that I really had not suspected felt it so badly.
>
> (AITKEN-SWAN 1977, p. 133)

There are doctors who believe that a request for an abortion puts the traditional doctor-patient relationship into a unique category, because the patient can make her own diagnosis that she is pregnant and can assess her personal situation. Others believe with equal conviction that if a doctor is to be asked to perform an abortion, then he or she must be allowed to exercise the clinical judgment of a professional as to whether such a procedure is warranted, medically, ethically and legally, and is "in the patient's best interest." In 1990, three eminent British doctors, sensitive to the need for abortion and well-known for allying themselves publicly with its defense, resigned from the Pro-Choice Alliance on precisely this issue. The Alliance proposed a letter to the press, urging new abortion legislation, which would "take the decision out of the hands of doctors and put it into the hands of women." Even the Dutch doctors who pioneered Holland's abortion clinics were adamant that, if they were to perform abortions, they had to be allowed to form their own judgments. "We are not plumbers," they said.[2] According to one liberal, Dr. Warren Hern, the context of abortion practice "is medical because women can die from pregnancy and it is medical because they can die from abortion."[3]

But vesting in doctors the power to determine "medical necessity," however creatively that is interpreted, is undoubtedly an expedient political defense. In Britain it has proved extremely hard for anti-abortion groups to attack the legislation in any substantial way. To do so first requires the creation of a mythology of "abortion on demand," with its connotations of trivial, selfish women, whimsically ordering up abortions in the same spirit as they would seek a face-lift. Whenever this accusation raises its head, defenders of abortion point instantly to the fact that the abortion decision must be made by two medical professionals, and women are not in a position to demand anything: the ruse falls flat. To be fair both sides are dissimulating—the law is flexibly framed, and for the well-off and articulate getting an abortion in Britain does not pose any real problems.

Of course, the concept of "medical necessity," and doctors' control is deeply flawed: it is objectionable from the point of view of women's autonomy to force them to make out a case which "fits the slot" and impugns women's capacity to decide an issue which is of central importance to their lives. It also creates a spurious distinction between abortions deemed medically necessary and those authorized on "social grounds." Many doctors (usually those hostile to women's reproductive rights) feel it is repugnant that there are "social grounds" for abortion, that is, reasons which fall outside a narrow definition of curative medicine. They keenly resent the way in which their professional status and reputation are being used by politicians to pass the buck on a controversial policy.

Legal Confusion, Unequal Access

At least in the smaller European countries with liberal laws, public health care funding and a population which is generally tolerant towards abortion, women who are unwillingly pregnant can be sure of getting a safe, early abortion. In Sweden and Denmark women can simply ask for an abortion in the first twelve weeks of pregnancy, without saying "I need to have my head examined" or having to explain their reasons to a doctor who is supposed to question them closely to determine if the reason is good enough. The United States, of course, concedes such a "right," but in name only, whereas the Swedish and Danish governments fund abortion services in public hospitals (Rolston and Eggert 1994). In other liberal countries, such as Holland, the law is disingenuously scant, but still nominally under medical control.

What speaks louder than the framework of the laws themselves is the readiness of such governments to commit public money to abortion services as a necessary part of a public health service.[4]

Elsewhere, bureaucratic hurdles can make a nonsense of legal abortion, putting it out of women's reach. In Zambia, for example, an abortion is only deemed legal if it has been authorized by three doctors, one of whom must be a specialist, *and* it must be performed in a hospital *and* the doctors must agree that the requisite medical indications are present. There is an acute shortage of doctors, many requests for abortion are refused, and illegal abortion continues to flourish (Liskin 1980).

Often, within one country, the laws are chaotically varied, as they are in Germany, the United States and Australia. From one province or state to another, abortion can be variously on request, highly restricted, free, expensive, available in specialist clinics, or only in state hospitals. Australia has it all. Whilst women's perception in many Australian states is that abortions are legal, routine procedures, Australian abortion law is still dominated by England's nineteenth-century statutes. Within the Australian federal gov-

---

LEGAL CONFUSION AND UNEQUAL ACCESS

In Tasmania, thanks to a feminist clinic which flies in a doctor from the mainland once a week, abortion is now available. But the circumstances in which abortion can be legally performed have never been tested in the courts. Most lawyers in the state think that protecting a woman's mental health would probably be legal, and most sympathetic doctors in Tasmania pursue this avenue, if they are prepared to consider abortion at all.

"Having asked the gynecologist . . . about getting an abortion, he replied 'It is against the law to do it'. Unless we could convince him there was a physical reason, or if I was able to convince a psychiatrist that I was unable, psychiatrically to survive a pregnancy, then he said there was no way under law that an abortion could be done. Not only wouldn't he do it, but he couldn't envisage anyone in Tasmania would—because, he said, no 'right thinking' gynecologist will break the law. I wasn't willing to go to a psychiatrist, that was simply ludicrous. I am as sane as anyone and I wasn't going to be labelled as a 'nut' even if it meant getting what I wanted. It just isn't right and I said so much. So Leon [husband] asked, 'What else can we do. Is there any other possibility?'

'Well yes,' said the gynecologist, 'you can go to Melbourne. That's the place to go. That's where everybody goes'."

Wendy Phillips, a thirty-year-old, married professional woman, living in Tasmania
Source: quoted from Ryan, Ripper and Buttfield 1994, p. 25

ernment system the states have their own, relatively independent criminal codes and make their own abortion laws.

In three states, populous New South Wales, Victoria and the sparsely populated, conservative state of Queensland, abortions are only legal by virtue of individual Bourne-type court decisions, given in cases involving criminal charges against doctors. It's different again in the state of South Australia, which passed abortion legislation in 1970, giving women more secure, but in reality quite limited, access to abortion. Elsewhere, such as in the island state of Tasmania, the old law has never been amended or tested, and the legalities are shrouded in doubt (Coleman 1988).

Australia has never had a *Roe v. Wade* case decided at a national level. Also, since 1974, most abortions have been paid for out of federal health funds, even when provided in private and non-profit clinics and hospitals. This funding has been continually challenged by anti-abortion forces, but the policy remains.

Frail and Tangled Web

For anyone contemplating a strategy of liberalization in abortion law the Australian scene is salutary and full of paradoxes. Throughout the 1970s and early 1980s most Australian politicians avoided the abortion issue by keeping their heads in the sand. The cross-currents of party politics had given the Catholic Church disproportionate power to block abortion reform. After court judgments in Victoria (1969) and New South Wales (1971) defined abortion as legal in certain conditions, the way was open for independent clinics to provide abortions on broadly interpreted health and social grounds. "Ironically, by preventing reform legislation in NSW [New South Wales] and Victoria, and thereby causing the matter to be resolved by the courts, the Catholic Church unwittingly opened up the possibility of abortion on demand" (Coleman 1988, p. 86).

In South Australia, however, in 1970 the state government passed its own, limited abortion legalization—strict time limits, available only to women with two months' residency in the state; two doctors must agree to indications similar to the British 1967 Act (Rathus 1994). The reform took the heat out of the simmering political conflict but public hospital facilities are limited and women have to wait, sometimes for weeks, sometimes until they are more than twelve weeks pregnant, by which time they are no longer entitled to help in South Australia and have to make the long journey to

Melbourne or Sydney (Ryan, Ripper and Buttfield 1994). Defenders of the state's laws have had to ward off parliamentary attacks, and defend the status quo with all its obvious imperfections. In political terms, however, what is most positive is the fact that the South Australian public sees abortion as a normal, legal part of public health provision—no longer anything to do with the criminal world.

By contrast, in New South Wales and Victoria, after the acquittals of doctors tried for performing illegal abortions more than twenty years earlier, specialist clinics were established, where women can get speedy, local-anesthetic abortions, more or less on a "neccessity" basis. Clinics also perform abortions after twelve weeks, often for women who have travelled half-way across the country because they cannot get help in their own state.

Queensland also, which has until recent years had a harsh anti-abortion government, now has independent clinics, following a Bourne-type acquittal in 1985 (Coleman 1988). In 1980, the puritanical right-wing Queensland government had drafted a Draconian bill not only outlawing almost all abortion, but even making it illegal to leave the state for an abortion. Although the bill was routed, the Queensland government did not give up. Five years later, two Queensland clinics, which had been set up in the wake of the legislative *débâcle,* were raided by police and patient files were seized. When the police announced that fourteen files had been selected for use in court, there was a national outcry, the state's Supreme Court eventually declared the police search warrants invalid and the files were returned. But although Queensland women have to pay for their abortions, as in the other two states where abortion depends on the precedent of a court case, the clinics are more or less self-regulated. What is different in Queensland is that the state's history of moral absolutism and animosity towards abortion (and other "progressive" social and sexual issues) means that many Queensland women *think* that they are breaking the law when they go into abortion clinics, even fearing that raids will happen again, despite a more liberal government now.

The frailty of the web which sustains legal abortion in Victoria, New South Wales and Queensland was exposed in 1994, when a New South Wales Supreme Court judge threw out a young woman's claim for damages against abortion-clinic doctors who failed to diagnose her pregnancy early enough for her to have an abortion. The judge said that her abortion would in any case have been illegal under the terms defined when a New South Wales doctor was acquitted of criminal abortion in 1972 (Neill 1994). (To add insult to the claimant's injury, the judge compared her to a bank robber trying to sue someone who had stopped him from robbing a bank.) It was a sharp reminder that access to abortion could be overturned by a judge's fresh interpretation and that, according to the letter of the law, abortion is still a crime. For weeks after the court case, pregnant women were ringing abortion clinics asking whether they could still legally get an abortion. The appeals and counter-appeals in this case, *CES vs. Superclinics NSW,* have now reached the ultimate court of appeal, the Australian High Court. Observers expect the judgment to have important implications not just for abortion law in the state of New Soth Wales, but possibly for other states as well.

Although Australia's vocal anti-abortion lobby has kept the brake on abortion law reform, the more extreme tactics of their U.S. counterparts have never gained a foothold. Australia is a highly irreligious society and there is consistent public support for liberal access to abortion. What is difficult for feminist campaigners is that there is a general complacency that access to abortion is never going to be a problem again for women in Australia. In reality, women crisscross the country in search of abortion, and many say that the worst aspect of getting an abortion is not the operation itself, but the distress of trying to find information amid secrecy and hostility and travelling to strange towns.

Is Repeal Better Than Reform?

The feminist Abortion Rights Network of Australia is contemplating a strategy which no other national movement has explored to such an extent. With the findings of the study of women's experiences of abortion services in three states, conducted by Lyndall Ryan and her colleagues, to back them up, many feminist Australians are calling for a complete repeal of abortion laws, decriminalizing the procedure and putting it on a par with other health care procedures and services. "There is no need for a law to say 'abortion is legal'," they say. "Women's judgement on this issue can be trusted . . . It should be covered, like all medical procedures, by the standard complaints mechanism for health care consumers, but it should not be singled out in any way."[5] The Ryan study itself recommends decriminalization of abortion, condemning the current regulation of abortion, within both the criminal code and the laws governing health services, as confusing and discriminatory.

Having laws which say that "abortion is illegal, unless . . ." giving women what sociologist Evert Ketting called an "immoral right" to abortion, stigmatizes the whole procedure and keeps it isolated from other reproductive health care services.[6] The Australian feminists believe that breaking the chains which link abortion, by law and in public perception, with criminality and "morals" would stimulate the provision of more equitable, sympathetic services, removing the fear of prosecution which inhibits doctors from providing abortion services (Women's Abortion Action Campaign 1994). Most of all it would signal an end to the state's interference with women's capacity to decide for themselves whether, and when, a pregnancy should be carried to term.

There are countries where abortion has already been taken out of the criminal code, notably China, but also Canada. (In Canada, however, the law is in almost as much chaos as it is in Australia.[7]) Abortion is governed like any other medical procedure—it is unlawful when undertaken by a medically unqualified person, or attempted without the free and informed consent of the woman (Cook 1989a). Some feminists in the United States, impatient with what they see as the mealy mouthed apologizing for abortion by pro-choice groups (as "a necessary evil") have revived the early feminist movement's demand for a complete repeal, rather than reform of the law (Baehr 1990). It is a bit like comparing alcohol and orange juice. Alcohol is regulated by laws concerning not only its production, but who can buy it and where. Orange juice is not regulated, except by public health requirements to check it is safe to drink.

Until the advent of fertility technology, abortion was the only medical procedure subject to criminal regulation. In 1967 with the Abortion Act in Britain, the state began to play a major role in its regulation. Before 1967, when it was broadly illegal, a decision to perform an abortion was simply up to the doctor concerned, provided he or she believed the operation to be medically justified. Many doctors in Britain resented the proposals of the 1967 reforms, precisely because they felt the state's regulations would hamper their clinical freedom. At present the law on abortion in Northern Ireland, where the 1967 Abortion Act does not apply, is in such chaos, so ambiguous, that many doctors are fearful of performing any abortions in case they land up in the criminal court; others are carrying out abortions, despite the legal risks. But for many women in Northern Ireland, the surest way to get an abortion is to cross the sea to England, in the same way that women from the Irish Republic are forced to do (Furedi 1995).

Reformers are divided about what is best for Northern Ireland. Some, such as the U.K.-based Abortion Law Reform Association, believe that women living in Northern Ireland are entitled to have the provisions of the

1967 Act available to them (Abortion Law Reform Association 1995). In some ways this would actually tighten up the law, because, for instance, two doctors would need to authorize the procedure, as the law in the rest of the United Kingdom requires. There is now the vexed question of the "peace process" and the distant possibility of closer ties between Northern Ireland and its southern neighbor, where abortion remains beyond the pale.[8] Some reformers who believe the 1967 Act is now outdated are arguing for Northern Ireland to recast its legislation along entirely different lines, perhaps like the French law. Others see the current law as potentially quite lenient and want the province's doctors to interpret "health" much more courageously and creatively (Furedi 1995).

The Irish Republic also faces the problem of framing a new law, in the wake of the political disaster of the "X" case. Tony O'Brien, now director of the U.K. Family Planning Association, and before that of the Irish Family Planning Association, believes that the simplest solution for Ireland would be to repeal the nineteenth-century (English) legislation and remove abortion from the criminal domain. "But they won't do it: they'll go for elaborate certification, Byzantine regulation of the tiniest details and there will be case after case in the courts" (Tony O'Brien, p.c. 12 June 1995).

Today, when some countries—Britain, for instance—actually have laws on abortion which are fairly liberal in practice, even if they are part of the criminal code, it is harder to see whether decriminalization would improve the reality of access to abortion.[9] It might have symbolic significance, for if there was enough of a public consensus to sustain it, it would send a clear message to women with unwanted pregnancies that their need for abortion was no more than that, and that ritual social shaming was no longer acceptable.

But the issue is a conundrum. It may make abortion both easier and harder to get, depending on the circumstances, as Australia's diverse state policies show only too clearly. Dutch sociologist Evert Ketting also argues that when a woman asks a doctor for an abortion, the parties to the dialogue are unequal, and the law may need to protect the weaker party—the woman—from being exploited, especially where health care is not publicly funded, or she is very young. If there is a law and it states that abortion can be performed on request, up to twelve weeks, then doctors are not able to deny women access to abortions, however vulnerable or inarticulate they may be. The law should be pragmatic and scant, in order to avoid what Ketting calls the "legal gymkhana."[10]

Abortion policies are anathema to politicians. Throughout the world they carefully ignore abortion unless it becomes so disruptive an issue that they have to defuse or contain it, in order to avoid being seen as ineffectual.[11] Today's politicians know that the anti-abortion lobby, whose power is totally disproportionate to their numbers—much like the American lobby for the right to own guns—are not about to soften their righteous rhetoric or steal away to obscurity. Action on abortion is a "no win" issue.

Eastern Europe: The Paradoxes of Transformation

The end of communism in the former Soviet Union and Eastern Europe is an object lesson in the dangers of complacency about legal abortion. With the exceptions of Romania and Albania—where abortion was strictly illegal under the former communist regimes—one country after another has taken steps to curtail women's access to abortion. As Barbara Einhorn, an expert in the problems facing women in Eastern Europe, points out:

> It is striking that abortion laws were one of the first pieces of state socialist legislation to come under attack, after the new democratic parliaments had restored private property rights in their drive to establish "the rule of law." In a context where politicians assert that the dire economic and political problems they face in the transition to democracy and the market make women's rights at best a luxury, at worst a frivolous extra in which they cannot afford to indulge, this attack on reproductive rights must count as one of the paramount paradoxes of the current transformation.
>
> (EINHORN 1994)

Within two years of the destruction of the Berlin Wall, Poland, Slovakia and Hungary had taken steps to clamp down on abortion. (The impact of the new laws in Poland is described in Chapter 3.) In Slovenia, a newly independent part of former Yugoslavia, abortion was the *only contested point* in the forming of the new constitution (Helsinki Citizens' Assembly Women's Commission 1992). The nationalist resurgence has triggered a celebration of the glories of the traditional patriarchal family and women's femininity. All over Eastern Europe, amid concern about falling birth rates, women are being urged to have babies, for the sake of the nation. It all has curious and disturbing echoes of the former Romanian dictator, Nicolae Ceausescu, who declared that giving birth was a woman's patriotic duty and declared the fetus "the socialist property of the nation." Abortion threatens the "biological substance of the nation," said Poland's bishops (Hadley 1994, p. 97). "Abortion Destroys the Nation's Blood," said anti-abortion slogans in Hungary. "Women are being told to bear children or else the Hungarian nation will die out"—but there is an unspoken racist sub-text—"lest the Hungarian nation be overrun with Gypsies." In the ethnic war in the former Yugoslavia, Serbian woman too were asked to produce for the war effort: "For every Serbian soldier fallen in the war . . . Serbian mothers must bear 100 more soldiers" (Einhorn 1994). Anti-abortion groups arrived to "counsel" survivors of the rape camps in the Balkan conflict—recognize your maternal instincts, they told the shattered women (Mertus 1993). In 1996 the Croation parliament passed a plan calling for "demographic renewal of the nation," which includes proposals to repeal the law allowing abortion. Already access to abortion has been severely curbed, not only by increasing the price to the equivalent of a month's salary, but also by some hospitals declaring that they have a "conscientious objection" to terminating pregnancy.[12]

In solidly Catholic Lithuania, a doctor who still provides abortions boasted that he had reduced the abortion rate. But he had not helped anyone with advice about preventing unwanted pregnancies: he had plastered the walls of his clinic with lurid, full color anti-abortion posters, with text in English, obligingly supplied by an American anti-abortion group. Efforts to set up a family planning association have run into trouble, with a concerted dirty tricks campaign by anti-abortion groups. The cost of abortions has risen, as has the cost of contraception. At the same time many women have seen national maternity benefits abolished, baby-food subsidies slashed and day-care facilities closed. The price of freedom and democracy has for many women in Eastern Europe been the loss of their reproductive rights, thanks to the concerted efforts of right-wing nationalists and the Roman Catholic Church (often the same people). The fragility of the laws and the speed with which women's rights have been demolished underline the need for abortion rights advocates everywhere never to be complacent.

Legal, accessible, safe, affordable—those are the barest elements of a policy for safe abortion. But an abortion service could be all those things and still either not accord women the chance to make their own decisions in a way which respects their judgment and integrity, or not offer them compassionate, respectful, high-quality treatment, within their communities. It takes more than a law to achieve that.

11

Reclaiming a Feminist Issue

To SOME PEOPLE, abortion is, above all, a human right (Kennedy 1995). To some it is a matter of the gravest moral significance; to some a preeminently medical matter; to some it is an essential element of women's self-determination and sexual equality. If you begin with the idea that abortion is an inseparable element of sexual politics and a question of liberating female heterosexuality from reproductive slavery, you are hardly likely to run over the same political or moral ground as if you begin by asking whether fetuses have or should have the same moral claims as women (Willis 1990). The perspectives seldom overlap: that's why arguments about abortion so often sound like people shouting at phantoms—there is an absolute abyss of division and almost no perceptible common ground.

For the anti-abortion movement the moral question is paramount, but it is also ready to enter the fray on medicine, science and even feminism. From a perspective underpinned by fetal personhood, ensuing strategies are fairly obvious and internally logical, whatever one might say about their correlation with reality. For those defending existing abortion policies or advocating more access to it, the strategy options are more diverse and complex. There is a price to be paid for investing too heavily or exclusively in the case for women's health or in abortion as a simple matter of individual rights. The values you invest on the starting line determine the way you are going to try to shape the contested territory.

This book has tried to avoid generalizations about "women's experiences" and so I offer no recommendation to women's health advocates, most of whom have been tussling with the issues in this book at far closer quarters and for many more years than I have. Of course, unwanted pregnancy is a shared biological and therefore universal "women's experience." But what makes a pregnancy "wanted" is not universal, that is, it is not the same all over the world. It is mediated by the social and cultural organization of the community in which a woman finds herself. What is shared, by women who feel that their pregnancy is unwanted, is the injustice of the dilemma. There is always going to be a tension between the core, feminist, universal aspects of seeking "control over one's own body" and transforming that into abortion policies which respect the diversity of communities and cultures in which women live their lives (Correa and Petchesky 1994).

A Moral Issue, Above All

First, the anti-abortion perspective: it is concise and clear. The moral issue is the eternal starting line, by dint of the conviction that the embryo/fetus is the moral equivalent not only of the child it will become, but also of an adult woman, unwillingly pregnant. If you believe this—and it is a question of faith; science does not help—everything else falls into place: abortion is murder and compromise is unthinkable. To abolish abortion, the anti-abortion lobby must either convince everyone that it is morally heinous—as awful as murder—or make it illegal; preferably both (Berer 1988).

In an effort to persuade the rest of us that forced motherhood is an acceptable corollary of fetal personhood, the anti-abortion movement has invested heavily in projecting the fetus as a symbol of innocence and hope. Incidental aids such as ultrasound, and other medical technology, have been exploited to the hilt to create what has become almost a cult of the fetus. Heart-rending stories about brain-dead pregnant women, injured in road accidents and kept alive, with the aid of aggressively interventionist life-support, to try to ensure that the fetal patient survives, reinforce our perception of pregnant women as mere vessels, carriers of precious fetal cargo. Such cases, as well as "custody disputes" over frozen embryos, raise incredibly complex and important ethical issues, but with the complicity of junk medical journalism, fetalism prevails unchallenged. It is very hard to argue for respect and compassion for women whose circumstances make them seek late abortions, or even early abortions, against this ever-constricting imagery of medical heroics, biotechnology and the lonely homunculus. And ever easier to depict women seeking abortions as cruel harpies, bent on wanton destruction of helpless life.

The moral status of the embryo/fetus is not the only moral issue for the opponents of abortion. Many would like to convince us that the purpose of heterosexual intercourse is solely reproduction, that it should take place only within marriage. Abortion leads to promiscuity, say the moralists, disconcerted not only about sexuality in general, but about what abortion implies about the right of women to enjoy "scot-free" sexual pleasure, as men have always done. In riposte, a banner carried at the 1989 *pro*-abortion demonstration in Washington, DC, hit the spot: "If abortion is a crime, fucking is a felony," it said.

The anti-abortion movement has made great headway with the moral issue. First, the idea that abortion is a tragedy, and is a deeply disturbing experience for all women, has gained a significant foothold. Secondly, there is now widespread public acceptance that abortion is pre-eminently about murder, killing, life, simply because one party to the dispute insists that it is. The media scarcely ever permit a "pro-abortion" campaigner access to a microphone without a right-to-life viewpoint being presented as "balance." This inevitably tips the "debate" straight into a contest of fetal rights versus women's rights, and morality. We are invited to counterpose morality and women's rights (Kirkby 1994b)

"Abortion Makes Women Ill"

Claiming a monopoly on morality, as defenders of the helpless and innocent fetus, is incontestably the kernel of the anti-abortion case. From there they do not hesitate to carry the morality banner into the arguments about abortion on the grounds of public and individual women's health. Simple points first: how can you possibly talk about health benefits of safe abortions, they ask, when one person—the fetus being contentiously that person—dies? If women are ready to kill their babies in order to benefit their so-called health, it follows that they must be heartless, immoral (and unwomanly).

Secondly, there has been an explosion in knowledge about embryonic and fetal development in recent years, often by dint of precisely the kind of research which the anti-abortion movement tries to stop. The impact of discovering, for instance, when electrical activity begins in the brain, how the fetus reacts to sounds, and so on, has created a mass of apparent scientific certainty which has been transformed into a juggernaut of moral claims for the fetal patient (McLean 1989a). Yet facts are just that, facts: knowing when electrical activity begins tells us nothing about the intrinsic value or moral status of the fetus. (For more about the stages at which the fetus has been accorded moral significance, see Chapter 4.) Nevertheless, medical and technological advances, such as the advent of ultrasound, prenatal diagnosis, and lowering the age at which premature babies can survive, have significantly constricted the moral framework of the abortion issue, especially the question of later abortions (Callahan 1986). These developments all invite us to view the fetus as an individual "patient," in whose interests doctors can override the interests of the woman. It has also fuelled a parallel track of "save the babies" court cases depicting women as the major threat to the health of their children and the womb as the most dangerous place for the innocent "unborn child." Women have undergone forced Cesarean deliveries or been jailed while pregnant because of alcohol or drug abuse problems. Yet at the same time as pregnant women are being harangued in restaurants for presuming to enjoy a glass of wine, millions of pregnant women in poverty receive no antenatal care at all (Pollitt 1990).

The anti-abortion lobby is unsurprisingly reticent about the health implications of unsafe abortion with its toll of countless women's deaths, injuries and illness. Instead, the anti-abortion literature states, abortions make women ill or mad or both: "Rarely are women warned of the psychological and physical consequences following abortion," said MP David Alton in the debates on his bill to restrict abortion, during which a new "medical" term, "post-abortion trauma," was integrated into the case against abortion. (The threat of infertility also continues to be a theme, despite the fact that it is predominantly *unsafe* abortion which endangers future fertility.) The fact that some women with unwanted pregnancies have a difficult time deciding what is best for them, and later regret that their circumstances were unfavorable to their continuing their pregnancies, is pounced on as evidence of post-abortion psychosis (McNeil 1991).

Feminists for Life?

Allegations of inevitable post-abortion grief have inspired the anti-abortion lobby to invoke feminism in their case against abortion! Not only is abortion purported to imperil women's health, but women are supposedly being exploited when they have abortions because they are forced by their sexual partners to do this. Feminist-for-a-day David Alton, obscuring the intentions of his bill, claimed:

> men too often leave women in the lurch, having used their sexuality without responsibility. Those who maintain that abortion is purely a woman's issue do women no service: it allows men to evade their responsibilities, and without changes in men's attitudes, *women will not be truly liberated.*
>
> (QUOTED IN STEINBERG 1991, HER EMPHASIS, AND MINE)

Groups such as Women Exploited by Abortion (known in Britain as Victims of Abortion) stoke up this line, often with the aid of groups rallying under such banners as "Feminists for Life," who see women who end unwanted pregnancies as more sinned against than sinning and blame the prevalence of abortion on oppressive social conditions, male chauvinism, feminism, lack of child care, racism, society's devaluation of child-rearing as a responsibility, and so on.

Of course abortion lets men "off the hook"—Alton and "pro-life" feminists are taking their stand on an essential feminist truth: that in a male-supremacist society, no choice a woman makes is genuinely free. "When having a child forces a young woman out of school and out of the labour market, the decision to terminate a pregnancy is in that measure a forced decision" (Greer 1993). But scratch beneath Alton's feminist veneer and you find abortion outlawed, women bearing children they do not want. And shotgun marriages. All in the name of making men face up to their responsibilities?

The minute women who have had abortions mention ambivalence, guilt or regret, the anti-abortion lobby triumphantly crystallizes these feelings as symptoms of permanent psychological trauma, as if the rest of us find decision-making about our lives, our futures, or our children's futures a blithe and simple enterprise in which ambivalence, guilt and regret never feature. The well-springs of shame and guilt are complex, and are shaped by history, politics, and religious and moral codes, however deeply personal and *unique* they feel. Whilst abortion may well be as much within the law as a visit to the dentist, many women having abortions carry in their heads the legacy of its deviance, and of the dirty, sinister, secret, backstreet association (Petchesky 1984, p. 368). And it is not only the legacy of history which stigmatizes the abortion experience. Running a gauntlet of pickets shrieking that "you are about to kill your baby" or meeting punitive doctors who reprimand you for "getting into trouble" hardly compares with a visit to the dentist either. It is little wonder that some women are troubled and upset, beyond the pressures of their own circumstances.

But why do women having abortions in Britain and the United States mention guilty feelings so much more often than Dutch women or women in Denmark? The reason is not so much that Dutch women are insouciant about abortion, as that they do not feel ashamed of having had sex, and it is the cultures of the United States and Britain which are all screwed up about sexuality. There is a link between the openness and permissiveness of social attitudes towards sex and teenagers' success in using contraception and avoiding unplanned pregnancy (Jones et al. 1986). Doctors in Dutch abortion clinics told me that it is women from Germany, where abortion is frowned on and the Catholic Church rails against all aspects of sexuality, who say they feel guilty about their abortions, much more than the Dutch women. In age and social class they are much like the Dutch patients, but they have met refusals from German doctors and have had to struggle to get themselves to Holland. Once they are back in Germany, many will have no one to talk to about their experience and the blanket of silence contains their sense of having done something terrible. For Irish women, it is a similar story of secrets and silence.

The notion that abortion will inevitably cause guilt and regret is sustained by the conservative assumption that it is instinctive for women to *want* to be mothers and harmful to them not to fulfill that role. And if selfless motherhood is a natural instinct, then it is not surprising, say the anti-abortionists, that women who thwart their maternal natures can expect to pay the price in tears and yearning. Unless of course they are in some way deviant—lesbians, women with disabilities or HIV/AIDS, black women, unmarried women—and their desire to bear children is deemed to be deviant or excessive: the categories can vary and the list is not exhaustive (Stanworth 1987a).

The act of abortion is a defiance of the ideology which defines women in terms of heterosexuality, marriage and motherhood.[1] When politicians and moral pundits condemn women for having abortions, they condemn them as deviants from the patriarchal norms of maternal self-sacrifice. In other words they call them selfish. Again and again, I have been struck by the theme of selfishness running through the abortion controversy at every level. A woman who has an abortion is depicted by the anti-abortion lobby as the ultimate hedonist, indulging her own convenience, for her own selfish reasons. If she does not suffer guilt, grief, ambivalence, but simply relief, she is in the dock for a decision "lightly taken" or "for using abortion as a form of contraception." How else can you justify requiring the consent of husbands for an abortion, as some states of the United States have attempted to do, calling it a pro-family measure?[2]

The anti-abortion case, be it moral, medical or purportedly feminist, rests on the assumption that the fetus is a person. It is a simple, unsubtle message, in whatever guise it appears. It also has the polemical merit of being tidy and self-contained—precisely what makes it unsuited for regulating the sprawling, contradictory nature of daily human life.

How Are Abortion Rights to Be Advocated?

If access to abortion is to be defended, legalized or in some way extended, the framing of the issues sets the trajectory for ensuing policies. Simply reacting to anti-abortion allegations, timidly blurring the edges of the arguments in the hope of winning allies in the "middle ground" is a dangerous game.

Whatever the moral issue is for advocates of the right to abortion, it can be assumed not to be that, from the instant of conception, the embryo or fetus must be valued as having the same moral claims and interests as a pregnant woman. Why then does the standard pro-choice line on abortion apologize for it as a "necessary evil"? The implication is that this "evil" and therefore repugnant act must, for various venal reasons, be tolerated. Such a defensive stance "conjures up exactly what is uncomfortable about abortion and hand[s] the moral high ground to the anti-abortionists" (Coward 1994).

There is another problem with implicitly conceding that, morally speaking, abortions are entirely to be regretted, always traumatic, never an ethical method of birth control. It implies that it should be the business of family planning to reduce abortion by almost any means, because anything is preferable to abortion. If there is more contraception or sterilization there will be less need for abortion, we are told. It sounds plausible enough. But in some developing countries, where abortion is illegal, this perspective has led to aggressive promotion of sterilization. For example, women who have just had babies are offered three days' rest in hospital instead of the usual twenty-four hours, if they consent to be sterilized. The reasoning is that more sterilization will mean less illegal and unsafe abortion. Also, as the director of a family planning organization in one Latin American country observed, "Its irreversibility puts the patient safely beyond any possible social, religious or marital conflict" (Hartmann 1987).

From a woman's perspective, if getting an abortion involves breaking the law and the only way to prevent future unwanted pregnancy is to take the drastic step of being sterilized or accepting long-acting contraception and its side-effects, what alternative has she got? From the family planning agency's viewpoint, her consent is a success; births prevented and possible unsafe abortion averted. But to her it is an intrinsically coercive policy which would make no sense at all if early abortion was not ostracized in the way it usually is. Defending abortion whilst excoriating it fails to challenge the framework of moral absolutism and can lead to coercive and paternalistic birth control policies.

Health: A Powerful Case to Answer

There is much to be said for basing the case for abortion on values of individual and public health. Women after all are determined and resourceful at ending unwanted pregnancies, and will do so legally if they can, but illegally if they must. Simply permitting abortion under the law is not enough. It does not in itself call forth a network of cheap affordable, safe services for women. Whereas defining unsafe abortion as an epidemic, and calling on governments to take steps to prevent the consequences of unsafe abortion on grounds of public health, as if it was malaria or tuberculosis or HIV/AIDS, imposes an obligation on governments to intervene and finance services and facilities. It also skirts round the morality maze, because abortion is defined as a health need. The concept of "need" in relation to abortion is anathema to the anti-abortion perspective. To them, nothing can justify such "murders" as need. Medicos and moralists, however, pass each other as ships in the night: their basic values and premises are destined never to meet.

Making a health issue of abortion may help bring doctors on board the campaigning alliance, and the political advantages of having heavyweight allies such as medical professionals are obvious. When, for example, the reforms of Britain's abortion laws were first proposed, the Royal College of Obstetricians and Gynaecologists was against any change, arguing, among other things, that women were "governed by the maternal instinct" and abortions would make them depressed. The British Medical Association was also pretty unenthusiastic. But as the more liberal law settled down, doctors backed it and their collective support considerably buttresses the public consensus that abortion is an acceptable procedure which should remain within the law. In a survey of family doctors in Britain in 1995, two thirds agreed that women should have the moral right to abortion and 16 per cent disagreed. The American Public Health Association is one of the few professional medical bodies in the United States to have taken (and maintained) a stand against abortion restrictions, which it did after weighing the health evidence: "The health risks from terminating a pregnancy within the first 16 weeks of gestation are from five- to ten-fold less than the risks from carrying the pregnancy to term. When the social criteria are added, the weight in favor of termination is still greater if the pregnancy is unwanted, if the woman is young or poor or single or all of these and if she already has a large family" (Susser 1992, p. 1323). By contrast, the Catholic Church hierarchy in Poland had little difficulty in co-opting the medical profession to its intensive campaign to outlaw abortion in Poland (Kulczycki 1995).

By leading the campaigns to criminalize abortion in the nineteenth century, the medical profession had ensured itself a key role in the political history of abortion. It was doctors who framed the issue as a medical matter, to thwart attempts by clergymen, lawyers and, not least, women from having a say in deciding who should be permitted an abortion (Luker 1984, p. 44). Doctors claimed the exclusive expertise to make not only technical decisions about women's physical suitability to continue a pregnancy, but also moral and social judgments about the likelihood of "good mothering." What is more, it is convenient for politicians to defer to the medicos—it absolves them of responsibility for participating in the moral fray. There is much to be said for defining abortion as a routine and usually very simple medical procedure, funded out of normal healthcare budgets and regulated by the same criteria to which other healthcare is subject (Ryan, Ripper and Buttfield 1994).

Doctors in Charge

But medical control of abortion has a downside for women. First, because doctors control access to abortion, women's role is only to present reasons which are good enough to win the doctor's approval. To the public eye, the woman as an active social agent, a decider, a person with the capacity to determine her own future, fades from view. To win public sympathy for abortion provision, hapless victims—"an overburdened mother, an unwed teenager, a woman with defective foetus, a sexual risk-taker"—are regularly displayed before the public gaze. What also disappears, curiously, is the act of heterosexual intercourse which heralded the crisis: talk of sexual risk-taking refers exclusively to women who take risks (Albury 1994, p. 47).

Secondly, with the breakneck pace of technological advance, there are very real dangers in relying on doctors to arbitrate on women's access to abortion. The opportunities for very frail and premature babies to be "saved by modern medicine" have pushed back the frontiers of fetal viability. "Technical viability" has become a key phrase in debates about the time limits for abortion. If the medical perspective on abortion is allowed to take precedence, focusing on doctors' ability to sustain life or not, this could lead to a devastating erosion of women's access to abortion. Who will discriminate between the potentially abortable "products of conception" and the potential cherished baby? Not pregnant women, is a fair bet. As Maureen McNeil points out, "this [technicization] shifts the focus of decision-making away from women who, in opting for or against abortion, make complex evaluations of their particular circumstances and of the social sustainability of new life (McNeil 1991, p. 156). Indeed, in a landmark medical commentary in 1995, doctors from Britain and the United States argued that a woman requesting a third trimester abortion for a fetal anomaly which these doctors had defined as not serious would "lack ethical authority." What's more, they said, when a doctor is "ethically obligated not to perform a procedure, refusal to perform the procedure is not coercion" (Chervenak 1995). Paying heed to "burdens on patients, parents, society, communities, institutions and health care professionals" was not the doctors' ethical concern. (Fetal anomalies defined by the doctors as "not serious," embraced all which did not entail certainty of early death or absence of cognitive development capacity: Down's Syndrome and spina bifida were thus deemed ethically unjustified for third trimester abortion.)

The other difficulty with a medical model of abortion is that doctors are supposed to authorize abortions for "medical" reasons. When so-called "social grounds" are hitched onto the list of indications for abortion, the resulting policy sits uneasily, however flexibly doctors choose to define health and well-being. The more specifically medical a law is, the more demeaning this can become, for both parties (Greenhalgh 1992). In some countries a woman and her doctor have to agree simply that a "severe emergency situation" exists, so there is less pressure to distort the woman's reality; in others, a woman does not have to make a case until she is more than twelve weeks pregnant. But cautious or beleaguered legislatures often try to appease the anti-abortion pressure groups by choreographing doctors and patients together in a tightly controlled and utterly hypocritical piece of make-believe.

The Fading of Feminism

How can women re-enter the abortion debate, which has come to be so dominated by intransigent moralism and double-edged science? "Every child a wanted child, every mother a willing mother: a woman's right to choose!" "Not the church, not the state, women must decide their fate!"—the slogans of the big London pro-abortion demonstrations of the 1970s and 1980s left no doubt that abortion was a feminist issue for the women who chanted them.

The archetypal slogan of feminist abortion campaigning is "A woman's right to choose." It is a common denominator of feminist politics, a simple, compelling but flawed demand. As the enthusiastic, militant campaigns for abortion of the 1960s and 1970s (mostly white) women's liberation movement painfully learned, "a woman's right to choose" was not a simple issue of women having the right to determine the outcome of unwanted pregnancies. To many black and Hispanic women in the United States, it sounded as if not merely abortion rights were being advocated, but abortions themselves. To many such women, in common with other poor working-class women, the prevalence of sterilizations on offer in public hospitals made them very suspicious of the motives of the campaigns for abortion.[3]

The idea of being free to choose abortion took a further knock when news began to seep out of China of appalling abuses of pregnant women, with forced abortions, sometimes late in pregnancy, and brutally coercive contraceptive policies. The last thing Chinese women needed, it seemed, was a right to choose abortion—what they needed was a right to refuse it. Finally, in India the advent of ultrasound technology seemed to be giving a fresh impetus to the preference for boys in Hindu families, with a huge rise in sex-selective abortions, fuelled by the notorious dowry system. The individualist concept of "a woman's right to choose" amounted almost to a solecism—and so the politics was gradually pushed forward to embrace a much wider concept of reproductive freedom and women's reproductive rights, making the fight against forced sterilization and for better maternal and child welfare and child-care services as important as access to abortion and safe contraception (Birke, Himmelweit and Vines 1990).

But that in itself took many years. In the immediate aftermath of the liberalizing of abortion laws in Britain and in the United States, many campaigning organizations simply packed up their banners and moved from the field of contest. And when the newly fledged anti-abortion movement emerged into the public domain as a real danger, especially in the United States, the main concern was to defend the existing laws on their own terms. Abortion as an essential plank of women's equality and sexual freedom faded from view.

In Europe also, whatever gains still had to be made for women, legal abortion seemed basically settled. The pro-life lobby in Europe was a resourceful and influential irritant, but its potency was insignificant compared to the behemoth which had been unleashed across the Atlantic. The laws themselves were not perfect, people reminded themselves from time to time, but public opinion backed women's access to legal abortion. An atmosphere of complacency crept in. Whenever the abortion issue became controversial, it was increasingly in terms of the medical and scientific parameters—late abortion, neonatal medicine, viability, and so on (McNeil 1991). Insisting that abortion is above all a feminist issue became an isolated, "extremist" position to maintain. A vocal strand of feminist thinking even began to echo the plangent regrets of the mainstream "pro-choice" organizations, defining a woman seeking abortion as the product of grim, driven desperation, committing violence against herself. "Of course, nobody likes abortion," they explained: "we just think there should be a choice." In 1995, high-profile U.S. feminist Naomi Wolf accused the pro-choice lobby of "dehumanizing" the fetus in order to champion women's right to abortion. She called for abortion to be recognized in a moral framework of "transgressions and redemption" (*Guardian,* 16 October 1995). The "right to choose" had to be earned, argued Wolf, by acts of atonement. "If one had to undergo an abortion, one could work to provide contraception, jobs, or other choices to young girls" (*Guardian,* 30 January 1996).

The mainstream "pro-choice" case today, espoused by family planning organizations world-wide and the big U.S. pro-choice organizations who dominate the defense of abortion, is that abortion is not a political question at all: it is a far more innocuous matter of personal, private choice which must be safeguarded to avert a return to the squalid horrors of illegal abortion. Such blandishments, aimed at damping down inflammatory notions such as women's rights, inadvertently bolster the perception of an abortion decision as a purely self-centered, self-indulgent and essentially ignoble act. It offers no challenge to the cultivated distaste for abortion, which the anti-abortion movement has done so much to foster.

Meanwhile the allure of the new reproductive technologies, giving a new edge to complex questions such as why women become mothers, and whether women can exercise any control over the new technology, captured the attention of much of the more vocal feminist movement. Despite a flurry of interest triggered by the arrival of RU 486, most feminist health advocates and analysts today are writing about either reproductive rights on a far larger canvas, or the new reproductive technologies and their implications for motherhood. Abortion has waned as an item of analytical fascination to feminist politicos. It also seemed to many feminists, especially in the United States, that now was not the time to insist on abortion as a woman's right and a necessary condition of her sexual freedom. Although they could see that abortion was in the front line of an explicitly anti-feminist attack from the New Right, which threatened not only abortion but almost everything women had gained in the 1960s and 1970s, the question of reproductive freedom seemed to have been reduced to defending the fragile, single-issue of "the choice" to have a legal abortion, the case for "choice" being much less strident and shrill-sounding than demanding "rights" (Fried 1990a).

When "easy" abortion came under attack—abortion on so-called social grounds—it was often expedient for "pro-choice" pressure groups to soft-pedal the "women's rights" aspect of abortion. They wanted to assuage the moral qualms of supporters who believed that there are some good "hard" reasons for *allowing* women to have abortions, and some reasons which should not be tolerated. The anti-abortion lobby has had considerable success in convincing the public that abortion is always morally problematic and of the validity of such distinctions. But the minute such arbitrary distinctions become admissible, it implies that someone other than the woman herself must judge whether or not the abortion is acceptable, and a woman's capacity to determine whether or not her pregnancy should continue has been compromised.

Reclaiming a Feminist Issue, Twenty-five Years On

From a pregnant woman's point of view these categories are a nonsense. There is only one reason for wanting abortion—unwanted pregnancy (Berer 1993b). Banning abortion declares, very forcefully, that women's reproductive role is paramount, motherhood is a God-given responsibility and not a chosen commitment. When the feminist case—that women's bodies are their own and it is up to them to decide when, and if, to have children—is allowed to drop beneath the horizon, we also lose sight of the fact that the impetus behind much of the anti-abortion movement is bolstering the ideology of motherhood itself.

"Women must decide their fate." That does not mean it is easy for them to "decide their fate." The sad feelings of *some* women in opting for abortion should not be belittled as artificially constructed by the oppressive influences of a patriarchal ideology. Some flat-out feminists seem to believe that the instant that women recognize how they have been brainwashed by "male-supremacist" notions of thwarted maternal instinct, that sadness will at once fade and it will mean no more than a trip to the dentist.[4] On the other hand, it does not serve women well to insist that an abortion is always to be regretted and sighed over. It is simply a fact that such choices have to be made in a society which is riven with oppression and inequality. No wonder women so often say of their abortions, "It was my only choice" (Rothman 1988).

A woman with a pregnancy which she does not welcome is at a crossroads, and whichever road she decides on there is no turning back. Such decisions crop up at other points of people's lives and, however positive the final choice may be, it may well be accompanied by sadness and even, for a while, grief, that circumstances could not be different. As the black American poet Langston Hughes says, "There's a certain amount of traveling in a dream deferred" (Hughes 1986, p. 270), and facing an unwanted pregnancy is an authentic confrontation with dreams, at least one of which has to be deferred, *whatever the outcome.* Why single out abortion as a uniquely momentous choice? Women face many decisions entailing gains and losses and it should be possible to acknowledge that, *for some women,* opting for abortion may be a very hard choice.

> The much discussed "ambivalence" of many women toward the *experience* of abortion (not the *right*) is a smokescreen that obscures a dense web of losses and sorrows relating to aging and childbearing and the precariousness of sexual relationships, as well as the longings for family ties and emotional commitment that a "baby" may symbolize.
>
> (PETCHESKY 1984, p. 368)

It can feel like a burden rather than a liberation to have to choose. Acknowledging that does not mean that abortion "exploits" women, thus handing game, set and match to the anti-abortion camp. Choosing abortion is sometimes a heavy burden, particularly after prenatal diagnosis of a congenital abnormality, for which the only "remedy" is a private decision to end the pregnancy (Rapp 1984). Women facing this dilemma are pulled and pushed by extraordinarily deep-seated pressures from a society which, on the one hand, expects motherhood to be an endless, selfless flow of spontaneous maternal love, but which, on the other hand, offers less and less meaningful support to people with disabilities and their families.

Claiming and defending women's rights to a legal, safe, affordable, accessible, compassionate and respectful abortion service cannot be pursued as a narrow, isolated issue. It has to take account of other struggles to change the conditions and the relationships which impinge on women's lives, especially when it comes to responsibility for pregnancy and for child-rearing. As the early history of the women's liberation movement, that is, the 1960s and 1970s, shows, it was the fight for legal abortion which in large measure galvanized the movement into existence and became emblematic of the struggle for women's reproductive freedom (Correa 1994, p. 69).

The relentless anti-abortion portrayal of abortion as a uniquely barbarous and squalid procedure, and of women who seek abortions as either selfish murderers, or dupes who will become psychotic when they realize what they have done, has put advocates of accessible abortion onto the defensive. Now both sides in the dispute take it for granted that abortion is morally problematic and a traumatic, negative, desperate decision for women. Feminists have a role to play in challenging this "awfulisation" of abortion, as some Australian feminists have termed it (Ryan, Ripper and Buttfield 1994). One way of reclaiming abortion as a normal element of a reproductive health service for women is to organize "speak-outs." In 1971 in West Germany, 300 women admitted in *Stern* magazine that they had had abortions. They did it in the United States too—a host of celebrities, including Whoopi Goldberg and Ursula Le Guin recounted their experiences of abortion (Bonavoglia 1991). And in 1993 the National Abortion Campaign organized a meeting in London where journalist Suzanne Moore and actress Janet Suzman were among those who declared, "I've had one . . ." (Moore 1993). Women speaking openly about having had an abortion is a challenge to the myth that abortion is something which only bad girls or child-haters do. It also gives the lie to the anti-abortion myth that everyone who has an abortion carries the memory like a hairshirt of remorse. Challenging the "awfulisation" of abortion is a vital task for a feminist abortion movement. Faint but unmistakable signs of a feminist element regaining ground in the international campaign for abortion came at the conference, "Abortion Matters," held in

March 1996 to mark twenty-five years of safe abortion in Holland. The so-called "Amsterdam Declaration" stated that abortion is first and foremost, "an issue of self-determination for women, and that it is deeply denigrating to woemen to suggest that they would irresponsibly resort to abortion when it becomes legal." The conference, of people from more than fifty countries involved in fighting for and providing abortion also condemned the stigmatization of women who have abortions.[5]

A Humanitarian Issue

What really counts for women is to know that a sympathetic and accessible service is there if needed, much like any other healthcare service. We desire high quality health care, we hope we don't need it, it's very simple. In her lucid exploration of "a woman's right to choose," Susan Himmelweit distinguishes between women having the right and the power to *decide* whether or not an abortion is appropriate for them, and creating a "humanitarian framework" in which such a decision can be made (Himmelweit 1988; see also Chapter 5). She stresses the woman's role as the actively nurturing agent and how impossible it is to expect good nurturing, in the broadest sense, to be carried out by a woman who is unwillingly pregnant. Rejecting the limitations of a narrow, rights-based, feminist case for abortion, which leaves unchallenged the lonely and privatised nature of what often feel to the woman like very hollow "choices," Himmelweit calls for what she terms a humanitarian perspective. This would not only make it possible to consider abortion as a routine part of reproductive health care, rather than simply as an abstract legal right for women, but it might also, one day, make it possible to open up a *reasoned* and respectful debate about the pressures on women which make them seek abortions in a range of different circumstances. At present, for instance, sex-selective abortions and abortions after diagnosis of fetal abnormality, raise a number of disturbing and important questions. It is, however, very difficult to debate the issues they raise without appearing to undermine or even condemn the women who opt for such abortions.

Himmelweit is venturing on to a minefield for feminism, beginning to question the morality of the reasons why women have abortions. When for the foreseeable future child-rearing is going to remain the province of mothers, it seems impossible to challenge a woman's decision to have an abortion without invoking something smacking of "maternal duty." That is why almost all feminist advocacy of a woman's rights to abortion in an unjust world centers on *her right to decide,* that is, the politics, and not the reasons for her decision. When the social conditions in which women work, choose and reproduce are transformed, it may be possible to bring the political and the moral closer together.

So the way abortion services are argued for or defended must vary. It may even be possible to challenge the moral case against abortion, as has Sister Ivone Gebara, a nun working in the slums of Recife, Brazil, who has bravely questioned the morality of the Vatican. Sister Ivone says that amongst the rapacious social inequalities of contemporary Brazil, forcing poor women to provide for undesired children was unbearable, unjust, in other words, immoral (Correa 1994, p. 73).

Strategies depend on local political topography. In some countries women's health advocates have had more impact on opinion about abortion by showing how illegal, unsafe abortion preys on women's health, and by not insisting on "women's rights" or even "human rights." Their strategy avoids presenting a target for the fetalist lobby to counterpose the "rights of the fetus." There is a lively debate underway between human rights lawyers, development pundits and women's health advocates about the advantages and disadvantages of arguing for women's reproductive health services (including abortion) on the grounds of universal human rights. Many nations have signed up under various United Nations Declarations, to documents such as the Convention on the Elimination of All Forms of Discrimination Against Women, and it might be possible to use this as a lever to improve access to abortion (Cook 1989b). Other activists and scholars have warned of the risks in this, observing how feminist-sounding rhetoric has been widely co-opted by conservative groupings, such as international population agencies, to embellish what remain narrow, quantitative goals (Correa and Petchesky 1994). They point out how adoption of human rights as a vehicle in which to push forward women's issues has made it easier "for nationalists and fundamentalists to object . . . to any international constitutional guarantees for women's reproductive rights, as interference in the collective human rights of their nations, which include the right to follow their own 'culture'."[6]

Pragmatic campaigning apart, the issue remains quintessentially a matter of women's reproductive and sexual freedom. That is what makes it a political issue, because in a male-dominated society women's dignity and freedom has to be fought for politically. The controversies of abortion may shift—prenatal diagnosis of fetal abnormality and fetal sex, HIV/AIDS,

RU 486 have all impinged in their different ways, and feminists have to take account of them. Abortion will never stop, whether it is banned by law or by the pope's denunciations: outlawing it will merely kill and injure more women. Handing out contraceptives or throwing bombs at clinics will not eliminate it either. It is not merely a method of last resort for women who can be dismissed as unlucky or plain foolish. Such distinctions only serve to perpetuate the legacy of shame surrounding abortion and compound women's emotional difficulties in seeking to end unwanted pregnancies.

Defenders of women's access to abortion cannot afford to ignore the connected issues of women's reproductive health, especially the imperfections of contraception: "as long as it remains possible for a woman to be pregnant without wanting to be, abortion will be a necessity and its denial a punishment of women—for having sex" (Petchesky 1984, p. 190).

Because I had had sex, someone thought I deserved to die.

(CERULLO 1990, p. 89)

Afterword

Introduction

In the year since this book was first published in the United States there have been some important developments around the world. What follows is an update on the topics covered in previous chapters.

For what I hope will be readers' convenience I have dealt with the developments not in order of their significance, but simply by following as closely as possible the order in which they appear in the main body of the book.

The United States

Surveying the last twelve months, it would be easy enough for the embattled defenders of abortion services in the United States to overlook the good news. They continue, after all, fighting tooth and nail in an overwhelmingly anti-abortion Congress and enduring persistent violence against abortion clinics. But it could all have been much, much worse.

The re-election of Democratic President Clinton in November 1996 meant that at the very least the President could be relied on not to rubber-stamp legislation hostile to abortion. Clinton's loyalty to the preservation of a woman's right to choose could hardly be described as staunch and fearless, but he is nonetheless an ally rather than an enemy, and that is something to be grateful for as the relentless attack on abortion rights continues unabated.

Abortion was not such a prominent influence on the 1996 presidential election campaign as in previous years: the Republicans succeeded in containing the forces of Christian fundamentalism within their ranks and not becoming hostage to their demands. Nevertheless the search for a running mate to Republican presidential contender Bob Dole was almost completely dictated by the need to find someone who would appease the anti-abortion militants. The resulting choice was rank outsider Jack Kemp, a man known to have publicly disagreed with Bob Dole on almost every matter except abortion itself.

It was to no avail—Clinton returned to the White House. But Congress remained solidly weighted against abortion rights and congressional opponents of abortion have spent the last year or so targeting specific late-term abortion procedures. By their own admission this is merely a tactic in their overall strategy to recriminalize abortion. It may yet provide, in the words of one observer, "an emotional crowbar which may finally prise a crack in the court's ruling" (i.e., the constitutional case of *Roe v. Wade,* which abortion rights activists have always used to challenge legislative attacks on abortion).[1]

Ralph Reed, leader of the powerful Christian Coalition, told the *New York Times* in March 1997 that he had discussed with House Speaker Newt Gingrich the possibility of scheduling a series of votes that would outlaw abortion by developmental stages. "That is, the House would first vote on a measure to outlaw all abortions in the ninth month. If that passed, it would vote to outlaw all abortions in the eighth month and so on."[2]

Meanwhile, the headlines have been dominated in the United States by congressional attempts to outlaw a specific late-term abortion procedure. Its critics call it "partial birth." Those who perform and defend it use its medical description, "intact dilatation and extraction" (or evacuation)—intact D&E for short. It is a rarely performed operation, and preventing it would hardly dent the overall American abortion statistics. According to the American Medical Association it accounts for one-tenth of one percent of all U.S. abortions.

But despite the fact that the term "partial-birth" is itself a campaigning tool, an invention of the anti-abortion lobby, rather than a medical term, the indisputably grisly nature of the procedure has greatly furthered the overall strategy of shifting public attention from the needs of the pregnant woman to the issue of the fetus. Briefly the procedure involves partially extracting a fetus, feet first, through the birth canal, piercing the barely visible base of the skull, and then draining out the contents of the skull in order that it collapses and the head can be pulled out.

It is not the only method of removing a fetus in the later stages of gestation and it is arguably not the most gruesome: others include dismemberment in the womb and piece-by piece extraction. Some doctors have stated that before beginning an intact D&E procedure they cut the umbilical cord to ensure that it is no longer alive; others give a lethal injection. But presumably not all do this, and the legislation before congress has always referred to the procedure in relation to a "living fetus." [3]

A summary of the controversy is that in the fall of 1996 both houses of the Congress passed a ban on the operation, before and after viability. This was vetoed, however, by Clinton because the only exception permitted was to save the *life* of the pregnant woman, and Clinton believed that there should also be safeguards to protect the pregnant woman's *health*. Once again, in March 1997 a similar bill passed easily through the House of Representatives and yet another White House–Congress showdown loomed. Anti-abortion sentiment in both Houses had hardened considerably since the November elections.

As the Senate prepared in May 1997 to debate the bill, Clinton announced that he would support a compromise measure, brokered by Roman Catholic Democratic senator Tom Daschle. Daschle's proposal was to restrict access to *all* late-term abortions after viability, except where the pregnant woman's health risked "grievous injury."

Clinton's undoubted aim in backing Daschle was to derail the Republican-backed version of the bill. But seeing that the Daschle proposal was also being supported, albeit with reluctance, by abortion rights defenders, most anti-abortion senators concluded that there must be something wrong with Daschle's bill and threw it out.

Indeed there was much wrong with the Daschle proposal: in banning an entire category of abortions, it would have been a small but significant incursion on the rights of women to end unwanted or troubled pregnancies, guaranteed by the historic 1973 Supreme Court *Roe v. Wade* judgment.

Days later, the Republican-backed bill was passed in the Senate by a large majority, aided marginally by the eleventh-hour support of the prestigious American Medical Association. Only a week before the AMA had been expressing neutrality on the bill, saying that politicians should keep out of clinical decision-making and that the wording was too vague and threatening to doctors. The anti-abortion lobby had spent US$1 million on advertising in eight states to sway wavering senators and had tightened up the technicalities of the bill slightly in order to win the AMA endorsement. But there were still not enough votes to prevent the President once again from being able to veto the bill, which he has vowed to do, calling it "unwise and unconstitutional."

The intractable controversy has been a minefield for the lobbying groups, as they try to engage public sympathy with their viewpoint. The one thing both sides agree on is the importance of getting their message across to the public. The abortions rights case was hardly helped in March when one of its leaders, Ron Fitzsimmons of the National Coalition of Abortion Providers, admitted that he had "lied through my teeth" and distorted statistics showing how rarely and when and for what reason the intact D&E method was used.[4] But despite intense media pressure, such as full-page ads in the national press by the National Conference of Catholic Bishops, polls continue to show that most Americans support abortion rights. But three-quarters have grave reservations about late-term procedures, and it is very clear that the anti-abortion lobby has been luridly focusing on these methods to drum up popular support for other anti-abortion measures. In vain, the defenders of abortion have issued details of the wrenching cases of couples who have learned late in the pregnancy, at twenty, twenty-six or thirty-one or more weeks, that there are severe fetal abnormalities such as encephalocele with severe microcephaly (a large portion of the brain having been formed outside the skull) or similar defects. The acres of fine print cannot contend with the graphic sensationalism of the simple term "partial-birth."

There have been admissions by the opponents of abortion about the difficulties of enforcing a ban on specific procedures. Mark Crutcher, leader of Life Dynamics, an anti-abortion group which specializes in taking legal action against abortion clinics, has stated that, "there is no way to enforce that law. . . . you are never going to see a prosecution of a partial-birth abortion. . . . the whole issue is a scam being perpetrated by people on our side of the issue for fund-raising purposes."[5] Crutcher was commenting on a court test of the ban in Michigan, which along with nine other states has already voted a ban on the particular procedure. In twenty-five other state legislatures a similar ban is under consideration, even though such laws may well have no practical effect other than causing fear and confusion.

The legislative gridlock is set to continue.

Other Battlegrounds

There have been other battlegrounds requiring update. More encouraging, for example, has been the slow progress toward making the abortion pill available in the United States (see The Abortion Pill—Mifepristone section below). But for thousands of women with unwanted pregnancies in the United States, abortion remains as out of reach as if *Roe v. Wade* had never been. For them, "the expense, location and shortage of services, burdensome legal restrictions and anti-abortion threats and violence create daunting barriers" (Fried 1997). It is low-income women, women of color (who comprise a disproportionate number of the poor) and young women who bear the brunt of restricted access. Even getting to a clinic presents a problem for many women. And clinic violence continues to ensure that visiting an abortion clinic can be a terrifying experience. One third of clinics are still facing serious violence, including death threats, arson and bombings. Non-violent disruption, including "sidewalk counselling" by protesters, also continues virtually unchecked after a recent Supreme Court ruling.[6]

One of the first things Clinton did in 1993 when he arrived in the White House was to reverse President Reagan's "Mexico City policy," which had banned aid to any international agencies which directly or indirectly funded abortions or gave advice on abortion as part of their services in developing countries (see pp. 12 and 168–69). The ban was so inclusively worded as to infringe the sovereignty of governments in their policies, but that never troubled the anti-abortion right wing in Congress.

In June 1997 a similar ban was voted for by the predominantly anti-abortion House of Representatives. It not only slashed the international family planning aid available via U.S. overseas aid, but was worded in such a way that it forbade any organization in receipt of U.S. aid from discussing abortion law or policy with governments, even in countries where it has been decided that abortion is legitimate. It also denied any money to UNFPA, the United Nations family planning organization, on the pretext of concern about China's coercive population control measures.

Finally, it is worth noting that the abortion rate in the United States seems to be falling. For many years it has been consistently higher than in many comparable European countries. But in 1994, the latest year for which figures are available, it dropped to 21 per 1,000 women of reproductive age, which as a percentage of live births brings it to its lowest level since 1976. The total number of abortions dropped from 1.5 million in 1992 to 1.4 million in 1994.

The drop is partly accounted for by changes in the profile of the population. Women under 30, who have markedly higher abortion rates than older women, make up a smaller proportion of American women than previously. But the teenage pregnancy rate—the figure that regularly spurs newspaper columnists into so much lamentation—is also falling; increased condom use is thought to be the main reason.

Almost six out of ten women having abortions in the United States blame their unwanted pregnancies on contraceptive failure (Alan Guttmacher Institute 1996). Nearly 90 percent of abortions take place before twelve weeks of pregnancy, with 99 percent within twenty weeks.[7]

The issue of access to abortion in the United States today illustrates in every detail the predictable discrimination that results from criminalizing or in any way impeding women's access to safe, legal, affordable abortion services. The lack of public funding for an operation which costs on average US $300 has a disproportionate effect on the poor and the young.

So much ground has been lost in political terms, too, as the defenders of abortion have retreated from the notion of abortion rights as an essential part of women's freedom. The main focus of the mainstream abortion rights campaigners is on the protracted technicalities of maneuvering and counter-maneuvering in Congress and in state legislatures, in a tortuous effort to prevent erosion of the *Roe v. Wade* principles. Nowadays, as the debate over late-term abortion clearly shows, the battle is waged almost entirely on the grounds of public health. The legality of abortion in general is defined as a question of "choice" or even "privacy." The notion of choice, as Marlene Gerber Fried (1997) points out, has little relevance to those who have no choices in their lives and whose voices are scarcely heard in the abortion debate. There has been little or no attempt to protect or reinstate the right of low-income women to have access to abortion "rights."

For years there has been no large-scale attempt to mobilize public support for the restoration of Medicaid funding for abortion operations, which has been banned on an annual basis for twenty years. The politics behind this ban on aid to poor women has been that public money should not be used for a purpose which is "repugnant." Implicitly it seems conceded by those campaigning to keep abortion legal that abortion is indeed universally repugnant, and therefore does not merit funding out of the public purse. Challenging the Medicaid ban becomes more and more difficult even, as in 1997, in the face of moves to make the funding restrictions permanent. There is similar wariness toward making any direct, ideological challenge to the conservative impetus behind, for instance, parental notification laws, which restrict the abortion rights of women below majority age and threaten their health and well-being in the name of patriarchal "family values" (Fried 1997).

Poland

"Poland's anti-abortion law is much more restrictive in real life than on paper, as women who have the right to a legal abortion are often refused one, even though they have the necessary certificates," says Wanda Novicka, leading campaigner for abortion in Poland (Novicka 1996b). Illegal abortion has been flourishing in Poland in the wake of the draconian 1993 anti-abortion law (see pp. 43–46). The clandestine operations are mostly performed by doctors, who risk up to two years in jail if they are caught and whose fees reflect the risk they are running. In the hospitals doctors are afraid to perform abortions, even when women have grounds for abortion within the narrow confines of the law. Opinion polls, however, have consistently shown that most Poles favor broad abortion rights.

The search for abortion continues to take women on long journeys. A clinic in Berlin reports about fifteen Polish women a week visiting for abortions and paying between US$400 and 1,300 for an operation.

There was a glimmer of hope for a few months that has now faded. Late in 1996 the Polish parliament passed a new, more liberal abortion law. Anti-abortion protesters came in buses from all over Poland. The leader of the Roman Catholic Church in Poland, Cardinal Jozef Glemp, declared that those who spoke "in favour of the death of the unborn . . . exclude themselves from the Church. There is no place for them at the altar" (Kozakiewicz 1997). But the law was signed by Poland's left-wing president, Alexander Kwasniewski, and became law in January 1997.

The new law's most significant extension allowed for abortion within the first twelve weeks of pregnancy if the woman had "difficult living conditions" or a "family situation." It also permitted abortions to be performed in private clinics. It is of course unlikely that many women "in difficult living conditions" would be able to afford private care, and from the record of the last few years, they could hope for little comfort from doctors in the public health service. Many public hospitals, for example, in the deeply Catholic south had announced flatly that they would not comply with the new law.

But hardly had the new law been on the statute books for a few months before it encountered a fresh challenge. In May 1997, on the eve of Pope John Paul II's arrival in Poland for a pilgrimage, the nation's constitutional tribunal decided in a 9–3 ruling that abortion was a violation of the democratic order.[8] The judges' ruling obliged parliament to reexamine the law within six months; a two-thirds vote was needed to overthrow it.

Stunned supporters of abortion rights observed that the decision, based on constitutional guarantees to the right to life, brought Poland as close as possible to becoming a clerical state. The ruling almost certainly means that abortion will once again become, with few exceptions, decisively illegal in Poland.

The Health Risks of Abortion

Breast Cancer

Health researchers continue to argue about whether or not having an abortion can increase a woman's likelihood of developing breast cancer (see pp. 55). In October 1996, Joel Brind, professor of endocrinology at the City University of New York, published a study that indicated a significant link between abortion and the disease. Given current abortion statistics and American women's overall lifetime risk of breast cancer (one in eight), the study estimated that an extra 24,500 cases of breast cancer could perhaps be attributed to abortion (Brind 1996).

Critics accused Brind of bias, given his long-standing public support for anti-abortion organizations. More significantly, Brind's work, which was based on an analysis of other studies and not on direct research, was criticized for putting too much faith in the quality of the previous research from which it drew its dramatic conclusions.

In January 1997, publication of a large, direct study, conducted on all Danish women born between 1935 and 1978, concluded that abortion does *not* generally increase the risk of breast cancer (Melbye 1997). The *British Medical Journal* observed that the scale of the study, involving 1.5 million women and information collected from registries, "may finally resolve the controversy surrounding the issue."[9] The study did show, however, that abortion performed after 12 weeks of pregnancy did seem to indicate a slightly greater risk of breast cancer.

Mental Health Hazards

Does having an abortion make a woman more likely to commit suicide than completing a pregnancy? Finnish researchers looking at the incidence of suicide after *pregnancy* concluded that suicides occur more commonly after abortion (Gissler et al. 1996). But their conclusions have been challenged and the debate about the effect of abortion on mental health continues.

Fetal Rights

While the United States was riven by the characteristically intemperate debate about "partial birth abortion," fetal rights and the rights of pregnant women have been tested in the more placid ambience of the English courts of law. In recent years, as doctors continue to intervene fairly aggressively in the process of childbirth, with increasing rates of cesarian sections, women have from time to time fought back in the courts. In a landmark case in 1997, judges made it clear that a woman cannot legally be made to undergo an operation against her will if she is competent to make that decision. Even if her decision causes birth defects or leads to death—her own or the baby's—no one has the right to intervene. In other words, they confirmed the law's view that the fetus has no rights until the moment of birth.[10]

Of course, as stated earlier (see Chapter 4), law and morality are not necessarily identical, but earlier cases of court-ordered cesarians were doing little to enhance the trust between doctors and women facing childbirth.

The Question of Viability

In 1997 in Britain a woman whose baby was born at twenty-three weeks' gestation asked for and got an official enquiry into her complaint that no help was offered to aid the child's survival. The doctors' decision not to intervene and to let the infant die was vindicated by the court hearing. Specialists in neonatal medicine have not significantly shifted their broad consensus that preterm infants born at twenty-five weeks or less are at very high risk of death and, if they do survive, have a high risk of serious disability (Koh 1997). For babies born at 23 weeks, the chances of survival are less than 5 percent. Although survival rates for babies born before twenty-eight weeks have improved, the proportion of those who have severe disabilities has not changed in recent years (Tin 1997).

The progress of this debate and the ethical dilemmas it creates for neonatal experts continues to impinge on the debate in Britain about the propriety of abortion after twenty-four weeks. This is the point at which abortion becomes illegal except to save the life of the pregnant woman, because it is now accepted, in terms of abortion law, as the cut-off point for viability. Abortion is however legal, at any gestation, when "there is substantial risk that if the child were born it would suffer from such mental or physical abnormalities as to be seriously handicapped." The very small number of abortions after twenty-four weeks (94 in 1994) shows that doctors are very cautious about sanctioning such procedures (Paintin 1997).

Rights for Fathers?

"Abortion test case shambles" declared the front page of one of Britain's leading newspapers in the midst of a series of tit-for-tat court hearings held to decide whether or not a woman in Scotland had the right to terminate a pregnancy against her estranged husband's will.

The couple had had a stormy two-year marriage and already had one child. They had parted amid mutual allegations that the other was an unfit parent and violent within the marriage. In May 1997, when the husband learned that his wife was pregnant and planning to ask for an abortion, he tried to get "custody" of the twelve-week-old fetus and succeeded in gaining an interim interdict. At the first court hearing to consider his plea the judge backed the wife and said the court could not frustrate operations approved within the terms of the 1967 Abortion Act. Abortion law in Britain does not allow abortion on request—two doctors must agreed that it is justifiable in terms of the woman's health, mental or physical.

But within twenty-four hours a second court forbade the abortion, pending an appeal to the House of Lords, Britain's supreme court. Anti-abortion commentators welcomed the new twist: "it takes two people for a baby to be conceived and once this is so, three people are involved," said one opponent of abortion in a typical comment.

A third court hearing covered arguments about the legal status of the fetus and the precedent set by two similar cases in the English courts, where men had failed to prevent abortions going ahead. The father's lawyer argued that the unborn child is entitled to his father's protection.

Finally, twelve days after the start of the legal battle, with the prospect of an appeal to the House of Lords, the husband abandoned the case without explanation. In a newspaper interview, the wife said that during the legal wrangling she had been made to feel like a killer and had contemplated suicide.

The abortion took place the next day, at the very limits of the time left for a simple, early abortion. Throughout the week newspaper columns were full of the polemic of a father's rights to be involved in the abortion decision and the difficulties which that creates. The outcome means that, as in England, a father or guardian in Scotland cannot protect a fetus in the womb. It is only the wish to thwart an abortion that has brought such cases to the law courts; a man has yet to use the law to try to force an abortion to take place. A moment's reflection on the absurdity of such a hypothetical scenario highlights the flaws of the "father's rights" argument.

The Abortion Pill—Mifepristone

In September 1996, the U.S. Food and Drug Administration declared that mifepristone, the pharmaceutical which makes it possible for women to have an abortion by medical means as opposed to surgical methods, was a safe and effective product. The decision was taken in a virtual bunker—a building surrounded by burly federal agents, bristling with metal detectors and other security equipment.

The FDA's action fell short of actual approval of mifepristone, more commonly known as RU 486 (see pp. 117–24). Before mifepristone can be used in the United States, in combination with the prostaglandin misoprostol, to terminate early pregnancies, the agency requires additional information from the holder of the U.S. patent rights, the Population Council, as to how the drug will be manufactured and labelled by the company which it has set up for the purpose. But it does mean that the trials of mifepristone that were conducted in the U.S. under the auspices of the Population Council met with rigorous FDA standards.

Hoechst, now the world's fourth largest drug company, had long been seeking to offload totally its ownership of the patent rights for mifepristone, making no secret of the fact. To the company, mifepristone had become nothing but a burden, literally more trouble than it was worth, netting a paltry US $3.4 million revenue in 1996. Additionally, threats of boycotts of its much more profitable medicines and agrochemicals had been made persistently by anti-abortion activists in the United States.

Passing the U.S. patent rights to the Population Council in 1994 had seemed the best way to shake off the boycott threats from American activists. The ruse would buy breathing time in the search for a company ready to take over rights for Europe. But suddenly in April 1997 Hoechst found itself once again under pressure from the American militants. Campaigners began buying full-page newspaper ads urging U.S. consumers not to use Allegra,

Hoechst's newly launched anti–hay fever treatment, whose annual U.S. sales were expected to top US $300 million over the next three years.

There was little surprise, therefore, when Hoechst announced soon after the ads appeared that, without any charge, it was transferring patent rights to make and sell RU 486 worldwide outside the U.S. to Dr. Edouard Sakiz, former chief executive of Roussel, and one of the pill's developers.

Dr. Sakiz had formed a new company, Exelgyn, to handle the drug, which is licensed for marketing only in Sweden, France, and Britain. As a one-product company, he told the press, he would not be vulnerable to boycotts. Most press analysis of the transfer was that boycott threats had forced Hoechst to make this move and "drop abortion pill."[11] Roussel-Uclaf, Hoechst's wholly owned French subsidiary, said it could not take the risk of continuing to make the drug, and industry experts said it was the first time a pharmaceutical company in the big league had given up rights to a drug which had been judged by regulators to be safe and effective.

Dr. Sakiz says any profits accruing from sales of mifepristone will be ploughed into research. And he accepts that he will now present a tempting target for anti-abortion campaigning, and even violence. He told *Le Monde,* "I will be a much easier target than a corporation. Edouard Sakiz has a house, an address. I risk being regarded as a Satan, or whatever you like. But in the end I reckon you cannot abandon such a promising product. . . . It is a magnificent French discovery which I don't want to see buried."[12]

Russia

According to the Ministry of Health in Russia, the abortion rate has dropped dramatically in the last few years, from 108 per 1,000 women of reproductive age in 1990 to 68 in 1996. Use of the Pill has doubled and there is much more information available to help women avoid unplanned pregnancies. It really seems possible to imagine for the first time that Russia may be able to move away from the "abortion culture" which prevailed in the post-Stalin Soviet Union. The shift from abortion to contraception has been so dramatic that it was not surprising to find that Planned Parenthood of America brought two of the Russian Family Planning Association's executives to congressional hearings in Washington in 1997 to try to dissuade U.S. lawmakers from cutting off family planning aid to international agencies whose work included abortion services (see above). More contraception, less abortion, was the Russians' unembellished theme.

The path in Russia is far from smooth. A burgeoning of extra-marital sexual activity, unprecedented access to pornography and soaring rates of sexually transmitted diseases such as syphilis are all features of post-communist Russia. Meanwhile traditionalists denounce sex education as an encitement to "promiscuity." Women working in the Russian Family Planning Association (RFPA), striving to reduce abortion rates by the provision of contraceptive services and information, have been publicly denounced as obsessed with sex and even labelled prostitutes. Christian fundamentalists have called the RFPA a "satanic institution" and it has been accused of killing Russia's sons. It remains to be seen whether the imminently expected AIDS epidemic, which health experts are now predicting as imminent, will help or hinder the RFPA's cause.

Holland

Ease of access to abortion in Holland has for many years been a matter of quiet public consensus, but with an undercover visit to an abortion clinic by an actress posing as a woman seeking an abortion, controversy reared its head.

The woman, who secretly filmed her experience, paid her visit on behalf of an evangelical Christian TV company, EO. The actress took her cue from the infamous case that the British pro-life movement had so exploited: she pretended that her pregnancy would inconvenience her plans for a skiing holiday. When the film was shown, it demonstrated exactly what the framework of Dutch abortion allows: for women themselves to decide whether or not their circumstances are such that they need to end a pregnancy.

The clinics took the TV company to court and judgment was resoundingly in their favor. The judge declared that the filming had been a violation of privacy, of the staff and more importantly of other patients who had been filmed secretly in the waiting rooms. Nevertheless, the broadcast prompted the minister of health to order an inquiry into the clinics' observance of the law.

The inspectors vindicated the clinics, but recommended a handful of minor changes in the way they kept their records. In future, for example, it will be possible to check how many women attended clinics seeking abortion but then changed their minds and did not actually undergo the operation.[13]

Despite this clear attempt by the Dutch anti-abortion movement to undermine positive attitudes to women's self-determination on the question of abortion, it seems that the Dutch public remains solidly positive, and the clinics are confident that with this support they can continue to provide a service that allows women to decide what is best for them.

Britain

With a general election in May 1997, it was inevitable that the attempt would be made to make abortion law an issue. In the months leading up to the election it seemed that fate had stepped in to hand the anti-abortion campaigners a bouquet of choice cases, which they could present to the British public as evidence of the abuse of abortion and of its brutality. Jack Scarisbrick, founder of the main British anti-abortion pressure group, Life, was described as "over the moon" at the public exposure of the 'barbarous' level that some doctors had reached.

It all began with news made public in August 1996 by gynecologist and professor Philip Bennett that one of his patients, whom he said was a single mother in "straitened circumstances" and pregnant with twins, was contemplating abortion of one of the sixteen-week-old fetuses. This released a storm of publicity in the British media. The tone was both judgmental and sentimental, but an elated Jack Scarisbrick greeted the row as a "defining moment" for his campaign. The anti-abortion lobby even pledged to give the woman £80,000 to change her mind. This promise of support was accompanied by equally persuasive menaces—attempts to get a High Court injunction preventing her from "doing away with her baby."

The whole affair took a new twist when Queen Charlotte's Hospital revealed in court that there could be no injunction because the woman had in fact already had the abortion a month before the public outcry. This bombshell was followed by the revelation that poverty was not at all the woman's problem; she was a well-off, married woman unable however to cope with the prospect of twins.

While pro-choice voices called for disciplinary action against Bennett for his breach of his patient's privacy and confidentiality, many were troubled by the medical ethics of such "selective abortion." But liberal opinion was summed up by Sir David Steel MP, architect of the 1967 abortion reform: "The anti-abortion organisations . . . are simply using the worrying case of the aborted twin to have another bash at the 1967 Abortion Act . . . It is quite intolerable that outside bodies should go to the courts and say 'We who know nothing about the case and know nothing about the mental state of this woman and her circumstances can second guess the doctors who know all the background.' "[14]

More was to come. The British media spotlight moved almost at once onto another fraught case: a 31-year-old woman pregnant with eight fetuses after taking fertility drugs. She was told that if she agreed to undergo early selective abortion of six fetuses, she might just stand a chance of delivering twins. But despite medical advice that she was risking her own life as well as that of her babies, Mandy Allwood announced that she was going to continue with her multiple pregnancy.

This time it was the patient herself who sought publicity, even hiring one of Britain's best-known publicity agents to handle the case. The agent at once declared that the more children Allwood produced alive the more money she would make in sponsorship deals—a kind of sliding price scale for fetuses.

In the face of this spectacle the anti-abortion lobby was calling for nature to take its course, despite the fact that this option threatened not only the woman's life, but the entire pregnancy. Allwood's boyfriend was quick to stoke the embers of the earlier "which twin?" row in his denunciation of selective abortion: "Which one would you choose first? It's too horrible to contemplate," he told the press.[15]

At nineteen weeks of pregnancy, the tragedy played itself out: "the loss of the fetuses was inevitable," said Allwood's doctors. The papers printed eight sonograms with the headline quote from Allwood: "I couldn't choose which to murder."[16]

Of course, selective abortion of multiple pregnancies does raise complex and sensitive ethical and psychological issues, but the stunt politics, which British gynecologist Wendy Savage condemned as "auctioning an unborn child," contributes nothing to the humane and rational discussion. However, with an election only months away, the question of abortion was firmly back in the headlines.

In the spring of 1997, Cardinal Thomas Winning, head of Scotland's Roman Catholic Church, made a fresh attack on "gynecological abbattoirs" and promised financial support from the church to women with unwanted pregnancies, in an effort to dissuade them from abortion. He had earlier attacked the leader of the Labour Party, Tony Blair, accusing him of washing his hands of the moral issue, and had even suggested that Scotland's 800,000

Catholics should consider their voting stance in the general election solely on the basis of candidates' stance on abortion.

In an effort to make abortion an election issue, anti-abortion campaigners fielded fifty candidates, in constituencies all over Britain, especially targeting districts where the main parties were in a close fight and their candidates were known to have liberal views on the question. "This nation is in denial about abortion," said a spokesman for the Pro-Life Alliance, announcing that in a TV election broadcast, the Alliance would be showing footage of a late abortion.

The anti-abortion "party manifesto" promised to outlaw all abortion, even after rape, except where the woman's life was at risk. It also opposed *in vitro* fertilization treatment, embryo research and euthanasia.

The fifty-candidates ploy was a gamble, clearly designed to swing the vote against pro-choice candidates in what was expected to be a photo-finish election. Not all anti-abortion supporters backed the tactic. One Roman Catholic politician said, "This has been tried time and time again. You get a derisory number of votes . . . and hand a weapon to your opponents who can say that only 500 people in the constituency are concerned about it [abortion]."[17]

Prophetic words: on 1 May 1997, at the general election, no anti-abortion candidates received more than 5 percent of the vote. In most places they did not achieve even 1 percent. They had achieved nothing like the publicity they hoped for, even when the public broadcasting companies refused to screen their election broadcast on the grounds that it contravened standards of public taste and decency to which they are bound to adhere. The film was part of the American film *Hard Truth,* showing the remains of aborted fetuses, which are claimed to have been found in the rubbish dump of a private clinic in Texas.

Of course, replied the Pro-Life Alliance in response to the broadcasting ban, "If this film is so horrific that we are not allowed to watch it, why on earth is . . . [abortion]. going on in this country 500 times in every single day?" If anyone required proof of the anti-abortion strategy of trying to mislead people into confusing late term abortion with all abortion, this dissimulating protestation surely was it.

Evidence of the concern women have about contraceptive safety and the importance of access to abortion as a back-up for contraceptive failure was clearly shown after a scare in October 1995 about the possible risks of thrombosis linked to certain brands of contraceptive pill (see Chapter 9, p. 175). In the year following the scare, abortions in Britain rose by a dramatic 14.5 percent. No conclusive proof could be given for blaming the Pill scare, but there is no other convincing explanation.[18]

Australia

The important legal case *CES v. Superclinics NSW* in which a woman claimed damages against abortion-clinic doctors who failed to diagnose her pregnancy, exposed the fact that legal access to abortion in some states of Australia was really quite ephemeral (see pp. 182–86). It was based on court rulings and not on laws debated and decided in parliaments. The woman's case—that she was forced into a pregnancy she had not wanted—was to be heard in the Australian High Court, but was settled out of court in 1996. Before news of the settlement came, however, it was clear that the stakes were seen as extremely high by at least some of those with an interest in the outcome. It became known that the Catholic-run private hospitals and the Roman Catholic bishops had filed a "friends of the court" application, seeking to address the court. This surprise move was hastily met with a counter application by the Abortion Providers Federation of Australia, and the stage was set for a clash of some significance.

Australian politicians breathed sighs of relief at news of the out-of-court settlement, which effectively kept abortion at bay as a political issue. It does not, however, resolve the muddle at the heart of the issue for abortion in Australia.

Word has meanwhile reached abortion rights activists in Australia that a similar case may be about to begin its protracted way through the legal system.[19]

South Africa

One of the world's most liberal abortion laws has been passed in South Africa. Under the former apartheid regime, abortion was very restricted and effectively discriminatory; access to safe, legal abortions was almost exclusively the preserve of white women. Estimates of backstreet abortion were around 400,000 a year, with as many as 45,000 women needing expensive hospital treatment for complications arising from unsafe abortion.

The law was not passed without strenuous protest from the Catholic Church. But with explicit personal support from President Nelson Mandela, the African National Congress Party made voting support for the Choice on Termination of Pregnancy Act a party matter, and it was passed in October 1996.

It allows termination of pregnancy, on demand, up to twelve weeks, and in certain circumstances with a doctor's consent, up to twenty weeks. Doctors unwilling to perform the operation are required by law to refer the patient to another doctor or risk a jail sentence of up to ten years. One especially interesting aspect of the reform is that in the first twelve weeks, specially trained midwives will be allowed to perform abortions as well as doctors. This is a completely new development and will be worth watching.

Commenting on the success of the reform, Dr. Abe Nkomo, a leading health campaigner in the African national Congress, commented (Dyer 1996):

The Choice on Termination of Pregnancy Bill replaces discrimination and death with equality and accessibility. Most importantly, it recognizes the right of every South African woman to make her own choices about her own body. It is a historic milestone on the road to women's emancipation. As a new law, based on tolerance, human kindness and alleviation of misery comes into being, let us for once rejoice—we are making progress.

Notes

1 *The United States*

1. For more on the effect of curbing access to abortion in the United States see Chapter 3; and for more on how it was done, see Chapter 9.

2. The *Roe* principle of the privacy of the abortion decision was also emerging as a poisoned chalice: if it's a private decision, why should the government pay for it? argued Hyde and his allies. Philosopher and jurisprudent Ronald Dworkin points out that deciding to continue a pregnancy is as much a private decision as deciding to have an abortion and it is illogical for the state to fund care for a woman who chooses one course of action in response to her pregnancy and not another (Dworkin 1993, p. 247).

3. This critique is not original, it is a summary of Rosalind Petchesky's convincing and far lengthier analysis in Petchesky 1984, pp. 249–52.

4. In an Iowa state election in 1978, a post-election survey showed that the successful Republican gained 25,000 votes solely due to his anti-abortion stance. With a meager turnout of 17 per cent, these votes were decisive (McKeegan 1992, p. 11).

5. Court judgments feature large in U.S. politics and the making of law. It was a decidedly liberal Supreme Court in 1973 which ruled on *Roe v. Wade*. By 1989, Republican presidents Reagan and Bush had seen to it, by their appointments to the nine-judge court, that liberals who retired were replaced with justices hostile to abortion (and to social reform in general). Anyone who could count up to nine could see that *Roe v. Wade* was very vulnerable (Tribe 1992).

6. Within minutes of the judgment each side appeared on television to denounce the outcome and attribute victory to their opponents, mindful no doubt of events after *Webster*. The verdict caused immense confusion. Opinion polls showed that the public, muddled and ambivalent as ever, believed the ruling meant that *Roe* was safe, and abortion rights home and dry. Yet in the wake of Casey the Supreme Court refused to hear a challenge to a Mississippi law which imposed a twenty-four hour waiting period between first see-

ing a doctor and the actual operation—a massive hurdle for poor women in a largely rural state (see Chapter 3)—and required women to be counselled with a scripted anti-abortion diatribe on fetal development as a condition of giving "informed consent."

7. For more on RU 486, see Chapter 7; for more on the "Mexico City policy," see Chapter 9 ("Clinton Moves with Speed to Reverse Bush Policies," *Wall Street Journal*, 25 January 1993).

8. Gingrich also proposed to remove all federal funding from clinics which provided subsidized contraception, cancer-screening facilities and treatment of sexually transmitted diseases to women on the breadline (*Daily Telegraph*, 24 February 1995).

9. *Front Lines Research* (1994) 1:3.

10. *Wall Street Journal*, 8 March 1996.

11. "In 1993 alone more than a hundred abortion bills were passed, introducing restrictions including mandatory waiting periods, pro-life biased counselling and parental consent requirements" ("US Anti-choice Groups Lose Ground," *IPPF Open File*, June 1994).

12. *1994 Clinic Violence Survey Report*, reported in *Reproductive Health Matters*, 6, Nobember 1995, pp. 164–65.

2 *Ireland and Germany*

1. Officially, around 4,000 women giving addresses in the Republic of Ireland obtain abortions in clinics in England and Wales, and that has been a steady figure for around five years. The real figure is doubtless far higher—some estimates put it as high as 15,000. See Chapter 3 for more on women's journeys in search of abortions.

2. Holden (1994) recounts in detail her terrifying experience and its effect on Ireland's abortion politics.

3. O'Reilly (1992). Emily O'Reilly charts the machinations of the Pro-Life Amendment Campaign and the organizations behind it, such as Opus Dei, the Knights of St. Columbanus and other fundamentalist bodies. These groups were well financed, well connected in Irish legal and medical circles, and with apparently unlimited access to Ireland's politicians. They were often supported by anti-abortion organizations in the United States, such as Father Paul Marx's Human Life International.

4. This condemnation came from none other than Peter Sutherland, the attorney-general of the very government which drafted the article (Solomons 1992).

5. The rape case itself did not come to trial until the summer of 1994, and ended with a plea of guilty and an admission that for more than two years the rapist had tried to pin the blame on the girl's young neighbor. The rapist was sentenced to fourteen years in prison but a year later this was reduced on appeal to four years. He could be released by 1997, with remission (Holden 1994, pp. 251–78).

6. "An Irish solution to an Irish problem" was how the then health minister for Ireland, Charles Haughey, described the government's proposed legislation on contraception, when he announced it in Parliament in 1978. The eventual 1979 Family Planning Act said contraceptives, including condoms, could be sold by chemists on prescription from GPs provided they were for "*bona fide* family planning purposes only." The law was con-

demned by the "divinely appointed guardians of morals," the Catholic hierarchy and the Church-inspired fundamentalists, and its eventual passage provoked them to campaign for the constitutional amendment on abortion, in order to "secure the sluice gates of every kind of immorality with the ultimate result of abortion" (O'Reilly 1992, p. 51).

7. There had been some dramatic landmarks in German abortion history, which made it an especially emotive political issue. The short-lived Weimar Republic of the 1920s had somewhat relaxed Bismarck's abortion laws, but when Hitler came to power, he proscribed abortion to all except "non-Aryans," who were encouraged to have abortions, and often brutally sterilized, in the name of "racial hygiene" (Mushaben 1993).

8. The 1972 East German abortion law stated that "the equality of women in education and vocation, in marriage and family, makes it necessary to leave it to the discretion of the women themselves to decide whether and when to have a child . . . women have the right to decide on their own responsibility on the number and timing of their children and shall be able to decide upon this through a termination of pregnancy" (Einhorn 1992).

9. Clements 1994. See Chapter 10 for more about the Memmingen trial.

10. The continuing legal uncertainty guarantees that German women will not have access to RU 486, the so-called abortion pill, because the drug's (German) manufacturer, Hoechst, has stipulated that a watertight abortion law and a public which manifestly tolerates abortion are preconditions to it marketing the drug in any given country. See Chapter 7 for more on RU 486.

3 *The Specter of the Backstreets*

1. In 1803 Parliament passed Lord Ellenborough's Act. Lord Ellenborough was an ultra-conservative lord chief justice who created as many capital felonies as he could think of in his catch-all crime statute. Punishments for abortion before quickening included whipping or fourteen years' exile to a penal colony; for abortion after quickening, the penalty was death.

2. It was the plight of women with too many children that excited the sympathies of the Birkett Committee (report published in 1937), as well as those of the early campaigners for abortion law reform in Britain, rather than that of the younger unmarried, single woman, finding herself pregnant for the first time (Cook 1989b).

3. Judge McNaghton said in his judgment: "I think those words [that the law allows termination of pregnancy for preserving the life of the mother] ought to be construed in a reasonable sense and, if the doctor is of the opinion on reasonable grounds and with adequate knowledge of the probable consequences, that continuing the pregnancy would make the woman a physical or mental wreck, the jury are quite entitled to take the view that the doctor who, under those circumstances and in that honest belief, operates is operating for the purpose of preserving the life of the mother" (Furedi 1995, p. 100).

4. The statistics quoted in the abortion polemic often took on a reality which was quite unjustified—they assumed the power of a talisman. The disputes continue almost thirty years later.

5. Koblinsky 1993, p. 133. Global figures about maternal deaths mask gross imbalances: whilst in countries of the North—the United States and Western Europe—a woman's risk of maternal death is around one in almost 2,000, in Africa it is one in 23. The health of mothers and children in Africa is worse than anywhere else in the world.

6. Population Action International 1993. Almost every child born to a mother who died in childbirth in rural Bangladesh was dead before his or her first birthday (Chen et al. 1974).

7. "Poland's Abortion Law in Court Test," *Guardian,* 3 April 1995. The judge found no evidence of pregnancy and acquitted the doctor (*The Lancet* [1995] Vol 346, p. 1356).

8. For more on the Church's efforts to turn Poland back towards medieval clericalism, see Hadley 1994 and Kulczycki 1995.

9. Phyllis Schlafly's view was cited in a pamphlet, published by Planned Parenthood of America, 1990, quoted in Blanchard and Prewitt 1993.

10. In fact, in recent years only two in a hundred unmarried women who give birth decide that adoption is the best course for their newborn children. If there was no legal abortion and no recourse to illegal measures in the United States there would have been 15 million children born in the decade 1980–90. Around 5 million of their mothers would have been living below the official poverty line; nearly 2 million of their mothers would have been under 18 years old. Would there have been enough adopters for 15 million children? (Russo, Horn and Schwartz 1992).

4 *The Fetus Factor*

1. The Hippocratic Oath, devised in the fifth century BC, required a doctor to promise not to give a woman a pessary for an abortion.

2. Moral boundaries may not coincide with law or politics. Indeed, the history of women's reproductive freedom is in many ways a travesty of the acclaimed moral principles of western society such as respect for personal autonomy and human rights. Technological change—especially in fetal medicine and in the care of premature babies—and the miasma of politics have had much more impact on what happens to women's reproductive rights in the real world (McLean 1989a).

3. Mary Ann Warren gives a lucid summary of the moral issues (Warren, 1991). See the sidebar on the stages of moral significance.

4. The limitation of taking on such a micro-exercise is that it offers no challenge to the overarching anti-abortion premise, namely that there are in theory moments along the path of fetal development at which one can attribute moral status to the fetus and, by dint of that, deny the pregnant woman's own moral agency.

5. The 1984 Unborn Children (Protection) Bill, sponsored by Enoch Powell MP.

6. The law has been moving steadily towards offering greater protection for unborn children, both in the United States and in Britain. In 1995 the English Court of Appeal decided that a man who stabbed his 26-week-pregnant girlfriend should have been charged with murder or manslaughter. Three weeks after the assault, the mother went into labor and at birth, the child was found to have been injured. The baby's subsequent death could not be directly linked to the stabbing, but rather to the premature delivery, and the ensuing legal controversy centered on whether any offense could be com-

mitted against a child unborn at the time of the act, since the law does not recognize a "person in being" until birth has taken place. The judges emphasized that their judgements were irrelevant to lawful abortion. Strictly speaking, this may be so, but the ruling clearly strengthens the legal status of fetuses and affects the ethical climate in which fetal rights are considered (*The Times,* 25 November 1995; *The Lancet,* Vol 346, p. 1622, 16 December 1995). The Scottish Law Commission is reviewing similar issues concerning claims for damages on behalf of pregnant women injured in road accidents.

7. There is a strong link between birthweight and a father's alcohol intake in the month before conception, and also evidence that tobacco damages sperm (Cefalo and Moss 1995, p. 236). Environmental factors, such as working with heavy metals, pesticides, paints and printing inks, may also damage sperm.

8. R. Goldstein 1988. Abortions after fifteen weeks account for just 4 per cent of the United States abortions and half the women who had such operations blamed the delay on their difficulties in scraping together the fee. Less than 0.5 per cent of abortions were after 20 weeks.

9. Forceps are sometimes used to crush and dismember the fetus in order to withdraw it through the cervix, while the woman has a general anesthetic; this method requires a high degree of specialist skill and is more often practiced outside the National Health Service. The other method is to expel the fetus by hormone-induced contractions, having usually first administered a lethal injection to the fetal heart, guided by ultrasound; the woman is conscious and the "labor" can be long and hard.

10. Clarke 1989/90; in 1988 *The Times* reported the case of a twenty-one-week-old fetus, diagnosed as suffering from a serious and rare birth defect, Ehlers-Danlos syndrome, delivered live in Carlisle's City General Hospital in July 1987 (*The Times,* 16 December 1988).

11. In Sweden and Denmark, both countries with liberal attitudes to late abortion, special care for babies with disabilities is exemplary.

5 *From Mortal Combat to Feminist Morality*

1. Women campaigning to prevent the virtual outlawing of abortion in Poland (see Chapter 3) said that defining abortion as a matter of women's rights seemed vulgar and selfish in Poland: access to abortion was better defended on social and economic grounds (Kulczycki 1995).

2. West 1990. Susan Faludi observes that the anti-abortion activists' handbook, *Abortion: Questions and Answers,* urges followers to borrow the feminist "right to our bodies" credo and apply it instead to aborted female fetuses: "the baby has to have a choice," they chant (Faludi 1992, p. 443).

3. What made women seeking abortions angry, according to a large Australian survey of their views, was being told that their reasons for needing an abortion were not good enough, being made to feel guilty for being pregnant, being made to feel they should be grieving when they felt simple relief, and feeling demeaned by the insistence that they should be counselled. If counselling is not required as a prelude to motherhood, why is it compulsory for an abortion? they asked (Ripper 1994).

6   A Woman's Right to Refuse

1. Chinese efforts have been almost exclusively directed at controlling women's fertility. Male resistance to contraception and to sterilization in particular has always been exceptionally forceful in China (and it is men who dominate the policy-making).

2. One careful study of attitudes and behavior resulting from the one-child policy has shown that while people favor sons, daughters are in fact also valued, and parents look to them for emotional support in old age, if not for financial security (Greenhalgh and Li 1993).

3. A team of researchers at the University of Adelaide, South Australia, reports that it has demonstrated that the London Gender Clinic techniques do not effectively separate male and female producing sperm (Vines 1994).

4. ITV, "Your Baby or Your Job," *World in Action,* 28 March 1994; *Independent,* 9 April 1994; *Guardian,* 7 June 1994, 19 October 1994, 24 December 1994, 14 February 1996.

5. "Abortions Test Case for Army," *Guardian,* 28 March 1994.

6. "£100,000 for Mother-to-be Fired by MoD," *Daily Telegraph,* 9 February 1995.

7. In Britain in 1990 the teenage pregnancy rate was 69 per 1,000 pregnancies; in Holland the comparable figure was 9 (Belleman 1993).

8. In 1995 a major piece of research into the cost-effectiveness of contraception calculated that every £1 spent on contraception "saves" roughly £11 in public spending on health and welfare services. Existing use of the National Health Service (NHS) family planning services prevents nearly 4 million unplanned pregnancies every year. It also estimated the average cost of an abortion to the NHS was £300, as opposed to the £1,000 price tag of a normal birth, and argued strongly that public money spent on contraception was a prudent investment, on social and economic grounds (McGuire and Hughes 1995).

9. Lader 1966, p. 156. Lader's scaremongering appeal to his implicitly white, middle-class readers is blatantly racist. He invites support for legal abortion as a means to tackle "the grim relationship between unwanted children and the violent rebellion of violent minority groups." More recently, a report published by the American College of Obstetricians and Gynecologists, full of debating tips for doctors wanting to defend public health spending on abortion, argues: "Children born to and raised by women who are refused abortion are often physically and mentally impaired, and have a high incidence of psychological disorder, delinquency, criminal behaviour and alcoholism. They are more likely to depend on public assistance" (Moore 1990, p. 12).

10. It happens in Australia too. "Many young Aboriginal women in the Northern Territory are being pushed into having an abortion by social workers and being sent from remote areas for an abortion which is often not what the young woman wants" (Kirkby 1994a).

7   New Controversies

1. Many business analysts point out that it would be impossible to make a boycott really bite, but Hoechst is unconvinced and the threats persist (*Wall Street Journal Europe,* 9 July 1994).

2. In certain circumstances women between thirteen and twenty weeks pregnant in Britain are now able to opt for medial abortion, using RU 486, or mifegyne as it is called in Britain (*Mifegyne Patient Information Leaflet,* Hoechst Marion Roussel, July 1995).

3. In both France and Britain, women requesting RU 486 are screened and no one who smokes or who is over 35 may be prescribed it. Likewise women with diabetes, liver or kidney problems, asthma or hypertension are refused this option (Holt 1992).

4. Hoechst Marion Roussel, personal communication 1996.

5. (1993) "Round Table on RU 486," *Women's Health Journal,* 2/93.

6. "Nun Wants Abortion Legalised in Brazil," *British Medical Journal,* 307 (1993), 8 December p. 1443.

7. Newburn 1993, p. 10. I am grateful to the National Childbirth Trust for their help with the summary of prenatal screening.

8. In 1976, a doctor in the United States observed, "American opinion is rapidly moving towards the position where parents who have an abnormal child may be considered irresponsible." This remark, by Dr. James Sorenson, associate professor of medical sciences at Boston University, was made in 1976, when prenatal testing had barely got into its stride, and the pressure on the welfare system had not yet brought it to the brink of breakdown. It is quoted in former U.S. president Ronald Reagan's book setting out his case against abortion and euthanasia (Reagan 1984).

9. "The choices surrounding prenatal diagnosis are a parent's nightmare," says social anthropologist Rayna Rapp in her restrained and heartrending account of her personal experience of a "bad result," and a decision to end a much wanted pregnancy at twenty weeks. "In a society where the state provides virtually no decent humane services for the mentally retarded, how could we take responsibility for the future of our dependent Down's Syndrome child?" (Rapp 1984).

10. The anti-abortion campaigners have not shied from making use of the explosion of genetic knowledge. Much pro-life literature has replaced its references to religion (oppose abortion because the fetus is an innocent soul) by setting fetal personhood in a biogenetic setting. "The unborn baby is a separate, unique individual. These are scientific facts. Deny them and you are flying in the face of modern genetics" (from a LIFE pamphlet, *Abortion and Human Rights,* quoted in Franklin 1991).

11. Rothman 1984, p. 30. Rothman's later book, *The Tentative Pregnancy* (Rothman 1988), shows dramatically how the amniocentesis procedure is altering how women feel about the experience of pregnancy.

12. Berer with Ray, 1993, Chapter 6. This is the only document that I have come across which deals with HIV/AIDS and abortion in any depth, and the account which follows owes a considerable debt to it. I am also grateful to Hope Massiah of Positively Women for her contribution to this section.

13. There is "a growing body of evidence that pregnancy has no discernible effect on the early progression of HIV disease in asymptomatic women," and "infection does not influence perinatal outcome" (Alger et al. 1993).

14. "Abortion and HIV-positive Women in Sub-Saharan Africa," *Reproductive Health Matters,* 2 (1993), p. 130.

15. "Abortion and HIV-positive Women in Sub-Saharan Africa."

8 *Contrasting Scenes*

1. Each year the countries of the former Soviet Union account for roughly 6.5 million legal abortions, a staggering proportion of the global total.
2. BBC "Russian Wonderland," 22 March 1995.
3. Author's interview with Dr. Inna Alesina, of the Russian Family Planning Association, London, 1995.
4. *IPPF Open File,* November 1995.
5. Direct action against the Dutch clinics is now confined to an annual demonstration, at which campaigners place little crosses on the ground. Picketing of clinics and harassment of patients has been stopped by an injunction, sought originally by the police, which prevents demonstrators coming within 200 meters of a clinic during working hours. The penalty is a hefty fine.
6. Before 1984, abortions were just as accessible in Holland, but the legal situation was in limbo.
7. For safer sex the Dutch message is "double Dutch": condom plus Pill.
8. Rosalind Petchesky points out that interpreting "maternal duty" in terms of a consumerist model of childbearing—children have a right to a certain standard of living, educational opportunities, and so on—is a powerful factor in abortion morality and cultural perceptions of contraception. "Today, not only most family planners but many ordinary people agree with John Stuart Mill's dictum 'that to bring a child into existence without a fair prospect of being able, not only to provide for its body, but instruction and training for its mind, is a moral crime, both against the unfortunate offspring and against society' " (Petchesky 1984, p. 371).
9. In 1979, a Royal Commission on the National Health Service noted that the two main areas of healthcare in which private services predominated, were abortion and nursing homes.
10. Professor McLaren was also one of the founding members of the Society for the Protection of the Unborn Child (SPUC), the organization which opposed the 1967 Act (Munday 1994).
11. It is impossible to quantify the cuts fully because the Department of Health stopped collecting statistics on family planning clinics.
12. There is now clear evidence that young people given high quality sex education in British schools start their sex lives later and are more responsible about contraception. (Mellanby, A. R., et al. (1995) "School Sex-education: An Experimental Programme with Education and Medical Staff," *British Medical Journal,* 311, pp. 414–17.)

9 *Weapons of War*

1. The accepted medical definition of pregnancy is the state of carrying an embryo or fetus which begins when the embryo, having travelled along the Fallopian tube, *becomes implanted in the lining of the uterus.* This generally takes place five to ten days after fertilization and many embryos (perhaps 40 per cent) fail to become implanted and are lost by menstrual discharge. A rise in certain hormones in the blood may be detectable before that stage, but if an embryo is not in the uterus, there cannot be, in current legal definitions, an abortion (Cook 1985).

2. Islamic religious texts are ambiguous on the morality of abortion and there is no hierarchy of interpretation in Islam—no supreme authority (Obermeyer 1994).

The Roman Catholic Church hierarchy comes down hard on its dissenters. In 1974, Bishop Medeiros of Boston condemned as an unfit mother a woman who had spoken at a public rally and declared herself "pro-choice." He forbade the baptism of her baby and when a Jesuit priest baptized the child on the steps of the church, he expelled the priest from the Jesuits. In 1984, an advertisement in the *New York Times* supporting Democratic (and Roman Catholic) vice-presidential candidate Geraldine Ferraro's pro-choice stance on abortion was printed with ninety-seven signatures, including the names of twenty-four nuns. The Vatican demanded that the Catholic signers retract or face dismissal from their congregation. The case of the "Vatican 24" alerted the U.S. media to the fact that Catholics did not unanimously oppose abortion. See also the dissent of Sister Ivone Gebara in Brazil, (Chapter 7).

3. The court decided that a challenge to Missouri's anti-abortion legislation, *Webster v. Reproductive Health Services,* was invalid. They did not overturn *Roe,* but they ruled that states could regulate abortion to the point where the rules imposed an "undue burden," on the pregnant women. As one dissenting judge observed, the Court, "with winks and nods and knowing glances," invited states to enact restrictions on abortion (Brodie 1994, p. 137).

4. Abortion is the only medical procedure where a conscience clause is permitted. Its existence legitimates the view that abortion is uniquely distasteful.

5. A U.S. constitutional amendment giving the fetus full legal rights from the moment of conception, never made it in the early 1980s.

6. The FBI defines terrorism as "the unlawful use of force or violence against persons or property to intimidate or coerce the government, civilian population or any segment thereof in pursuance of political or social objectives" (Radford and Shaw 1993, p. 145).

7. In 1993, Rescue America even sent its leader, Don Treshman, to Britain, to "defend the rights of British children." He told the press that there was no difference between running an abortion clinic and a concentration camp and was deported, because the home secretary, Kenneth Clarke, considered his presence in Britain was "not conducive to the public good." Treshman said that the "blood of mangled British babies" was on [Mr. Clarke's] hands."

8. "Pope Denounces Abortion and Euthanasia as 'Culture of Death'," *Guardian,* 31 March 1995.

9. *British Medical Journal,* 301 (1995), pp. 1025–6. 22 April.

10. So says Bill Price of United Texans for Life, quoted in *Family Planning World,* November/December (1993), p. 13.

11. Women Living Under Muslim Laws, a network founded in 1984 in response to the persecution in various countries of women who questioned the application of Islamic law to women, registered their deep concern at the growth of fundamentalism, which regards women as "community or national property needing pious male protection from unholy outsiders or infectious 'devious new ideas' in a fast changing world." They also challenged the feasibility of an individualized reproductive rights perspective for women living in communities where their wider human rights are ignored in the name of "Islamic" family codes (Women Living Under Muslim Laws 1994).

12. The opportunities and dangers for women world-wide in the light of the politics of Cairo are analyzed in Hartmann 1994, p. 47; Hartmann 1995, pp. 205–6; Smyth

1995; and Richter and Keysers 1994. There were also critics, including women's health advocates, regretting the fact that the conference was hijacked by the Vatican and forced into close combat on such a narrow range of topics. What happened to the *development* in International Conference on Population and Development? they asked. And the environmental lobby felt even more excluded: "The future of the planet barely got a mention at Cairo," reported *New Scientist* on 17 September, adding disparagingly that "the impact of more people on the environment and economic development was *eclipsed by arguments over women's rights*" (my emphasis).

13. *Newsletter of the International Conference on Population and Development,* No. 19 (1994).

14. In 1916 C. V. Drysdale of the Malthusian League expressed the hope that "the greatest care will be taken to avoid any confusion between the results of prevention of conception on the one hand and of abortion or attempted abortion on the other, as the whole subject has been seriously obscured by such confusion" (Brookes 1988).

15. Requena 1970. Avoiding pregnancy and childbirth sets in chain a complex series of factors affecting the abortion rates. To give just one example, young sexually active women, at the most fertile stage of their lives, tend to become fertile more quickly after abortion than after childbirth, putting them at risk much sooner of a repeat contraceptive failure (Greenwood and Young 1976).

16. "The safest approach to fertility control is to use the condom and to back it up by abortion in case of method failure" (Ory 1983, p. 62).

17. In the months that followed a 10 per cent increase in the abortion rate at Britain's largest independent abortion provider, British Pregnancy Advisory Service, showed that many women had stopped taking their pills and risked unplanned pregnancy (British Pregnancy Advisory Service, 1996).

18. The Indian government minister responsible for the family planning program of the 1970s, and the excesses of the sterilization camps, was unusually outspoken about abortion. He complained of the illogicality of "motivating" Indian women to want small families and then denying them abortion when contraception failed (Chandrasekhar 1974).

10   *The Pitfalls of the Law*

1. In 1983, sixty people—doctors, clinic staff, patients and patients' partners—were arraigned in a Ghent court, but were acquitted amid huge protests (Donnay et al. 1993).

2. Author's interview with Dr. Willem Boissevain and Dr. Paul Bekkering, Arnhem, Holland, April 1994.

3. There are a number of ways in which medical control can be justified. Hern states, "a woman seeking an abortion is making a circumstantial self-definition of pregnancy as an illness for which she considers the appropriate treatment to be an abortion." He points out that "in Western culture pregnancy has traditionally been defined as normal and the desire to terminate a pregnancy as pathologic," which is why in many abortion policies, "a woman who wants an abortion must need to have her head examined" (Hern 1984, p. 9).

4. In Holland abortions are not funded from the general health budget, but by a special fund for Exceptional Medical Expenses, and there are critics who point out that this

would make abortion funding potentially vulnerable if there was a change of public and political attitudes towards abortion (Stimezo 1992).

5. *Newsletter for Abortion Rights Network of Australia,* 2:1 (1994).

6. Ketting points out that many laws liberalizing abortion are couched in anti-abortion rhetoric, citing the French law, which allows abortion on request up to twelve weeks for a woman in "a situation of distress," but states that the law "guarantees the respect of every human being from the commencement of life," and warns that abortion must not constitute a means of birth control (Ketting and Praag 1986).

7. In 1988 Canada's Supreme Court struck down the previous abortion law as unconstitutional (and in doing so decriminalized abortion), and ordered the government to devise a new law. Attempts to do so have failed and women's access to abortion depends on where they live (Brodie, Gavigan and Jenson 1992).

8. "Major Gives Reassurance on Abortion": British prime minister John Major told an all-party group of MPs from the province that there would be no change to the abortion laws: the MPs feared that abortion would be *liberalized* (*Irish Times,* 25 February 1995).

9. In June 1995 a MORI poll found that two thirds of adults in Britain agree or strongly agree that a woman should have abortion on request, provided she has discussed it with her doctor and though carefully about it (*Abortion Review,* no. 57, Summer 1995).

10. Author's interview with Evert Ketting, Utrecht, April 1994.

11. In Mexico, despite tireless campaigning by women's groups and health organizations which have left politicians in no doubt about the grave public health consequences of illegal abortion, and conservative concern about population growth, successive governments have refused to support any liberalization of abortion (Elu 1993).

12. "Support Women's Access to Safe and Legal Abortion in Croatia," leaflet from Women's Global Network for Reproductive Rights, March 1996.

11 *Reclaiming a Feminist Issue*

1. The only exception to this is the decision to have an abortion after a diagnosis of fetal abnormality, or when a wanted pregnancy becomes compromised by illness or injury which is life-threatening to the woman.

2. There are some striking exceptions, of course, for when women are HIV-positive or when fetuses are found to be abnormal (or in some cases female), it is women who *decline* to have abortions whom society condemns as selfish. "Be sensible," these women are told, usually by the medical profession or social workers, both professions heavily infused with the ideology of maternal responsibility.

3. What's more, across the Third World, the energies of the agencies dedicated to controlling global population growth were translating into increasingly aggressive methods of hormonal contraception, which could not be reversed at will by women who used them—injectables, implants and sterilization itself (Hartmann 1987).

4. "For women feelings about abortion would seem to be inseparable from the profound conditioning that has told us we are supposed to have babies and feel guilty for sex that bears no consequences, that we are supposed to prioritize others over ourselves whatever their ontological status or lack thereof" (Chancer 1990, p. 114).

5. Amsterdam Declaration on Abortion, Amsterdam: Stimezo, 1996.
6. Yuval-Davis 1995. Part of the problem is that it is hard even for feminists to agree exactly what the term "reproductive rights" means. In Arabic there is no equivalent, in other cultures it has connotations variously of social needs, citizenship, or "a good life." An International Reproductive Rights Research Action Group has been set up to explore what "reproductive rights" means in different social conditions and cultural settings. Rosalind Petchesky, author of *Abortion and Woman's Choice* (1984), is its co-ordinator (Petchesky and Weiner 1990).

Afterword

1. *The Guardian,* 21 May 1997.
2. *New York Times,* 23 March 1997, quoted in memorandum by NARAL (National Abortion and Reproductive Rights League), 22 April 1997.
3. In Britain, the advice of the Royal College of Obstetricians and Gynaecologists is that measures should be taken to ensure that the fetus is not alive before proceeding on any abortion after twenty-one weeks (*Termination of Pregnancy for Fetal Abnormality in England and Wales and Scotland* [London: Royal College of Obstetricians and Gynaecologists, 1996]).
4. "A Bitter New Battle Over Partial-Birth Abortions." *Newsweek,* 17 March 1997.
5. "State abortion Law Tough to Enforce," *Detroit Free Press,* 15 April 1997.
6. "Abortion Foes Win 'Up Close'" *International Herald Tribune,* 20 February 1997.
7. It is worth noting, in relation to the intemperate accusations of lying which have marked the debate about late-term abortion, that no national data exist on abortions after twenty weeks. The Alan Guttmacher Institute, one of the main sources for abortion statistics, notes that data collection has become much more difficult in the face of the fear and violence engendered by clinic protests (Alan Guttmacher 1996).
8. "Abortion Could be Illegal Again in Poland After Court Rules Law is Unconstitutional," *International Herald Tribune,* 30 May 1997.
9. *British Medical Journal,* 18 January 1997.
10. "Foetus Has No Rights, Say Caesarian Case Judges," *The Guardian,* 27 March 1997.
11. *Financial Times,* 9 April 1997.
12. "Un medicament avec lequel on ne doit pas faire de l'argent" *Le Monde,* 9 April 1997.
13. Jany Rademakers, research fellow at NISSO (National Institute of Social Sexological Research), Utrecht, personal communication, April 1997.
14. *The Guardian,* 8 August 1996.
15. *The Lancet,* 348, 31 August 1996, p. 605.
16. *Daily Mirror,* 3 October 1996.
17. *The Guardian,* 30 December 1996.
18. "Abortions Up 14pc after Pill Warning" *The Guardian,* 21 February 1997.
19. Margaret Kirkby, Abortion Rights Network of Australia, personal communication, June 1997.

Glossary

abortifacient Any substance or device used to achieve an abortion.

abortion The termination of a pregnancy before the fetus is viable, that is, capable of life outside the womb. Spontaneous abortions, or miscarriages, are those which are not deliberately provoked. Induced abortions are carried out by various methods and can be legal or illegal, self-induced or performed by someone other than the woman.

amniocentesis A prenatal test for genetic abnormalities (see sidebar on prenatal tests in Chapter 7).

Cesarean section A baby who cannot be delivered vaginally for whatever reason, must be delivered by Cesarean section; an incision is made in the wall of the womb allowing the baby to be lifted out.

chorionic villus sampling A prenatal test for genetic abnormality (see sidebar on prenatal tests in Chapter 7).

curettage The traditional western method of abortion, which can be traced back 4,000 years to ancient Egypt, involves dilating the cervix—the neck of the womb—and scraping the lining of the womb with a sharp curette to remove the contents. Thus the method is referred to as D&C.

conception Not a true medical term, and should properly be called fertilization—the moment of fusion between the sperm and the egg. It is the moment at which the genetic package is assembled, but it is not possible to tell at this stage whether there will be one individual or twins.

ectopic pregnancy A pregnancy in which the embryo begins to grow elsewhere than in the womb. Usually it is in one of the Fallopian tubes and, if undiagnosed, can lead to a rupture of the tube.

embryo A fetus before it looks recognizably human, up to around ten weeks of pregnancy.

fetus The term used after about ten weeks of pregnancy, up to the point of birth.

gestation The length of the pregnancy in time. A pregnancy is dated from the first day of the last menstrual period. Thus when a pregnancy is reported to be at ten weeks, eight weeks have elapsed since fertilization.

implantation   The stage at which the embryo becomes embedded in the lining of the womb. It is especially significant in contraception/abortion law because devices such as the IUD, which work by preventing implantation, are in current medical/legal definitions not abortifacients, but contraceptives. Strictly speaking they are contragestives, as is the "morning-after" pill, which has a similar effect.

miscarriage   A spontaneous and involuntary termination of pregnancy.

neonatal   The period up to one month from birth.

pregnancy   The state of carrying an embryo or fetus which begins when the fertilized egg or embryo becomes implanted in the lining of the womb. This generally takes place five to ten days after fertilization. Before that stage, a rise in certain hormones can be detected in the blood, but many embryos fail to implant and are lost. Until the embryo has become implanted, there cannot, in current legal definitions, be an abortion.

prenatal diagnosis   Summarized in Chapter 7.

"quickening"   The moment when the pregnant woman feels fetal movement for the first time—usually between sixteen and twenty-two weeks.

trimester   The term given to each of the three stages of pregnancy; the first trimester is up to twelve weeks, the second up to twenty-four weeks, the third up to birth.

viability   A highly contentious term, used by doctors to described the stage at which a fetus, if delivered, can be capable of surviving outside the womb, with or without medical help. The current limit of viability is determined by the development of the lungs.

If You Think You Are Pregnant . . .

And you don't want to be . . . act fast.

- If your period is more than ten days late, get a pregnancy test.
- If you are pregnant, make an appointment to see your doctor or a family planning center.

You will get another test, and if you request an abortion you will be assessed to see if you meet the legal conditions. Your doctor may refer you to a local hospital, which is the point at which delays may really start.

If there is a long delay or you feel you are not getting the sympathetic help you want, you may decide to go to a private or charitable clinic.

Alan Guttmacher Institute
120 Wall St.
New York, NY 10005
212-248-1111

National Abortion and Reproductive Rights Action League
1156 15th St., N.W., Suite 700
Washington, DC 20005
202-973-3000

National Abortion Federation
1436 U St., N.W.
Washington, DC 20009
202-667-5881
Abortion Hotline
800-772-9100

Planned Parenthood® Federation of America, Inc.
810 Seventh Avenue
New York, NY 10019
212-541-7800
http://www.ppfa.org/ppfa
For an appointment with the Planned Parenthood health center nearest you,
    call 800-230-PLAN.

References

Abortion Law Reform Association (ALRA) (1995) *Model Abortion (Amendment) Bill,* London: ALRA.

Adler, N., H. David et al. (1990) "Psychological Responses after Abortion," *Science,* 248: pp. 41–44.

Adler, N., H. David et al. (1992) "Psychological Factors in Abortions: A Review," *American Psychologist,* 47: 10, pp. 1194–2104.

Aird, J. (1990) *Slaughter of the Innocents: Coercive Birth Control in China,* Washington, DC: AEI Press.

Aitken-Swan, J. (1977) *Fertility Control and the Medical Profession,* London: Croom Helm.

Alan Guttmacher Institute (1993) *Abortion in the United States: Facts in Brief,* New York: Alan Guttmacher Institute.

Alan Guttmacher Institute (1994) *Clandestine Abortion: A Latin American Reality,* New York: Alan Guttmacher Institute.

Alan Guttmacher Institute (1996) *Induced Abortion: Facts in Brief,* New York: Alan Guttmacher Institute.

Alberman, E., D. Mutton, R. Ide et al. (1995) "Down's Syndrome Births and Pregnancy Terminations in 1989 to 1993: Preliminary Findings," *British Journal of Obstetrics and Gynaecology,* 102, pp. 445–47.

Albury, R. (1994) "Speech and Silence in Abortion Debates in Australian Parliaments," in ARNA, *Abortion: Legal Right, Women's Right, Human Right: Proceedings of the First National Conference of Abortion Rights Network of Australia,* Windsor, Queensland: ARNA.

Alger, L. S., et al. (1993) "Interactions of Human Immunodeficiency Virus Infection and Pregnancy," *Obstetrics and Gynecology,* 82, pp. 787–96.

Amnesty International (1995) "Women in China: Imprisoned and Abused for Dissent," *AI Index,* ASA/17/29/95, September/October, pp. 6–8.

Anderson, C., K. Kaltenhaler et al. (eds) (1993) *The Domestic Politics of German Unification,* London: Lynne Rienner Publ. Inc.

Arditti, R., R. D. Klein and S. Minden (eds) (1984) *Test-tube Women: What Future for Motherhood?* London: Pandora.

ARNA (Abortion Rights Network of Australia) (1994) *Abortion: Legal Right, Women's Right, Human Right: Proceedings of the First National Conference of Abortion Rights Network of Australia,* Windsor, Queensland: ARNA.

Baban, A., and H. P. David (1994) *Voices of Romanian Women: Perceptions of Sexuality, Reproductive Behavior and Partner Relations during the Ceaucescu Era,* Bethesda, Md.: Transnational Family Research Institute.

Baehr, N. (1990) *Abortion without Apology,* Boston: South End Press.

Baird, D. (1994)"Medical Abortion in Britain," *British Journal of Obstetrics and Gynaecology,* 101:5, pp. 367–8.

Balakrishnan, R. (1994) "The Social Context of Sex-selection and the Politics of Abortion in India," in G. Sen and R. Snow (eds), *Power and Decision: The Social Control of Reproduction,* Boston: Harvard University Press.

Barabosa, R. M. and M. Arilha (1993) "The Brazilian Experience with Cytotec," *Studies in Family Planning,* 24:4, July–August pp. 236–40.

Bardhan, P. (1988) "Sex Disparity in Child Survival in Rural India," in Srinavasan, T. and P. Bardhan (eds), *Rural Poverty in South Asia,* New York: Columbia University Press.

Bayer, R. (1989) "The Suitability of HIV-positive Individuals for Marriage and Pregnancy," *Journal of the American Medical Association,* 261:7, 17 February, p. 993.

Bayer, R. (1994) "Screening and Treating Women and Newborns for HIV Infection: Ethical and Policy Issues," *Reproductive Health Matters,* no. 4, p. 87–92.

BBC (1995) "Russian Wonderland," 22 March.

Beard, W. and P. W. Nathanielsz (eds) (1976) *Fetal Physiology and Medicine,* London: W. B. Saunders.

Belleman, S. (1993) "Let's Talk about Sex," *Guardian,* 19 November.

Benshoof, J. (1993) "Beyond Roe, After Casey: The Present and Future of a 'Fundamental' Right," *Women's Health Issues,* 3:3, pp. 162–70.

Berer, M. (1988) "Whatever Happened to 'A Woman's Right to Choose'?" *Feminist Review,* no. 29 (Spring), pp. 24–37.

Berer, M. (1993a) "Abortion in Europe from a Woman's Perspective," in International Planned Parenthood Federation, *Progress Postponed: Abortion in Europe in the 1990s,* London: IPPF.

Berer, M. (1993b) "Overcoming Ambivalence about Abortion," *Planned Parenthood in Europe,* 22:3, pp. 2–3.

Berer, M. with S. Ray (1993) *Women and HIV/AIDS: An International Resource Book,* London: Pandora.

Bewley, S., and R. H. Ward (eds) (1994) *Ethics in Obstetrics and Gynaecology,* London: Royal College of Obstetrics and Gynaecology Press.

Birke, L., S. Himmelweit and G. Vines (1990) *Tomorrow's Child: Reproductive Technologies in the 90s,* London: Virago.

Birth Control Trust (1991) *Abortion: An Introduction,* London: Birth Control Trust.

Birth Control Trust (1994a) *Briefing: Do Late Abortions Cause Pain to the Fetus?* London: Birth Control Trust.

Birth Control Trust (1994b) *Running an Early Medical Abortion Service,* Proceedings of a conference organized by the Birth Control Trust, 22 April 1993, London: Birth Control Trust.

Blanchard, D. and T. J. Prewitt (1993) *Religious Violence and Abortion: The Gideon Project,* Gainesville: University Press of Florida.

Boa, E. and J. Wharton (eds) (1994) *Women and the 'Wende': Social and Cultural Reflections of the German Unification Process,* Amsterdam: Rodopi.

Bok, S. (1976) "Ethical Problems of Abortion," in T. Shannon (ed.), *Bioethics,* New York: Paulist Press.

Bonavoglia, A. (ed.) (1991) *The Choices We Made,* New York: Random House.

Boschmann, H. (1994) "Abortion in Cairo: Failure or Victory?" *Women's Global Network for Reproductive Rights Newsletter,* 47 (July–September) pp. 8–9.

Boylan, C. (1992) "The Hardest Labour of All," *Guardian,* 25 November.

Bradley, J., N. Sikazwe and J. Healy (1991) "Improving Abortion Care in Zambia," *Studies in Family Planning,* 22:6, pp. 391–94.

Brewer, C. (1978) "Induced Abortion after Feeling Foetal Movements: Its Causes and Emotional Consequences," *Journal of Biosocial Science,* 10:2, pp. 203–8.

Brind, J., V. M. Chinchilli, W. B. Severs *et al.* (1996) "Induced Abortion as an Independent Risk Factor for Breast Cancer: A Comprehensive Review and Meta-analysis," *Journal of Epidemiology and Community Health,* 50, pp. 481–96.

British Pregnancy Advisory Service (1996) *Outcome of Contraceptive Pill Announcement,* Solihull: British Pregnancy Advisory Service.

Brodie, J. (1994) "Health versus Rights: Comparative Perspectives on Abortion Policy in Canada and the United States," in G. Sen and R. Snow (eds), *Power and Decision: The Social Control of Reproduction,* Boston: Harvard University Press.

Brodie, J., S. Gavigan and J. Jensen (1992) *The Politics of Abortion,* Toronto: Oxford University Press.

Bromham, D. (1993a) "Are Current Sources of Contraceptive Advice Adequate to Meet Changes in Contraceptive Practice?" *British Journal of Family Planning,* no. 19, pp. 179–83.

Bromham, D. (1993b) "Knowledge and Use of Secondary Contraception among Patients Requesting Termination of Pregnancy," *British Medical Journal,* 306, pp. 556–7.

Brookes, B. (1988) *Abortion in England: 1900–1967,* London: Croom Helm.

Browne, S., A. Ludovici and H. Roberts (1935) *Abortion: A Debate,* London: George Allen and Unwin.

Browner, C. (1979) "Abortion Decision Making: Some Findings from Colombia," *Studies in Family Planning,* 10:3, pp. 96–106.

Butler, J. D., and D. F. Walbert (eds) (1992) *Abortion, Medicine and the Law,* 4th edn, New York: Facts on File.

Callahan, D. (1976) "Abortion: Some Ethical Issues," in T. Shannon (ed.), *Bioethics,* New York: Paulist Press.

Callahan, D. (1986) "How Technology Is Reframing the Abortion Debate," *Hastings Center Report,* February 16:1 pp. 33–43.

Callahan, S., and D. Callahan (eds) (1984) *Abortion: Understanding Differences,* New York: Plenum Press.

Cefalo, R., and M. Moos (1995) *Preconceptional Health Care,* St. Louis: Mosby.

Centers for Disease Control and Prevention (1995) "US Public Health Service Recommendations for Human Immunodeficiency Virus Counseling and Voluntary Testing for Pregnant Women," *Morbidity and Mortality Weekly Report,* 44:RR–7, pp. 1–14.

Cerullo, M. (1990) "Hidden History: An Illegal Abortion in 1968," in M. Fried (ed.), *From Abortion to Reproductive Freedom: Transforming a Movement,* Boston: South End Press.

Chalker, R., and C. Downer (1992) *A Woman's Book of Choices: Abortion, Menstrual Extraction and RU-486,* New York: Four Walls Eight Windows.

Chancer, L. (1990) "Abortion without Apology," in M. Fried (ed.), *From Abortion to Reproductive Freedom: Transforming a Movement,* Boston: South End Press.

Chandrasekhar, S. (1974) *Abortion in a Crowded World,* London: George Allen and Unwin.

Chen, L., et al. (1974) "Maternal Mortality in Rural Bangladesh," *Studies in Family Planning,* 5:11, pp. 334–41.

Chervenak, F. A., L. B. McCullough and S. Campbell (1995) "Is Third Trimester Abortion Justified?" *British Journal of Obstetrics and Gynaecology,* 102, pp. 434–5.

Clarke, L. (1989/90) "Abortion: A Rights Issue?" in R. Lee and D. Morgan (eds), *Birthrights: Law and Ethics at the Beginning of Life,* London: Routledge.

Clements, E. (1994) "The Abortion Debate in Unified Germany," in E. Boa and J. Wharton (eds), *Women and the 'Wende': Social and Cultural Reflections of the German Unification Process,* Amsterdam: Rodopi.

Coelho, H. (1991) "Selling Abortifacients over the Counter in Fortaleza, Brazil," *The Lancet,* 338, p. 247.

Cohen, S., and N. Taub (eds) (1989) *Reproductive Laws for the 1990s,* Clifton, NJ: Humana Press.

Coleman, K. (1988) "The Politics of Abortion in Australia: Freedom, Church and the State," *Feminist Review,* no. 29 (Spring), pp 75–95.

Conlon, R. (1994) "The Reality of Abortion for Irish Women: An Analysis of the Pregnancy Counselling Service Offered by the Irish Family Planning Association," unpublished thesis, University College, Dublin.

Conner, E. M., R. S. Sperling et al. (1994) "Reduction of Maternal-Infant Transmission of Human Immunodeficiency Virus Type 1 with Zidovudine Treatment," *New England Journal of Medicine,* 331, pp. 1173–80.

Cook, R. (1985) "Legal Abortion: Limits and Contributions to Human Life," in R. Porter and M. O'Connor (eds), *Abortion: Medical Progress and Social Implications,* Ciba Foundation Symposium 115, London: Pitman.

Cook, R. (1989a) "Abortion Laws and Policies: Challenges and Opportunities," *International Journal of Gynecology and Obstetrics,* Supplement 3, pp. 61–87.

Cook, R. (1989b) "Reducing Maternal Mortality: A Priority for Human Rights Law," in S. McLean (ed.), *Legal Issues in Human Reproduction,* Aldershot: Gower.

Cook, R., and D. Grimes (eds) (1992) "Anti-progestin Drugs: Ethical, Legal and Medical Issues," special issue of *Law, Medicine and Health Care,* 20:9 Fall.

Copelon, R. (1990) "From Privacy to Autonomy: The Conditions for Sexual and Reproductive Freedom," in M. Fried (ed.), *From Abortion to Reproductive Freedom: Transforming a Movement,* Boston, South End Press.

Corea, G., et al. (eds) (1985) *Man-made Women,* London: Hutchinson.

Correa, H. (ed.) (1993) *Unwanted Pregnancies and Public Policy,* Commack, NY: Nova Science.

Correa, S. (1994) *Population and Reproductive Rights: Feminist Perspectives from the South,* London: Zed Books and DAWN.

Correa, S., and R. Petchesky (1994) "Reproductive and Sexual Rights: A Feminist Perspective," in G. Sen, A. Germain and L. Chen (eds), *Population Policies Reconsidered: Health, Empowerment and Rights,* Boston: Harvard University Press.

Corrin, C. (ed.) (1992) *Superwomen and the Double Burden: Women's Experience of Change in Central and Eastern Europe and the Former Soviet Union,* London: Scarlet Press.

Council on Scientific Affairs, American Medical Association (1992) "Induced Termination of Pregnancy Before and After *Roe v Wade*," *Journal of the American Medical Association,* 268:22, pp. 3231–39.

Coward, R. (1994) "The Big Issue: Abortion," *Guardian,* 16 September.

Craig, B. H., and D. M. O'Brien (1993) *Abortion and American Politics,* New Jersey: Chatham House Publishers.

Croll, E., D. Davin and P. Kane (1985) *China's One-child Family Policy,* London: Macmillan.

Dagg, P.K.B. (1991) "The Psychological Sequelae of Therapeutic Abortion—Denied and Completed," *American Journal of Psychiatry,* 1481, pp. 578–85.

Daling, J., K. Malone, L. Voigt, E. White and N. Weiss (1994) "Risk of Breast Cancer among Young Women: Relationship to Induced Abortion," *Journal of the National Cancer Institute,* 86:21, pp. 1585–92.

David, H. (1992) "Abortion in Europe 1920–91: A Public Health Perspective," *Studies in Family Planning,* 23:1, pp. 1–22.

David, H., and A. Titkow (1994) "Abortion and Women's Rights in Poland," *Studies in Family Planning,* 25:4, pp. 239–42.

Davin, D. (1985) "The Single-child Family Policy in the Countryside," in E. Croll, D. Davin and P. Kane, *China's One-child Family Policy,* London: Macmillan.

Davis, A. (1990) "Racism, Birth Control and Reproductive Rights," in M. Fried (ed.), *From Abortion to Reproductive Freedom: Transforming a Movement,* Boston: South End Press.

Davis, S. (1988) *Women under Attack: Victories, Backlash and the Fight for Reproduction Freedom,* Boston: South End Press.

De Crespigny, L., with R. Dredge (1990) *Which Tests for My Unborn Baby?* Melbourne: Oxford University Press.

Department of Health (1991) *The Health of the Nation,* London: HMSO.

Dixon-Mueller, R. (1988) "Innovations in Reproductive Health Care: Menstrual Regulation Policies and Programs in Bangladesh," *Studies in Family Planning,* 19:3, pp. 129–40.

Dixon-Mueller, R. (1990) "Abortion Policy and Women's Health in Developing Countries," *International Journal of Health Services,* 20:2, pp. 297–314.

Dixon-Mueller, R. (1993) "Abortion Is a Method of Family Planning," in R. Dixon-Mueller and A. Germain, *Four Essays on Birth Control Needs and Risks,* New York: International Women's Health Coalition.

Dixon-Mueller, R., and A. Germain (1993) *Four Essays on Birth Control Needs and Risks,* New York: International Women's Health Coalition.

Donnay, F., A. Bregentzer et al. (1993) "Safe Abortions in an Illegal Context: Perceptions from Service Providers in Belgium," *Studies in Family Planning,* 24:3, pp. 150–62.

Donovan, P. (1995) *The Politics of Blame: Family Planning, Abortion and the New Poor,* New York: Alan Guttmacher Institute.

Downey, G., J. Dumit and S. Traweek (eds) (1995) *Cyborgs and Citadels: Anthropological Interventions into Techno-humanism,* SAR/University of Washington Press.

Doyal, L. (1995) *What Makes Women Sick: Gender and the Politics of Health,* London: Macmillan.

Driscoll, C. (1970) "The Abortion Problem," *Women: A Journal of Women's Liberation,* Winter.

Du Plessix-Gray, F. (1991) *Soviet Women Walking the Tightrope,* London: Virago.

Dworkin, R. (1993) *Life's Dominion,* London: HarperCollins.

Dyer, M. (1996) "A New Deal for South African Women," newsletter of Abortion Rights Action Group, Vlaeberg, South Africa, November.

Dytrych, Z., Z. Matejcek et al. (1975) "Children Born to Women Denied Abortion," *Family Planning Perspectives,* 7:4, pp. 167–71.

Einhorn, B. (1992) "Emancipated Women or Hard-working Mothers?" in C. Corrin (ed.), *Superwomen and the Double Burden: Women's Experience of Change in Central and Eastern Europe and the Former Soviet Union,* London: Scarlet Press.

Einhorn, B. (1994) "Gender Issues in Transition: The East Central European Experience," *European Journal of Developmental Research,* 6:2, pp. 119–40.

Elu, M. (1993) "Abortion Yes, Abortion No, in Mexico," *Reproductive Health Matters,* 1:1, pp. 58–66.

Faludi, S. (1992) *Backlash,* London: Vintage.

Family Planning Association (1966) *Abortion in Britain,* London: Pitman.

Farrant, W. (1985) "Who's for Amniocentesis? The Politics of Prenatal Screening," in H. Homans (ed.), *The Sexual Politics of Reproduction,* Aldershot: Gower.

Finkle, J., and B. Crane (1985) "Ideology and Politics at Mexico City: The United States at the 1984 International Conference on Population," *Population and Development Review,* 11, pp. 1–28.

Fost, N., D. Chudwin and D. Wikler (1980) "The Limited Moral Significance of 'Fetal Viability'," *Hastings Center Report,* December 10:10, pp. 10–13.

Fox, M., and J. Murphy (1992) "Irish Abortion: Seeking Refuge in a Jurisprudence of Doubt and Delegation," *Journal of Law and Society,* 19:4, pp. 454–66.

Frank, P., R. Mcnamee, P. Hannaford, C. Kay and S. Hirsch (1991) "The Effects of Induced Abortion on Subsequent Pregnancy Outcome," *British Journal of Obstetrics and Gynaecology,* 98, pp. 1015–24.

Franklin, S. (1991) "Fetal Fascinations: New Dimensions to the Medical-scientific Construction of Fetal Personhood," in S. Franklin, C. Lury and J. Stacey (eds), *Off-centre: Feminism and Cultural Studies,* London: HarperCollins Academic.

Franklin, S., C. Lury and J. Stacey (1991a) "Feminism and Abortion: Pasts, Presents and Futures," in S. Franklin, C. Lury and J. Stacey (eds), *Off-centre: Feminism and Cultural Studies,* London: HarperCollins Academic.

Franklin, S., C. Lury and J. Stacey (eds) (1991b) *Off-centre: Feminism and Cultural Studies,* London: HarperCollins Academic.

Fried, M. (1990a) "Transforming the Movement: The Post-Webster Agenda," in M. Fried (ed.), *From Abortion to Reproductive Freedom: Transforming a Movement,* Boston: South End Press.

Fried, M. (ed.) (1990b) *From Abortion to Reproductive Freedom: Transforming a Movement,* Boston: South End Press.

Fried, M. (1997) "Abortion in the U.S.: Barriers to Access," *Reproductive Health Matters,* 9, May, pp. 36–44.

Furedi, A. (ed.) (1993) *Medical Abortion Services: European Perspectives on Anti-Progestins,* Report of a conference held in Frankfurt, Germany, 5 and 6 December 1992, London: IPPF.

Furedi, A. (ed.) (1995) *The Abortion Law in Northern Ireland,* Belfast: Family Planning Association Northern Ireland.

Furedi, A., and M. Tidyman (1994) *Women's Health Guide,* London: Health Education Authority.

Gallagher, J. (1987) "Eggs, Embryos and Foetuses: Anxiety and the Law," in M. Stanworth (ed.), *Reproductive Technologies: Gender, Motherhood, and Medicine,* Cambridge: Polity Press.

Gallagher, J. (1989) "Fetus as Patient," in S. Cohen and N. Taub (eds), *Reproductive Laws for the 1990s,* Clifton, NJ: Humana Press.

Gammon, M. D., J. E. Bertin, M. B. Terry (1996) "Editorial: Abortion and the Risk of Breast Cancer: Is There a Believable Association?" *Journal of the American Medical Association,* 275:4, pp. 321–22.

Garcia, J., R. Kilpatrick et al. (eds) (1990) *The Politics of Maternity Care,* Oxford: Oxford University Press.

Germain, M., M. A. Krohn et al. (1995) "Reproductive History and the Rise of Neonatal Sepsis," *Paediatric Perinatal Epidemiology,* 9:1, pp. 48–56.

Gilchrist, A., P. Hannaford et al. (1995) "Termination of Pregnancy and Psychiatric Morbidity," *British Journal of Psychiatry,* 167: pp. 243–48.

Gilligan, C. (1982) *In a Different Voice: Psychological Theory and Women's Development,* Cambridge, Mass.: Harvard University Press.

Gissler, M., E. Hemminki and J. Lonnqvist (1996) "Suicides after Pregnancy in Finland 1987–94: Register Linkage Study," *British Medical Journal,* 313, 7 December, pp. 1431–34.

Glasier, A. (1993) "Provision of Medical Abortion in the UK—Organisation and Uptake," in A. Furedi (ed.), *Medical Abortion Services: European Perspectives on Anti-Progestins,* Report of a conference held in Frankfurt, Germany, 5 and 6 December 1992, London: IPPF.

Gold, R. B. (1984) "Ultrasound Imaging During Pregnancy," *Family Planning Perspectives,* 16:5, pp. 240–3.

Gold, R. B. (1990) *Abortion and Women's Health: A Turning Point for America?* New York: Alan Guttmacher Institute.

Goldstein, R. (1988) *Mother-love and Abortion,* Berkeley and Los Angeles: University of California Press.

Gorna, R. (1994) *Women Like Us,* London: Positively Women.

Gould, C., and M. W. Wartofsky (eds) (1976) *Women and Philosophy,* New York: Capricorn.

Gow, D. (1992) "German Row over Abortion Reform to Go to Court," *Guardian,* 27 June.

Gow, D. (1993) "Anger at German Abortion Ruling," *Guardian,* 29 May.

Grant, L. (1993) "Too Little, Too Late," *Guardian,* 5 July.

Greaves, D., M. Evans, D. Morgan et al. (1992) "Bioethics in the United Kingdom and Ireland: 1989–1991," in B. A. Lustig (ed.) *Bioethics Yearbook,* Vol. 2, Dordrecht: Kluwer Academic publishers, pp. 127–52.

Green, J. (1993) "Ethics and the Late Termination of Pregnancy," *The Lancet,* 342, p. 1179.

Green, J. (1995) "Obstetricans' Views on Prenatal Diagnosis and Termination of Pregnancy: 1980 Compared with 1993," *British Journal of Obstetrics and Gynaecology,* 102, pp. 228–32.

Green, M. (1993) "The Evolution of US International Population Policy 1965–92: A Chronological Account," *Population and Development Review,* 19, pp. 303–22.

Greenhalgh, P. (1992) "The Doctor's Right to Choose," *British Medical Journal,* 305, 8 August, p. 371.

Greenhalgh, S. (1994) "Controlling Births and Bodies in Village China," *American Ethnologist,* 21:1 pp. 3–30 (February).

Greenhalgh, S., and J. Li (1993) *Engendering Reproductive Practice in Peasant China: The Political Roots of the Rising Sex Ratios at Birth,* Research Division Working Papers no. 57, New York: The Population Council.

Greenwood, V., and J. Young (1976) *Abortion in Demand,* London: Pluto Press.

Greer, G. (1993) "To Give Freely Is to Get Shafted," *Guardian,* 23 September.

Habgood, J. (1995) "The Meaning of Life—and Death," *Independent,* 20 April.

Hadley, J. (1994) "God's Bullies: Attacks on Abortion," *Feminist Review,* no. 48 (Autumn), pp. 94–113.

Hall, M. (1990) "Changes in the Law on Abortion," *British Medical Journal,* 301, 17 November pp. 1109–10.

Hall, R. (ed.) (1970) *Abortion in a Changing World,* New York: Columbia University Press.

Hartmann, B. (1987) *Reproductive Rights and Wrongs,* New York: Harper and Row.

Hartmann, B. (1994) "Consensus and Contradiction on the Road to Cairo," *Women's Global Network for Reproductive Rights Newsletter,* 47 (July–September) pp. 10–11.

Hartmann, B. (1995) "The Cairo 'Consensus': Women's Empowerment or Business as Usual?" *Geojournal,* 35:2, pp. 205–6.

Hausknecht, R. U. (1993) "Methotrexate and Misoprostol to Terminate Early Pregnancy," *New England Journal of Medicine,* 333:9, pp. 537–40.

Helsinki Citizen's Assembly Women's Commission (1992) *Reproductive Rights in East and Central Europe,* Prague: Helsinki Citizen's Assembly.

Henifin, M. S., R. Hubbard and J. Norsigian (1989) "Prenatal Screening," in S. Cohen and N. Taub (eds), *Reproductive Laws for the 1990s,* Clifton, NJ: Humana Press.

Henshaw, S. (1990) "Induced Abortion: A World Review," *Family Planning Perspectives,* 22:2, pp. 76–79.

Henshaw, S. K. (1995a) "Factors Hindering Access to Abortion Services," *Family Planning Perspectives,* 27:2, pp. 54–87.

Henshaw, S. K. (1995b) "The Impact of Requirements for Parental Consent on Minors' Abortions in Mississippi," *Family Planning Perspectives,* 27:3, pp. 120–2 (May/June).

Hern, W. (1984) *Abortion Practice,* Philadelphia: J. P. Lippincott.

Hern, W., and B. Corrigan (1980) "What about Us? Staff Reactions to D & E," *Advances in Planned Parenthood,* 15, pp. 3–8.

Hillier, S. (1988) "Women and Population Control in China," *Feminist Review,* no. 29 (Spring), pp. 101–13.

Himmelweit, S. (1988) "More than 'A Woman's Right to Choose'?" *Feminist Review,* no. 29 (Spring), pp. 38–56.

Holden, C. (1989) "Koop Finds Abortion Evidence 'Inconclusive'," *Science,* 243, pp. 730–31.

Holden, W. (1994) *Unlawful Carnal Knowledge: The True Story of the Irish 'X' Case,* London: HarperCollins.

Holmes, H. B., B. Hoskins and M. Gross (eds) (1981) *The Custom-made Child?* Clifton, NJ: Humana Press.

Holmgren, K. (1992) "Women's Evaluation of Three Early Abortion Methods," *Acta Obstetrica et Gynecologica Scandanavica,* 71:199, pp. 616–23.

Holt, R. (1992) "RU486/Prostaglandins: Considerations for Appropriate Use in Low-resource Settings," in R. Cook and D. Grimes (eds), "Anti-Progestin Drugs: Ethical, Legal and Medical Issues," in *Law, Medicine and Health Care,* Fall, 20:9, pp. 169–83.

Homans, H. (ed.) (1985) *The Sexual Politics of Reproduction,* Aldershot: Gower.

Hook, E. (1994) "Prenatal Sex Selection and Autonomous Reproductive Decision," *The Lancet,* 342, 1 January, p. 56.

Hubbard, R. (1984) "Personal Courage Is Not Enough: Some Hazards of Childbearing in the 1980's," in R. Arditti, R. D. Klein and S. Minden (eds), *Test-tube Women: What Future for Motherhood?* London: Pandora.

Hubbard, R. (1994) "The Politics of Fetal/Maternal Conflict," in G. Sen and R. Snow (eds), *Power and Decision: The Social Control of Reproduction,* Boston: Harvard University Press.

Hughes, L. (1986) "Montage of a Dream Deferred," in *Selected Poems,* London: Pluto.

Hunt, L. (1995) "Abortion Most Desperate," *Independent,* 21 March.

Hye-Jin, H. (1996) "Unwelcome Daughters—Son Preference and Abortion in South Korea," *Women's Global Network for Reproductive Rights Newsletter,* 53, January–March, pp. 16–17.

International Planned Parenthood Federation, *Progress Postponed: Abortion in Europe in the 1990s,* London: IPPF.

ITV (1994) "Your Baby or Your Job," *World in Action,* 28 March.

Jacobson, J. (1988) "Choice at Any Cost," *World-Watch,* 1:2.

Jacobson, J. (1990) *The Global Politics of Abortion,* Worldwatch Paper 97, Washington, DC: Worldwatch Institute.

Jaggar, A. (1976) "Abortion and a Woman's Right to Decide," in C. Gould and M. W. Wartofsky (eds), *Women and Philosophy,* New York: Capricorn.

"Jane," (1990) "Just Call Jane," in M. Fried (ed.), *From Abortion to Reproductive Freedom: Transforming a Movement,* Boston: South End Press.

Jankowska, H. (1993) "The Reproductive Rights Campaign in Poland," *Women's Studies International Forum,* 16:3, pp. 291–96.

Jeffreys, D. (1995) " 'Jane Roe' Has Switched Sides," *Independent,* 24 August.

Jenkins, A. (1961) *Law for the Rich: A Plea for the Reform of the Abortion Law,* London: Gollancz.

Johnsen, D. (1987) "A New Threat to the Pregnant Woman's Autonomy," *Hastings Center Report,* 17:4, pp. 33–40.

Johnsen, D. (1992) "Shared Interests: Promoting Healthy Births without Sacrificing Women's Liberty," in J. D. Butler and D. F. Walbert (eds), *Abortion, Medicine and the Law*, 4th edn, New York: Facts on File.

Johnson, A., P. Townshend, P. Yudkin, D. Bull, A-R. Wilkinson (1993) "Functional Abilities at Age Four Years of Children Born before 29 Weeks of Gestation," *British Medical Journal*, 306, 26 June, pp. 1715–18.

Johnson, K. (1993) "Chinese Orphanages: Saving China's Abandoned Girls," *Australian Journal of Chinese Affairs*, 30, pp. 61–87.

Jones, E., et al. (1986) *Teenage Pregnancy in Industrialised Countries*, New Haven: Yale University Press.

Kelly, J., et al. (1994) "The Effect of HIV/AIDS Intervention Groups for High-risk Women in Urban Clinics," *American Journal of Public Health*, 84:12, pp. 1918–22.

Kennedy, H. (1995) "Human Rights and Reproductive Choice," a speech given at a meeting held in London in memory of the Late Jo Richardson MP, 26 April 1995.

Kenny, M. (1983) "Abortion Examined: Male and Female Attitudes," *The Tablet*, 25 June.

Ketting, E. (1994) "Is the Dutch Abortion Rate Really that Low?" *Planned Parenthood in Europe*, 23:3 pp. 29–32.

Ketting, E., and P. van Praag (1986) "The Marginal Relevance of Legislation Relating to Induced Abortion," in J. Lovenduski and J. Outshoorn (eds), *The New Politics of Abortion*, London: Sage.

Ketting, E., and A. Visser (1994) "Contraception in The Netherlands: The Low Abortion Rate Explained," *Patient Education and Counselling*, 23, pp. 161–71.

Kirkby, M. (1994a) "Abortion Down Under," *Women's Health Newsletter*, no. 23 (August).

Kirkby, M. (1994b) "The Politics of 'Deserving Case' vs Women's Right: Abortion Rights Campaigning in Australia," in ARNA, *Abortion: Legal Right, Women's Right, Human Right: Proceedings of the First National Conference of the Abortion Rights Network of Australia*, Windsor, Queensland: ARNA.

Klein, R., J. Raymond and L. Dumble (1991) *RU 486—Misconceptions, Myths and Morals*, Melbourne: Spinifex Press.

Koblinsky, M. (ed.) (1993) *Health of Women: A Global Pespective*, Boulder, CO: Westview Press.

Koh, T.H.H.G. (1997) "Counselling Parents of Extremely Premature Babies," *Lancet*, 349, 25 January, p. 289.

Kommers, D. (1993) "The Basic Law under Strain: Constitutional Dilemmas and Challenges," in C. Anderson, K. Kaltenhaler et al. (eds), *The Domestic Politics of German Unification*, London: Lynne Rienner Publ. Inc.

Konner, M. (1993) *The Trouble with Medicine*, London: BBC Books.

Kozakiewicz, M. (1997) "Poland—the Struggle for 'Free Choice' Continues," *Choices*, 26: 1, pp. 18–20.

Kulczycki, A. (1995) "Abortion Policy in Postcommunist Europe: The Conflict in Poland," *Population and Development Review*, 21:3, pp. 471–505.

Lader, L. (1966) *Abortion*, Indianapolis: Bobbs-Merrill.

Lader, L. (1991) *RU486: The Pill That Could End the Abortion Wars and Why American Women Don't Have It*, Reading, MA: Addison-Wesley.

Lafleur, W. (1992) *Liquid Life: Abortion and Buddhism in Japan*, Princeton: Princeton University Press.

Lawson, A., and D. Rhode (eds) (1993) *Politics of Pregnancy: Adolescent Sexuality and Public Policy,* New Haven: Yale University Press.

Li, V., G. C. Wong et al. (1990) "Characteristics of Women Having Abortions in China," *Social Science of Medicine,* 31:4, pp. 445–53.

Liskin, L. (1980) "Complications of Abortion in Developing Countries," *Population Reports,* Series F, no. 7, Baltimore: Population Information Program, The Johns Hopkins University.

Londono, M. (1989) "Abortion Counseling: Attention to the Whole Woman," *International Journal of Gynecology and Obstetrics,* Supplement 3, pp. 169–74.

Lovenduski, J., and J. Outshoorn (eds) (1986) *The New Politics of Abortion,* London: Sage.

Luker, K. (1984) *Abortion and the Politics of Motherhood,* Berkeley and Los Angeles: University of California Press.

Lunneborg, P. (1992) *Abortion: A Positive Decision,* New York: Bergin and Garvey.

Lustig, B. A. (ed.) (1992) *Bioethics Yearbook,* Vol. 2, Dordrecht: Kluwer Academic Publishers.

McDonnell, K. (1984) *Not an Easy Choice: A Feminist Reexamines Abortion,* Toronto: Women's Press.

McGuire, A., and D. Hughes (1995) *The Economics of Family Planning Services,* Cheltenham: Contraceptive Alliance.

Macintyre, S., and S. Cunningham-Burley (1993) "Teenage Pregnancy as a Social Problem: A Perspective from the United Kingdom," in A. Lawson and D. Rhode (eds), *Politics of Pregnancy: Adolescent Sexuality and Public Policy,* New Haven: Yale University Press.

McKeegan, M. (1992) *Abortion Politics: Mutiny in the Ranks of the Right,* New York: The Free Press Maxwell Macmillan International.

Mackinnon, C. (1991) "Reflections on Sex Equality under Law," *Yale Law Journal,* 100, pp. 1281–1328.

McLean, S. (1989a) "Women, Rights and Reproduction," in S. McLean (ed.), *Legal Issues in Human Reproduction,* Aldershot: Gower.

McLean, S. (ed.) (1989b) *Legal Issues in Human Reproduction,* Aldershot: Gower.

McLean, S. (1994) "Moral Status (Who or What Counts?)," in S. Bewley and R. H. Ward (eds), *Ethics in Obstetrics and Gynaecology,* London: Royal College of Obstetrics and Gynaecology Press.

McNeill M. (1991) "Putting the Alton Bill in Context," in S. Franklin, C. Lury and J. Stacey (eds), *Off-centre: Feminism and Cultural Studies,* London: HarperCollins Academic.

Marteau, T. M., M. Plenicar and J. Kidd (1993) "Obstetricians Presenting Amniocentesis to Pregnant Women: Practice Observed," *Journal of Reproductive and Infant Psychology,* 11, pp. 3–10.

Mason, K. (1989) "Abortion and the Law," in S. McLean (ed.), *Legal Issues in Human Reproduction,* Aldershot: Gower.

Melbye, M. et al. (1997) "Induced Abortion and the Risk of Breast Cancer," *New England Journal of Medicine,* 336, pp. 81–85.

Mertus, J. (1993) *Meeting the Health Needs of Women Survivors in the Balkan Conflict,* New York: The Center for Reproductive Law and Policy.

Mihill, C. (1994) "Clinics Defend Abortion Stance," *Guardian,* 19 August.

Mintzes, B. (ed.) (1992) *Women's Perspectives on the Use and Development of Contraceptive Technologies*, Amsterdam: Women and Pharmaceuticals Group, Health Action International.

Moore, K. G. (ed.) (1990) *Public Health Policy Implications of Abortion*, Washington, DC: American College of Obstetricians and Gynecologists.

Moore, S. (1993) "Abortion: I Have, Have You?" *Guardian*, 3 September.

Mosher, S. (1994) *A Mother's Ordeal*, London: Little, Brown and Co. (UK).

Munday, D. (1994) "The Development of Abortion Services in England and Wales," in D. Paintin (ed.), *Abortion Services in England and Wales*, London: Birth Control Trust.

Mushaben, J. (1993) "Concession or Compromise: The Politics of Abortion in United Germany," paper given at the annual meeting of the American Political Science Association, September 1993.

Naamane-Guessous, S. (1993) "Traditional Methods Still Widely Used," *Planned Parenthood Challenges*, 1, pp. 14–16.

National Abortion Rights Action League (NARAL) (1992) *Facing a Future without Choice*, report of National Commission on America without Roe, New York: NARAL.

National Women's Health Network (1989) *Abortion Then and Now: Creative Responses to Restricted Access*, Washington, DC: National Women's Health Network.

Neill, R. (1994) "A Woman's Right to a Life," *The Australian*, 23–4 April.

Newburn, M. (1993) "Testing Times," *New Generation*, 12:1, March, pp. 10–11.

Newcomb, P. A., B. E. Storer, M. P. Longnecker et al. (1996) "Pregnancy Termination in Relation of Risk of Breast Cancer," *Journal of the American Medical Association*, 275:4, pp. 283–87.

Newsletter of Abortion Rights Network of Australia (1994) 2:1.

Novicka, W. (1993) "Ban on Abortion in Poland," *Women's Global Network for Reproductive Rights Newsletter*, no. 43 (April–June), p. 15.

Novicka, W. (1995) "Consequences of the Anti-abortion Law in Poland," *European Network for Women's Right to Abortion and Contraception Newsletter* (Winter) pp. 4–10.

Novicka, W. (1996a) "The Effects of the Anti-abortion Law in Force in Poland Since March 16, 1993," Report No. 2, Warsaw: Federation for Women and Family Planning.

Novicka, W. (1996b) "The Effects of the Anti-abortion Law in Poland," *Entre Nous*, no. 34/35, December, pp. 13–15.

Obermeyer, C. M. (1994) "Reproductive Choice in Islam: Family State and Women's Options," in G. Sen and R. Snow (eds), *Power and Decision: The Social Control of Reproduction*, Boston: Harvard University Press.

Office of Population Censuses and Surveys (1995) *Abortion Statistics: Legal Abortions Carried Out under the 1967 Abortion Act in England and Wales, 1992*, Series AB, no. 19, London: HMSO.

Ooms, T. (1984) "A Family Perspective on Abortion," in S. Callahan and D. Callahan (eds), *Abortion: Understanding Differences*, New York: Plenum Press.

O'Reilly, E. (1992) *Masterminds of the Right*, Dublin: Attic Press.

Ory, H. (1983) "Mortality Associated with Fertility and Fertility Control," *Family Planning Perspectives*, 15, pp. 57–62.

Outshoorn, J. (1986) "The New Politics of Abortion," in J. Lovenduski and J. Outshoorn (eds), *The New Politics of Abortion*, London: Sage.

Paintin, D. (1985) "Legal Abortion in England and Wales," in R. Porter and M. O'Connor (eds), *Abortion: Medical Progress and Social Implications*, CIBA Foundation Symposium 115, London: Pitman.

Paintin, D. (ed.) (1994) *Abortion Services in England and Wales*, London: Birth Control Trust.

Paintin, D. (1997) "Abortion after 24 Weeks," *British Journal of Obstetrics and Gynaecology*, 104, April, pp. 398–400.

Patel, V. (1989) "Sex-determination and Sex Preselection Tests in India: Modern Techniques for Femicide," *Bulletin of Concerned Asian Scholars*, 21:1, pp. 2–10.

Petchesky, R. (1984) *Abortion and Woman's Choice*, London: Longman.

Petchesky, R. (1987) "Foetal Images: The Power of Visual Culture in the Politics of Reproduction," in M. Stanworth (ed.), *Reproductive Technologies: Gender, Motherhood, and Medicine*, Cambridge: Polity Press.

Petchesky, R., and J. Weiner (1990) *Global Feminist Perspectives on Reproductive Rights and Reproductive Health*, New York: Hunter College.

Phoenix, A. (1990) "Black Women in the Maternity Services," in J. Garcia, R. Kilpatrick et al. (eds), *The Politics of Maternity Care*, Oxford: Oxford University Press.

Phoenix, A. (1991) *Young Mothers?* Cambridge: Polity Press.

Pollitt, K. (1990) "Tyranny of the Foetus," *New Statesman*, 30 March.

Pons, J., et al. (1991) "Development after Exposure to Mifepristone in Early Pregnancy," *The Lancet*, 338, 21 September, p. 763.

Popov, A. (1990) "Sky-high Abortion Rate Reflects Dire Lack of Choice," *Entre Nous*, 16, pp. 5–7.

Popov, A. (1994) "The USSR," in B. Rolston and A. Eggert (eds), *Abortion in the New Europe: A Comparative Handbook*, Westport, CT: Greenwood Press.

Population Action International (1993) *Expanding Access to Safe Abortion: Key Policy Issues*, Washington, DC: Population Action International.

Porter, R., and M. O'Connor (eds) (1985) *Abortion: Medical Progress and Social Implications*, CIBA Foundation Symposium 115, London: Pitman.

Powledge, T. (1981) "Unnatural Selection: On Choosing Children's Sex," in H. B. Holmes, B. Hoskins and M. Gross (eds), *The Custom-made Child?* Clifton, NJ: Humana Press.

Pro-Choice Alliance (1993) *Survey of Abortion Patients*, London: Pro-Choice Alliance.

Punnett, L. (1978) "Menstrual Extraction: Politics," *Quest*, 4:3, pp. 48–60.

Quindlen, A. (1994) "Holy Right and Mainly Wrong," *Guardian*, 7 July.

Rademakers, J. (1993) "Teenage Pregnancy and Contraceptive Behavior in The Netherlands," in H. Correa (ed.), *Unwanted Pregnancies and Public Policy*, Commack, NY: Nova Science.

Radford, B., and G. Shaw (1993) "Antiabortion Violence: Causes and Effects," *Women's Health Issues*, 3:3, pp. 144–51.

Rapp, R. (1984) "XYLO: A True Story," in R. Arditti, R. D. Klein and S. Minden (eds), *Test-tube Women: What Future for Motherhood?* London: Pandora.

Rapp, R. (1995) "Real-time Fetus: The Role of the Sonogram in the Age of Monitored Reproduction," in G. Downey, J. Dumit and S. Traweek (eds), *Cyborgs and Citadels: Anthropological Interventions into Techno-humanism*, SAR/University of Washington Press.

Rathus, Z. (1994) "Legal Challenges in Changing Australia's Abortion Laws," in ARNA, *Abortion: Legal Right, Women's Right, Human Right: Proceedings of the First National Conference of the Abortion Rights Network of Australia*, Windsor, Queensland: ARNA.

Reagan, R. (1984) *Abortion and the Conscience of the Nation,* Nashville, TN: Thomas Nelson.

Report of the Committee of Enquiry into Human Fertilisation and Embryology (1984) Cmnd 9314 [Warnock Report].

Requena, M. (1970) "Abortion in Latin America," in R. Hall (ed.), *Abortion in a Changing World,* New York: Columbia Press.

Rich, A. (1976) *Of Woman Born,* New York: W. W. Norton.

Rich, F. (1995) "The Far-right Bombers Aren't New to the Job," *International Herald Tribune,* 2 May.

Rich, V. (1994) "China's New Law on Maternal and Infant Health," *The Lancet,* 344, 12 November, p. 1355.

Richter, J., and L. Keysers (1994) "Towards a Common Agenda? Feminists and Population Agencies on the Road to Cairo," *Development,* 1, pp. 50–5.

Ripper, M. (1994) "Changes Needed in Abortion Service Provision: Perspectives of Women and Service Providers in Three States," in ARNA, *Abortion: Legal Right, Women's Right, Human Right: Proceedings of the First National Conference of Abortion Rights Network of Australia,* Windsor, Queensland: ARNA.

Rocha, J. (1995) "Illegal Use of Ulcer Drug in Abortions 'Causes Handicap'," *Guardian,* 3 February.

Roggencamp, V. (1984) "Abortion of a Special Kind: Male Sex Selection in India," in R. Arditti, R. D. Klein and S. Minden (eds), *Test-tube Women: What Future for Motherhood?* London: Pandora.

Rolston, B., and A. Eggert (eds) (1994) *Abortion in the New Europe: A Comparative Handbook,* Westport, CT: Greenwood Press.

Rosenfield, A. (1992) "RU 486," *American Journal of Public Health,* 82:10, pp. 1325–6.

Rosoff, J. I. (1989) " 'Hard Cases' and Reproductive Rights," in S. Cohen and N. Taub (eds), *Reproductive Laws for the 1990s,* Clifton, NJ: Humana Press.

Rothman, B. K. (1984) "The Meanings of Choice in Reproductive Technology," in R. Arditti, R. D. Klein and S. Minden (eds), *Test-tube Women: What Future for Motherhood?* London: Pandora.

Rothman, B. K., (1987) "The Abortion Problem as Doctors See It," *Hastings Center Report,* 17:1, p 36.

Rothman, B. K. (1988) *The Tentative Pregnancy,* London: Pandora.

Rothman, L. (1978) "Menstrual Extraction: Procedures," *Quest,* 4:3, pp. 44–48.

Rowland, R. (1985) "Motherhood, Patriarchal Power, Alienation and the Issue of 'Choice' in Sex-preselection," in G. Corea et al. (eds), *Man-made Women,* London: Hutchinson.

Russo, N., J. Horn and R. Schwartz (1992) "United States Abortion in Context: Selected Characteristics and Motivations of Women Seeking Abortions," *Journal of Social Issues,* 48:3, pp. 183–202.

Ryan, L., M. Ripper and B. Buttfield (1994) *We Women Decide: Women's Experiences of Seeking Abortion in Queensland, South Australia and Tasmania 1985–1992,* Adelaide: Flinders University.

Ryan, M. (1987) "Illegal Abortions and the Soviet Health Service," *British Medical Journal,* 294, 14 February, pp. 425–6.

Sachdev, P. (1993) *Sex, Abortion and Unmarried Women,* Westport, CT: Greenwood Press.

Saha, A., W. Savage and J. George (1992) *The Tower Hamlets Day Care Abortion Service Study,* London: Doctors for a Woman's Choice on Abortion.

Savage, W. (1985) "Requests for Late Termination of Pregnancy—Tower Hamlets 1983," *British Medical Journal*, 290, 23 February, pp. 621–623.

Savage, W. (1995) "Medical Aspects of Legal Abortion," in A. Furedi (ed.), *The Abortion Law in Northern Ireland*, Belfast: Family Planning Association Northern Ireland.

Schonhofer, P. S. (1991) "Brazil: Misuse of Misoprostol as an Abortifacient May Induce Malformations," *The Lancet*, 337, 22 June, pp. 1534–5.

Sen, G., and R. Snow (eds) (1994) *Power and Decision: The Social Control of Reproduction*, Boston: Harvard University Press.

Sen, G., A. Germain and L. Chen (eds) (1994) *Population Policies Reconsidered: Health Empowerment and Rights*, Boston: Harvard University Press.

Shannon, T. (ed.) (1976) *Bioethics*, New York: Paulist Press.

Shapiro, R. (1987) *Contraception: A Practical and Political Guide*, London: Virago.

Singer, P. (ed.) (1991) *A Companion to Ethics*, Oxford: Blackwell.

Singer, P. (1993) *Practical Ethics*, Cambridge: Cambridge University Press.

Smith, A. (1988) "Late Abortions and the Law," *British Medical Journal*, 296, p. 446.

Smith, W. (1993) "Medical Abortion—Widening the Choice for Women in the UK," in A. Furedi (ed.), *Medical Abortion Services: European Perspectives on Anti-Progestins*, report of a conference held in Frankfurt, Germany, 5 and 6 December 1992, London: IPPF.

Smyth, I. (1995) *Population Policies: Official Responses to Feminist Critiques*, London: The Centre for the Study of Global Governance, LSE.

Solomons, M. (1992) *Pro-Life: The Irish Question*, Dublin: Lilliput Press.

Sommers, P. M., and L. S. Thomas (1983) "Restricting Federal Funds for Abortion: Another Look," *Social Science Quarterly*, 6:2, pp. 340–6.

South, J. (1985) "And at the End of the Day Who Is Holding the Baby?" *New Statesman*, 15 November.

Speckhard, A., and V. Rue (1992) "Postabortion Syndrome: An Emerging Public Health Concern," *Journal of Social Issues*, 48:3, pp. 95–119.

Srinavasan, T., and P. Bardhan (eds) (1988) *Rural Poverty in South Asia*, New York: Columbia University Press.

Stanworth, M. (1987a) "Reproductive Technologies and the Deconstruction of Motherhood," in M. Stanworth (ed.), *Reproductive Technologies: Gender, Motherhood and Medicine*, Cambridge: Polity Press.

Stanworth, M. (ed.) (1987b) *Reproductive Technologies: Gender, Motherhood, and Medicine*, Cambridge: Polity Press.

Staunton, D. (1994) "Kohl's Young Crusader Sparks Feminist Fury," *Observer*, 27 November.

Stephenson, P., M. Wagner, M. Badea and F. Serbanescu (1992) "Commentary: The Public Health Consequences of Restricted Induced Abortion—Lessons from Romania," *American Journal of Public Health*, 82:10, pp. 1328–30.

Steinberg, D. L. (1991) "Adversarial Politics: The Legal Construction of Abortion," in S. Franklin, C. Lury and J. Stacey (eds), *Off-centre: Feminism and Cultural Studies*, London: HarperCollins Academic.

STIMEZO (1992) *Abortion in the Netherlands: The Facts*, Utrecht: STIMEZO.

Susser, M. (1992) "Induced Abortion and Health as a Value," *American Journal of Public Health*, 82:10, pp. 1323–4.

Thomson, J. J. (1971) "A Defence of Abortion," *Philosophy and Public Affairs*, 1:1, pp. 47–66.

Thoss, E., and J. Baross (1995) "Germany," in A. Furedi (ed.), *The Abortion Law in Northern Ireland*, Belfast: Family Planning Association Northern Ireland.

Tin, W., U. Wariyar and E. Hey (1997) "Changing Prognosis for Babies of Less than 28 Weeks," *British Medical Journal*, 314, 11 January, pp. 107–11.

Tisdall, S. (1993) "Storm Troopers of the Burning Red Line," *Guardian*, 3 April.

Tomforde, A. (1993) "Dilemma for Women in United Abortion Law," *Guardian*, 12 August.

Tooley, M. (1983) *Abortion and Infanticide*, Oxford: Clarendon.

Torres, A., P. Donovan et al. (1986) "Public Benefits and Costs of Government Spending for Abortion," *Family Planning Perspectives*, 18:3. May/June, pp. 111–18.

Tribe, L. (1992) *Abortion: The Clash of Absolutes*, New York: W. W. Norton.

Turque, B., and B. Cohn (1995) "Foster Follies," *Newsweek*, 20 February.

Vines, G. (1994) "Sperm-sorting Fails to Separate Boys from Girls," *New Scientist*, 4 June, p. 8.

Walker, M. (1994) "Abortion Loses its Capital A with the Antis," *Guardian*, 21 September.

Warren, M. (1985) *Gendercide: The Implications of Sex-selection*, Totowa: Rowman and Allanheld.

Warren, M. (1991) "Abortion," in P. Singer (ed.), *A Companion to Ethics*, Oxford: Blackwell.

Wertz, D. C., and J. C. Fletcher (1989) "Fatal Knowledge? Prenatal Diagnosis and Sex-selection," *Hastings Center Report*, 19:3.

Wertz, D. C., and J. C. Fletcher (1993) "Prenatal Diagnosis and Sex Selection in 19 Nations," *Social Science of Medicine*, 37, pp. 1359–66.

West, R. (1990) "Taking Freedom Seriously," *Harvard Law Review*, 104, pp. 43–106.

Westoff, C. (1981) "Abortions Preventable by Contraceptive Practice?" *Family Planning Perspectives*, 13 (September–October) pp. 218–23.

Willis, E. (1990) "Putting Women Back into the Abortion Debate," in M. Fried (ed.), *From Abortion to Reproductive Freedom: Transforming a Movement*, Boston: South End Press.

Wilmoth, G., and M. de Alteris (1992) "Prevalence of Psychological Risks Following Legal Abortion in the United States: Limits of the Evidence," *Journal of Social Issues*, 48:3, pp. 37–66.

Wilt, J. (1990) *Abortion, Choice and Contemporary Fiction*, Chicago: University of Chicago Press.

Women Living Under Muslim Laws (WLUML) (1994) *Women's Reproductive Rights in Muslim Communities and Countries: Issues and Resources*, WLUML Dossier for Non-governmental Forum, International Conference on Population and Development, Cairo, 1994, Grabels, France: WLUML.

Women's Abortion Action Campaign (WAAC) (1994) *Medical Negligence and the Law on Abortion in NSW*, Sydney: WAAC.

Women's Health Journal (1994) 4:94.

Woodside, M. (1966) "The Woman Abortionist," in Family Planning Association, *Abortion in Britain*, London: Pitman.

World Health Organization (1992) *Women's Health across Age and Frontier*, Geneva: World Health Organization.

World Health Organization (1994) *Abortion: A Tabulation of Available Data on the Frequency and Mortality of Unsafe Abortion,* 2nd edn, Geneva: World Health Organization.

World Health Organization (1995) *Complications of Abortion,* Geneva: World Health Organization.

Yuval-Davis, N. (1995) "Women and Transversal Politics," *Journal of Women against Fundamentalism,* no. 6 (Spring).

Zagano, P. (1994) "RU 486: A Lot of People, a Lot to Answer For," *USA Today,* 20 May.

Index